55°

U. S. S. R.

DERBENT

BATUM

BAKU

BUKHARA

CASPIAN SEA

85 Ft. Below Sea Level

ARDEBIL

TABRIZ

Urmia

REZAIYEH

MAHABAD

MESHED

35°

TEHERAN

18,400

KHURASAN

E L B U R Z   M T S.

MAZANDERAN

AFGANISTAN

I R A N

Z A G R O S   M T S.

ISFAHAN

YEZD

L U T

S E I S T A N

KIRMAN

30°

KHUZISTAN

ABADAN

SHIRAZ

F A R S

PAKISTAN

ARABIA

PERSIAN GULF

O M A N

RAILWAYS

Indian	5' 6"	+—+—+—+
Russian	5'	+—+—+—+
Standard	4' 8.5"	+—+—+
Iraq	3' 3.4"	+—+—+
Palestine	3' 5.4"	+—+—+

MOUNTAIN AREAS

0   100   200   300   400   500

MILES

50°

55°

R.L.Williams

The United States and Turkey and Iran

THE AMERICAN FOREIGN POLICY LIBRARY

SUMNER WELLES, EDITOR

DONALD C. MCKAY, ASSOCIATE EDITOR

The United States and Britain

BY CRANE BRINTON

The United States and the Near East

BY E. A. SPEISER

The United States and the Caribbean

BY DEXTER PERKINS

The United States and Russia

BY VERA MICHELES DEAN

The United States and South America
The Northern Republics

BY ARTHUR P. WHITAKER

The United States and China

BY JOHN KING FAIRBANK

The United States and Scandinavia

BY FRANKLIN D. SCOTT

The United States and Japan

BY EDWIN O. REISCHAUER

The United States and France

BY DONALD C. MCKAY

The United States and Turkey and Iran

BY LEWIS V. THOMAS
AND RICHARD N. FRYE

THE
UNITED STATES
AND
Turkey and Iran

By

Lewis V. Thomas
and
Richard N. Frye

HARVARD UNIVERSITY PRESS
Cambridge, Massachusetts
1951

IN MEMORIAM

WALTER LIVINGSTON WRIGHT, Jr.

1900–1949

CONTENTS

INTRODUCTION, *by the Honorable Sumner Welles*   xi

The United States and Turkey

PREFACE   3

1. Introductory   5

2. Land and People   11
    1. Frontiers   11
    2. Geography   18
    3. Natural Resources: Agriculture   23
    4. Minerals   27
    5. Inhabitants   28
    6. Transportation and Communications   32
    7. Étatism   34

3. The Legacy of the Past   38
    1. The Peasant and History   38
    2. Non-Peasant: Ruling Group   41
    3. Westernization   47

4. Atatürk's Turkey   58
    1. Turkey for the Turks   58
    2. New Turks for a New Turkey   71

5. Inönü's Turkey   88

6. Turkey Today   113
    1. Turkey's Social Order   113
    2. The Turks' View of Themselves   123
    3. The Turks' View of the World   126
    4. Religion   135

7. The United States and Turkey   139

APPENDIX I. General Information about Turkey — 153

APPENDIX II. The Turkish Constitution — 156

APPENDIX III. Suggested Reading — 167

The United States and Iran

PREFACE — 173

1. Introductory — 175

2. The Country and the People — 179
   1. Land of Extremes — 179
   2. People of Extremes — 183

3. Government and Social Classes — 193
   1. The Court and the Shah — 193
   2. The Parliament and Bureaucracy — 195
   3. The Landed Aristocracy — 197
   4. The Army — 198
   5. Labor and the Middle Class — 198
   6. The Religious Leaders — 200

4. Religion and Law — 202
   1. The Official Religion — 202
   2. Law — 205
   3. Religious Minorities — 207

5. Character, Culture, and History — 209
   1. The Arts — 210
   2. Literature — 212
   3. The Glory that Was Iran — 213

6. The Impact of the West — 218

7. Reza Shah Pahlevi — 223

8. World War II and Its Aftermath — 229

9. The United States and Iran — 245

10. The Present and the Future — 259

Contents

APPENDIX I. The Supplementary Fundamental Laws to the
Constitution: Articles 1 and 2   272

APPENDIX II. Irano-Soviet Treaty of 1921: Articles 5 and 6   274

APPENDIX III. The Anglo-American-Soviet Declaration
Concerning Iran, Teheran, December 1, 1943   276

APPENDIX IV. General Information about Iran   277

APPENDIX V. Suggested Reading   279

INDEX   285

Maps

Middle East—U. S. A.   10

Iran: Minorities and Tribes   189

INTRODUCTION

If any American foresaw a generation ago what the freedom and welfare of Turkey and of Iran were going to mean to the American people in this year of 1951, he must either have possessed prophetic powers or else have had a unique measure of vision as to the future course of world affairs.

Until very recent years both nations seemed to the average American to be exceedingly remote. Both were alien to the sphere of direct United States interests. There was little political or commercial contact. By far the larger part of our diplomatic relations revolved around the activities of the missionaries or educators who had gone to the two countries for purely altruistic purposes.

How different has the situation now become! The demand for the withdrawal of Soviet troops from Iranian territory after the conclusion of the Second World War became the chief issue in the sessions of the Security Council of the United Nations in the spring of 1946. The satisfactory outcome of the controversy constituted the first great victory of the United Nations and the first conclusive proof that collective security through the United Nations can be achieved. The success of the United Nations preserved the independence of Iran.

The dispute focused the attention of the American people upon Iran. A year later, with the adoption of the so-called Truman doctrine of aid to Greece and Turkey, the American people realized as never before how important the safety of Turkey had become to their own safety.

Today we see a new threat of Soviet intervention in Iran. Front page articles in the American newspapers are giving us in full detail every development during this period of renewed unrest and of political upheaval in Iran, when the oil supplies upon which the defense and economy of Great Britain so largely depend are in danger of being cut off. We are daily obtaining a clearer understanding of the vital importance of the Middle East to us here in the Western Hemisphere.

Most Americans now see clearly that the maintenance of world peace will in no small measure hinge on the ability of the Turkish and Iranian peoples to preserve their integrity and freedom and to resist successfully the increasing pressure which emanates from Moscow.

By writing this book Mr. Thomas and Mr. Frye have done much to make it possible for American public opinion better to know the history, the economy, the political and strategic problems, and the nature of being of these two ancient nations which have so suddenly become of such great significance to the security of the United States. We can learn from these pages how fundamental is the opposition of the Turkish people to all that Soviet Communism implies. We can appreciate what real and rapid progress the Turkish people have been making along the road to an advanced democratic and representative government. We can convince ourselves without difficulty of their adamant determination to resist aggression from whatever source it may come. We have the opportunity to appreciate more sympathetically the basic reasons for the protracted political unrest in Iran, and the nature of the economic remedies that must be undertaken if the living standards of the masses of the Iranian people are successfully to be raised as one sure means of promoting social and political stability. We can find out in full detail just what course American policy has taken with regard to both nations during the Second World War and during the postwar years, and decide for ourselves whether that policy has been wise and whether it has been efficiently carried on.

This volume on Turkey and Iran could hardly have been published at a more appropriate moment. I am confident that it will prove to be of outstanding value as a means of promoting a wider and more accurate comprehension in the United States of an all-important aspect of this country's foreign relations.

Sumner Welles

THE UNITED STATES AND TURKEY

by

LEWIS V. THOMAS

PREFACE

In the summer of 1948 Walter Livingston Wright, Jr., Professor of Turkish Language and History at Princeton University and former President of the Istanbul American Colleges, revisited Turkey to gather material for a volume to appear in this series. At the time of his death, May 1949, Professor Wright had completed only the rough draft of a small part of the proposed book. This, together with his notes, has been at my disposal but was not near enough to completion to be utilized directly. My debt to Dr. Wright is rather for the privilege of years of almost daily discussions with him, at Istanbul, Washington, and Princeton, years when he was teacher, chief, and incomparable friend. Much that may be called good in this book stems directly from him. The imperfections are all my own.

I wish also to acknowledge deeply felt gratitude to students, teachers, and friends in Turkey, western Europe, and my own country, to the Rockefeller Foundation for a postwar fellowship (1947) and a travel grant (1949), and—beyond all others—to my wife and son who have uncomplainingly shared a seminomadic life. Not least are my sincere thanks to the Editor and Associate Editor of this series and to the staff of the Harvard University Press.

Lewis V. Thomas

Princeton University
December 18, 1950

1. Introductory

When the thoughtful American voter, never more perplexed than today, runs his eye across the world map, few areas are more puzzling than the general region whose natural center is Turkey. To Turkey's north and west the Balkan countries, apart from American-supported Greece, are obscured behind the Iron Curtain, with Tito's communist Yugoslavia currently an exception as problematical as it is enigmatic. To Turkey's south and east is the central Moslem area—Iran, the independent Arab states, and the small, newly established Jewish enclave of Israel. These lands are obscured by no Iron Curtain, but their comparative accessibility only serves to heighten awareness of the perplexing state of flux which prevails throughout them.

Every map-reader knows that the natural routes, land and sea, which join these many countries, from the Danube to the Persian Gulf and the Nile, and from the Caspian and Black Sea to the Aegean and Mediterranean, must invariably cross Turkey, and also that the Straits Area—Istanbul (Constantinople) city, the Bosporus-Marmara-Dardanelles waterway, and the easy passages from Europe to Asia at Istanbul and Gallipoli—would inevitably form one of humanity's most important crossroads, if only political conditions permitted. Today, however, as has happened frequently in the past, political conditions emphatically do not so permit. Hence Turkey's current importance to her various neighbors is not that of a functioning crossroads, but of a potentially vital crossroads. Nonetheless all those neighbors must take Turkey's present stand and future plans into their own most vital calculations, whether of friendly or of hostile intent.

One consequence is measurably to increase Turkey's own sense of isolation from all her neighbors. She has successfully averted falling behind the Iron Curtain, and she apparently gives every indication of a wholehearted resolve never to fall behind it if she can possibly avoid it. Hence her relations today with Russia and with Russia's Balkan puppets are as strained as well might be expected. In the case of each of these neighbors, moreover, there is mutual antipathy with Turkey, today stronger than ever, because it is deep-rooted in history and so reflects and reinforces tensions and aversions centuries old. Against Greece, Turkey's position is somewhat different, for she has formally maintained astonishingly good relations with Greece since the bitterness of the early 1920's, and Greece in her turn has for the most part fully reciprocated and fully reciprocates today. It is true that these Turkish-Greek "good relations" are almost entirely formal in nature and that the vast majority of the people of each country unquestionably, and at times vocally, harbors an aversion for the other party. But even so, given the prevailing trend of events and national antipathies characteristic of this whole region of the globe, Turkish-Greek amity can be regarded only as an encouraging phenomenon by any observer except one who hopes to improve his fishing by further troubling the waters.

To turn to Turkey's relations with her Asiatic neighbors, the essential point to note is a misconception of our own, namely that we, far more than the facts warrant, still regard the Turks as basically "non-European" and as fundamentally west-Asiatic, as being an integral part of the Moslem world. This misconception is well summed up in the still unfulfilled nineteenth-century west-European slogan: "Drive the Turks out of Europe" (and so back into Asia where they "belong"). In sober fact, since at least the fourteenth century the Anatolian Turks have in many respects really been as "European" as "Asiatic," if indeed these omnibus adjectives have any meaning at all in this connection, while today Turkey certainly does not regard herself as solely or even primarily a Moslem country. Her relations with, and her concern for, her Arab and Persian Moslem neighbors are much less close, cordial, or compelling than western European and American theorizing ordinarily assumes.

Turkey today is and wants to be surprisingly self-contained and isolated from her neighbors. This is one of the major facts about Turks which should first arrest the eye of the American who sets out to appraise the modern Middle East * and America's chances therein.

---

* We have used the now more popular term "Middle East" instead of "Near East" in this book. In American usage the terms are synonymous and include the Arab World, Israel, and Afghanistan, as well as Turkey and Iran.

The average thoughtful American is, of course, not unaware of modern Turkey. If nothing else, her successfully neutral role in World War II and her importance in subsequent attempts to contain Russian territorial expansion have often brought her to his attention. It is probably fair to assume that such an American observer of the world today "knows" that Turkey is a Republic, that the modern Turkish state was erected by an exceedingly vigorous and colorful figure named Atatürk, and that most of the inhabitants of the country today are Turks, inasmuch as the Armenians and Greeks who once abounded there have meanwhile disappeared, the former having been "massacred" and the latter "driven into the sea" while Smyrna burned. To this stock, compounded of information and misinformation, our American observer is likely to add some recollection of the "million Turkish bayonets" our press frequently reported as barring Hitler's expansion to the southeast, and also a subconscious conviction, perhaps Hollywood-born, that Turkey is largely desert, its picturesqueness much enhanced by camels, and its population of a distinctly swarthy hue. In addition, he could likely also recall that Atatürk is reported to have made everyone wear hats or take off veils, take last names, use the Latin alphabet, say "Istanbul" instead of "Constantinople" and "Ankara" instead of "Angora," and generally modernize himself in a hurry. Then, if our American friend has been frequenting certain self-consciously "liberal" circles of his fellow countrymen, he doubtless also holds the belief that Turkey is really a "dictatorship" and a police-state, more or less successfully disguised, and that "Fascist" is not much too strong a term to apply to the case, but he may have some trouble in squaring all this with the further news that the President of the Republic was defeated in the election of May, 1950. Finally, too, he must account for the fact that Turkey, despite her cautious course of neutrality during World War II, has since then not only withstood all Russian pressures upon her but has even taken a measure of initiative in attempting to render active aid to anti-Soviet forces at a time when those forces, in Korea, were patently at a great disadvantage. These all are considerations which may be expected to come to the well-read American's mind when Turkey is mentioned.

Naturally, in such a composite impression, some elements are entirely false, some half false, and others quite correct. It is precisely because of the elements of truth which this picture contains that its total effect is disastrously misleading. If the only disaster involved

were the injustice to modern Turkey which such misinformation entails, there would be no reason why anyone but the emotionally pro-
Turkish American—and few Americans indeed are strongly pro-
Turkish—should try to set down the facts and to encourage responsible fellow-Americans to draw their own conclusions. But there are
further considerations which bear directly on America's interests, and
the duty of presenting those considerations is the task which the
present book attempts. The approach is certainly "pro-Turkish," if
by this one implies rational readiness to stop belaboring the Turks
for the sins, real and fancied, of their fathers and to judge them for
what they are, and for what they have to offer to the United States
today. But it is scarcely pro-Turkish in any sentimental fashion.
Sometimes Turks will find it offensive. What is said here, however, is
addressed specifically and directly to the American reader with a
sincere hope that the result may be a small contribution towards
furthering America's interests, hopes, and ideals.

Outstanding characteristics which first impress the student who
carefully contrasts Turkey with her neighbors today are: (1) Turkey's comparative strength, (2) her internal stability, and (3) her
marked steadiness in international dealings. One must never forget
that these characteristics are only *relative*, relative to the situation
and the norms which prevail in the eastern Mediterranean, and that
when measured against the great powers, Turkey today is by no
means absolutely strong, unusually well-knit as a national unit, or
possessed of an unclouded horizon in her international dealings. To
understand her weak points as well as her strong points and so attempt both to appraise what it is that Turkey can and does offer the
United States as well as what the United States can, does, and should
offer Turkey, we obviously must first assess her total resources as of
today, developed and undeveloped, and then gain some understanding
of how the past, recent and remote, conditions the modern scene and
the Turks who move across it. In so far as we may, also, we should
investigate what it is that the modern Turks say and think about
themselves, their neighbors, and the rest of the world, paying specific
attention to their attitudes towards as well as their relations with the
people and the government of the United States. We cannot strike a
reliable balance until we have made a critical inventory. The first
general questions we must answer are: What does Turkey amount to
today? What are her resources? What is the nature of her popula-

tion? What of her installed and operating industrial plant? With what success is she exploiting the resources and equipment which she now has, and what specific plans has she for increasing the effectiveness of that exploitation?

Once we have in hand reliable answers to these questions—reliable but not necessarily complete, for as we shall see, the nature of the case does not always admit of complete answers—we shall be in better position to advance towards our final goal, a balanced appraisal of what Turkey does and might mean to the United States.

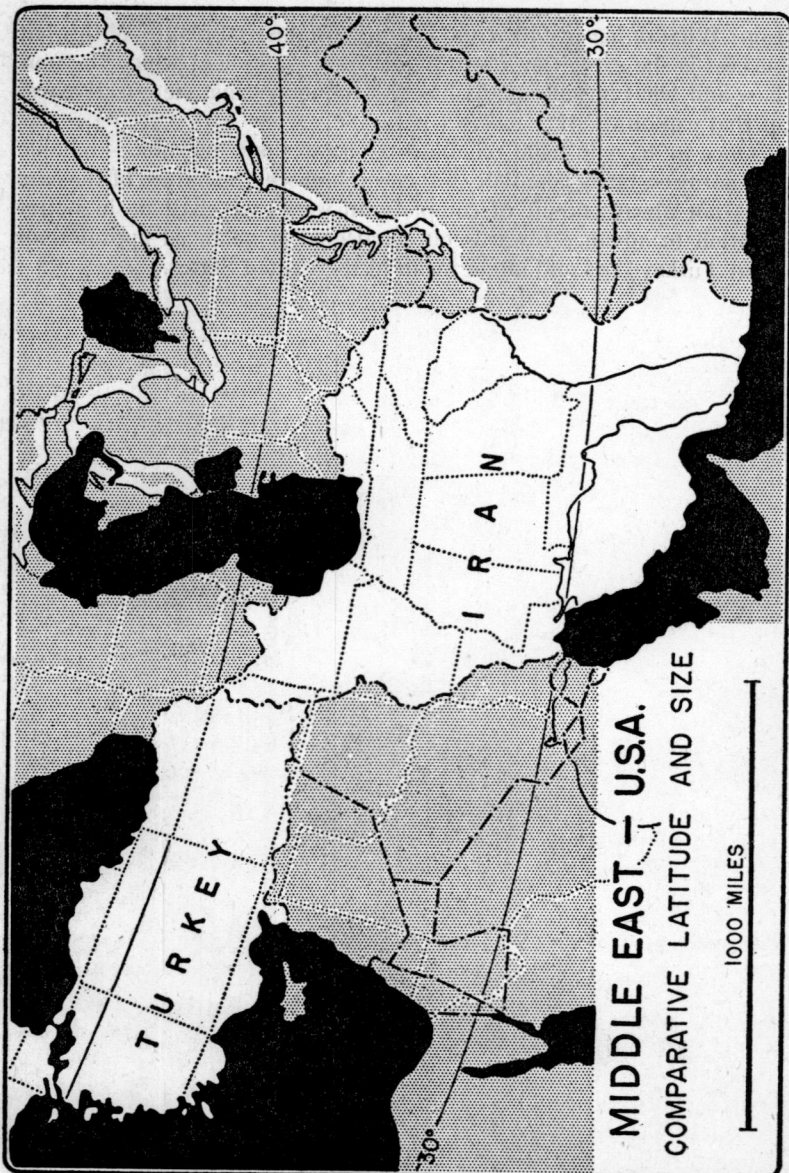

MIDDLE EAST – U.S.A.
COMPARATIVE LATITUDE AND SIZE

1000 MILES

2. Land and People

A bird's-eye survey of Turkey leaves the typical newcomer with the impression of a land bigger, more empty and barren, more backward, and more forbidding than he had expected to see. Turkey's area, in fact, is just under 300,000 square miles, somewhat larger than Texas and somewhat smaller than Pennsylvania, Maryland, Virginia, West Virginia, Kentucky, Ohio, Indiana, and Illinois taken together. Thus Turkey is definitely a large country by western European standards, and ranks as one of the middle-sized countries of the entire globe.

Although the impression at one's first bird's-eye survey is principally one of barrenness and emptiness, closer examination speedily reveals that this will not suffice for many of Turkey's smaller divisions and subdivisions. Indeed, the final conclusion after a more careful exploration of the entire country is that it exhibits such sharp contrasts, geographically and climatologically speaking, that no nationwide generalizations will hold beyond the mere statement that the land is extremely varied in nature, including within its frontiers a startling assortment of scenery and climate which would unquestionably make it a tourist's paradise if travel conditions permitted.

1. FRONTIERS

Only about three one-hundredths of the total area is "Turkey in Europe" (called *Trakya*, eastern Thrace), the vast bulk of the land comprising the peninsula of Asia Minor, or Anatolia. On the north, west, and southwest of Anatolia, the shores of the Black Sea, the Aegean, and the eastern Mediterranean give Turkey well-defined frontiers. The Black Sea coast is particularly forbidding: for its entire length, from the Russian frontier just southwest of Batum to the entrance of the Bosporus a few miles north of Istanbul (some 860 miles in all), there is no really good all-weather natural harbor, and indeed the dangers of these waters of the southern Black Sea have been proverbial since the recorded beginnings of navigation. Turkey's western and southern coasts, from the exit from the Dardanelles on the north, bearing southward and then east along the Mediterranean to the Syrian frontier below the cities of Iskenderum (Alexandretta) and Antakya (Antioch), are as different from her Black Sea coasts as could be imagined. Here, along the Aegean, the coast line abounds in natural harbors, the chief of which is Izmir (Smyrna), traditionally the region's principal center of export. It is true that once one leaves the Aegean and heads east, keeping to the north of Cyprus, Turkey's southern coast again becomes more forbidding, but this is amply compensated when one finally reaches the magnificent Gulf of Iskenderun, by all odds the finest natural roadstead in the entire eastern Mediterranean.

The maintenance of navigational services and the defense of these extremely long coasts—the total length of Turkey's frontage (including islands) on salt water being almost 4500 miles—represent a real problem. It is certainly complicated by the circumstance that numerous islands in the Aegean, some of them less than three miles from the Turkish mainland and most of them comparatively close to her coast, are not under Turkish sovereignty but belong to Greece. One can well understand that responsible authorities in Turkey should view this situation with much the same misgivings with which Americans would regard the possession of a number of Nantuckets and Martha's Vineyards, not to mention Long Islands, by any power other than ourselves. This being the case, Turkey's self-restraint in refraining from pressing the question of these islands, despite more than one opportunity to do so, is an impressive illustration of that steadiness in international dealings which we have already mentioned as one of her outstanding attributes in the eyes of the careful observer.

Whatever problems of trade and defense Turkey's sea frontiers may pose are today insignificant when compared with those connected with her land frontiers. Her boundaries on land touch six other sovereign states: in Europe, Bulgaria and Greece; in Asia, Syria, Iraq, Iran, and the Soviet Union, the common frontier with the last-mentioned state being technically divided into a frontier over against Soviet Armenia and then, to the north and west, another over against

Soviet Georgia. None of these land frontiers, whose aggregate length is approximately 1650 miles, can be called a "satisfactory" natural frontier. Otherwise phrased, no one of these frontiers represents the militarily most advantageous or the economically most sensible demarcation, but in each case the line as established today marks a compromise which when it was made was wholly satisfactory to none of the parties involved.

Turkey's frontier with Bulgaria, about 125 miles, from the Black Sea to the Merich (Maritsa) River, runs for the most part through rugged, broken country and is traversed by no railroad and by relatively few lines of communication of any sort. The same river also forms Turkey's frontier with Greece, starting at a point some nine miles west of Edirne (Adrianople) and descending to the Aegean Sea (about 125 miles). An outstanding peculiarity of this Greek-Turkish frontier is its relationship with the railroad which runs from Istanbul to Edirne and thence, this being Turkey's sole direct rail connection with Europe, to Sofia and Belgrade, a sub-line having branched off south of Edirne to provide a connection through Greek Thrace to Salonika. When the Istanbul-Edirne-Sofia railroad was constructed, in Ottoman times, it was laid out to cross the Maritsa some distance south of Edirne, and then to run northwest, skirting the river's right bank. This arrangement, however, eventually allowed treaty makers to devise a line which has ever since plagued all parties concerned.

When traveling from Istanbul to Edirne by Turkish train today, one leaves Turkey, enters Greece, and then reënters Turkey at Edirne station, across the river from the city. If, then, one proceeds on from Edirne to Sofia, one once again must enter Greece in order finally to get to Bulgaria. The customs problems and various difficulties caused by this frontier snarl came out clearly indeed in the second World War when, with the Germans holding Greece, it was actually necessary to have Axis permission in order to make the trip Istanbul-Edirne.

All this, although illustrative of the generally unsatisfactory nature of Turkey's frontiers, is of course not now of major importance, nor does there appear to be any likelihood that its nuisance value will be strong enough to bring the Bulgars, Greeks, and Turks to effect an amicable adjustment. One would judge it more likely that Turkey will eventually build another line for a few kilometers along her side of the Maritsa. Meantime, a detour via Salonika can furnish a through-connection with western Europe.

In a sense, the Turkish-Greek frontier situation is duplicated by the railroad problem which marks the Turkish-Syrian frontier. Here the famous Baghdad railroad (Istanbul-Ankara-Adana-Aleppo-Baghdad) leaves Turkey at Meydanekbez, as one travels south, to descend through Syria to Aleppo. It then doubles back to the northeast, reentering Turkey at Chobanbey. Thenceforward, as one proceeds east, the southern edge of the railroad line itself marks the Syrian-Turkish frontier until the town of Nusaybin is reached. Here the railroad reënters Syria, turning southeast towards the Iraqi frontier which it finally crosses some distance northwest of Mosul. Thus, to travel or ship by rail from Ankara to, for example, the Turkish city of Mardin, it is again necessary to leave and then reënter Turkey, meantime traversing a portion of Syria.

Apart from this inconvenience, however, the Turkish-Syrian frontier today does not offer any major problem. A portion of that frontier was redrawn, in Turkey's favor, in 1939 following the Turkish-French declaration of mutual assistance in which France as mandatory of the Levant States allowed Turkey to annex the hitherto French-mandated Sanjak of Alexandretta which was subsequently renamed the Hatay (Hittiteland) by the Turks. The circumstances of this transfer of territory are sufficiently notorious to be known to all students of the modern Middle East. In brief, at the end of the first World War, France succeeded in having the Sanjak of Alexandretta, whose principal importance then as now was comprised in the city of Antioch and the port of Alexandretta (the latter connected by rail with the Turkish rail system but not directly with the Syrian system), included in her Levant States mandate, that is to say, "in Syria." The population of this Sanjak region was very mixed as to "peoples," quite *à la Macédoine,* but at this time Arabs predominated, with Turks running them a good second.

With the stabilization of the Republic of Turkey, it eventually became a basic article of Turkish faith that the Republic was satisfied with her existing frontiers and that the state would neither cherish nor tolerate any irredentism or *revendications* of any sort. This has, as we saw in the case of the Greek Islands, contributed greatly to the steadiness in international dealings which so markedly characterizes modern Turkey. From the very start, however, it was made plain by Ankara that Alexandretta Sanjak was an exception and that Turkey would eventually claim it if ever circumstances permitted. In fact, as early as 1921, Turkey had agreed to the Sanjak's inclusion in the Syrian mandate only on condition that it should have its own special regime so that its large Turkish minority would never be subject directly to the rule of an Arab nationalist Syria. This condition was entirely agreeable to the French with their Levantine policy of divide and then divide again to rule, and when in 1936 France finally permitted Syria to move at least one step closer to the attainment of true self-government, she was again glad to set up a special League of Nation's commission which (1937) was to supervise the election of a local Sanjak assembly wherein representation was to be granted proportionately to the various peoples of the territory. The creation of such an assembly was not welcomed by the local Turks nor by the Turkish Republic, for the Turks of Alexandretta were still well below forming a majority of the inhabitants of the Sanjak. There then followed a comedy of sophistry, every move in which was intensified by consciousness on all sides of Italy's menacing attitude in the eastern Mediterranean. Finally "arrangements," which eventually included the arrival of Turkish troops with French consent, produced a Turkish majority and in 1939 the territory became an integral part of the Turkish Republic.

The aftermath of Turkey's "redemption" of the Hatay is, of course, rather bitter. The French can contend that Turkey unblushingly exploited France's peril to get what she wanted. The Syrians can and do say that France most wrongly gave away what should have remained inviolable Syrian-Arab soil, and that the Turks were guilty of attenuated aggression at the most or of selfish unfriendliness at the least. So far as the matter concerns France, it is now only academic, and although the Syrians certainly "remember the Sanjak" and at times wave their grievance as a politically convenient bloody flag, the whole issue for Syria is of secondary importance in comparison with other problems which now confront her. Syrian resentment against Turkey, though alive, is not likely to become of tangible consequence in the foreseeable future, as long as Syria remains a free agent.

As for the Turks, they can honestly maintain that on economic and strategic grounds the territory concerned should have been theirs from the start, that on "ethnic" grounds they had about as good a claim as did anyone else, and above all that they never made the least secret of their resolution to "redeem" the Hatay whenever they could. They also point out that the means which they used to get it were short of force and were no more questionable than those frequently resorted to by powers which have long advertised themselves as far more "civilized" than Turkey. Meantime, the Turks have Iskenderun port and Antioch city, and except for that portion of the Sanjak's population, particularly the Armenians, who emigrated before the transfer took place, it would be hard to maintain that anyone is the worse off for the change. Indeed, most of the Sanjak inhabitants now view the change as desirable and advantageous.

Apart from the Hatay problem, the situation today along the 490-odd-mile Turkish-Syrian frontier, although it can scarcely be compared to that prevailing along the Canadian-American line, is still probably the Middle East's closest approach to such a utopian state of affairs. It is also a smuggler's utopia.

From the point where the Baghdad railroad veers south, the Turkish-Syrian frontier proceeds east until it intersects the Tigris. There Syria ends and Iraq begins. Turkey's frontier with Iraq (approximately 235 miles) runs for the most part through high and rugged mountains and is crossed by no railroad and by few roads or tracks of any description. The location of this boundary is a legacy of the lengthy and acrimonious dispute between Turkey on the one hand and Britain and Iraq on the other which for several years embittered the relations of all three and which, generally speaking, represented a distinct reverse for Turkey, but a reverse which she accepted in good part and has since made no serious effort to recoup. The Turkish-Iraqi frontier runs through Kurdistan, a most backward region which has in the last three decades been the scene of frequent disturbances both on the Iraqi and the Turkish sides of the boundary. That Turkey's share of the Kurdish problems seems now to be on its way to a laudable and lasting solution will appear as we proceed, and the reader will find evidence to justify the conclusion that the Turkish-Iraqi frontier today gives little likelihood of becoming in itself the seat of important difficulties.

The same general characterization—a ruggedly mountainous frontier region marked by comparative stability and quiet except for ephemeral and inconsequential local disturbances—serves to describe the Persian-Turkish frontier. It runs from the northeastern corner of Iraq in a generally northernly direction to the Aras (Araxes) River. This frontier traverses the mountains east of Lake Van, eventually curving eastward to include the two main summits of Mount Ararat (Turkish Ağrï Dağ) within Turkey's boundaries. It is crossed by a number of important land routes, especially the age-old Trabzon-

Tabriz transit road which passes from Turkey into Persia just south of the town of Doğu Bayazit, but by no railroad. The nations which face each other across the 290-odd miles of this Rocky Mountain-like frontier region have in the past felt little respect or liking for each other, but in these latter times by mutual consent they have firmly tabled differences, impelled to this by their overwhelming mutual preoccupation with their northern neighbor, Soviet Russia.

Turkey's Russian frontier, from its commencement at the junction point of Iran, Turkey, and Soviet Armenia, directly east of Mount Ararat, ascends the Aras River to that stream's important right-bank affluent, the Arpa, and then mounts the Arpa north to almost opposite the city of Leninakan. On the Russian side of this part of the frontier runs a railroad, and back from it stands the recently important Armenian center of Erivan. The only railroad which crosses the Soviet-Turkish frontier, however, comes directly from Leninakan and then proceeds (Russian gauge) southwest to the Turkish city Kars which, with Ardahan, is currently claimed by the Soviets. From the intersection of frontier and railroad, the boundary bears more to the west, advancing for the most part with no regard for watersheds or for other natural features, until it finally reaches the Black Sea just south of Batum. In its course through the mountainous country south of Soviet Georgia it quite arbitrarily divides, on the Turkish side, a large share of Batum's natural hinterland from that city, on the Russian side.

The tensions and precautions which prevail along this line beggar description. Throughout the region Russian sentry-points are closely spaced. In places where the nature of the soil and the soil cover make this feasible, the Russians actually rake the ground before sunset each night during the snow-free months of the year, so that the next morning telltale foot-tracks will reveal whether anyone has successfully slipped across. Despite Russian precautions, there is an intermittent trickle of escapees into Turkey here, most of them drawn from those Armenians who a few years ago elected to return from their various non-Soviet havens to what they believed would be a national refuge and a semi-autonomous homeland in the Soviet Armenian Republic. These individuals now risk the perils of an attempt to escape the Soviet Union and throw themselves on the mercies of their traditional enemies, the Turks.

With her frontier over against Russia we have terminated the circuit of Turkey's long and vulnerable land frontiers, gaining as we circumambulated the country not only a more accurate conception of its size and of the ruggedness of many of its geographical features, but also some notion of the perplexing historical heritage which does so much to divide Turkey from, and so little to unite her with, her numerous neighbors.

2. GEOGRAPHY

When we next attempt to describe what lies within the frontiers we have inspected, we run the risk of obscurity. Turkey's geographical structure has left many a writer and many a reader floundering in despair. It has been likened to everything from an upside-down cake pan to a well-worn pork-pie hat. We begin with the land's central and fundamental feature, the great Anatolian plateau, a vast, roughly oval plateau area stretching from Eskishehir and Afyonkarahisar on the west to Kayseri (Caesarea) and beyond on the east, and from the mountain ranges which parallel the Black Sea on the north to Konya (Iconium), Karaman, and Ulukïshla on the south.

This large tract has an average elevation of 3000 feet above sea level, or even slightly more. Aside from one stream, the Kïzïl Irmak (Halys) which swings in sickle fashion clockwise from north of Kayseri to the Black Sea, the watercourses which cross the plateau are of negligible importance, although some become raging torrents in the season of melting snows. Much of the plateau, in fact, does not drain to the sea at all, and the central region is occupied by large salt marshes and a Tuz Gölü (salt lake) which varies in size from year to year according to the amount of run-off. Many sizable stretches of the plateau's floor are quite flat and featureless, although even here the rising and setting sun brings out colors reminiscent of the Grand Canyon, but the entire plateau unit is so much larger than the eye's reach that at no single point on its floor does one get any impression of the essential structure of the whole. Apart from this, moreover, great tracts of the plateau floor are themselves extremely broken country, ranging all the way from precipitous canyons to steepish rolling hills and quite respectable mountains. Mount Erjiyas (Argaeus), south of Kayseri, is one of the principal landmarks of western Asia. This combination of factors serves further to conceal from the traveler the real design of the plateau formation which he is crossing.

In no matter what direction one goes, however, one eventually comes to the edge of the plateau and then encounters its rising lip, for the whole is ringed with mountains. Upon leaving the plateau floor, the climb up to the saucer rim is not ordinarily very strenuous, but once one attains the very rim, then comes the long and steep descent to the coastal plains and the sea on the north, west, and south. And whether one moves towards the Black Sea, the Aegean, or the Mediterranean, the general configuration of the land is similar. Rugged mountains in one range or several parallel ranges bar the way from the plateau-saucer's rim down to the coastal plain, but once these have been passed the plain itself is a marvel of fertility, especially in contrast to the more arid high plateau so recently left behind.

In the north, the coastal ranges skirting the Black Sea are precipitous but can easily be passed in many places. The descent on the northwest, via Eskishehir and along the Sakarya (Sangarius) River, is the easiest of all from the central plateau, and these routes, of course, lead directly to the Straits Area and so afford an easy passage on into the Balkan valleys which connect with central Europe. On the west, where prolongations of Turkey's Black Sea coastal ranges and her Mediterranean coastal ranges squeeze inwards toward each other, the result is a complicated mountain system descending gradually to the Aegean. This system is broad and wearisome to traverse, but its valleys generally tend from east to west and so offer many easy passages and are not serious impediments to commerce. Further down, on the southwestern rim of the plateau, the mountains which descend to the sea are much more troublesome than those behind Izmir, but here too there is at least one frequented route, that leading south to the Mediterranean port of Antalya (Adalia, Attaleia). East of this Antalya road are the majestic Taurus Mountains, and then the Anti-Taurus, which rise between the Mediterranean and the central plateau. They form a mountain barrier which has served since history began as one of the most important and effective of all obstacles to mankind's passage. Through this stupendous mountain country one good way, and one good way alone, leads down to the fertile plains of Cilicia, today the province of Adana (or Seyhan). One leaves the plateau at Ulukĭshla and proceeds through awe-inspiring gorges to Pozantĭ; here the ways fork. By road the traveler continues through the famous Cilician Gates, but by rail goes slightly more to the east and through an impressive series of tunnels until at last, by either route, he emerges into the Cilician plain where stand Adana and Tarsus, the city of St. Paul.

Such is the essential structure of the Anatolian plateau and, north, west, and south, of its surrounding mountains and the coastal plains beyond them. When, however, one advances across this plateau to the east, there is no drop to a coastal plain and a shining sea; instead, one enters ever more complicated systems of mountains, smaller and higher plateaus, narrow, breath-taking valleys, raging mountain streams and placid alpine lakes. When one has continued east to a point about two-thirds of the way from the Aegean to the Russian frontier, one encounters the Euphrates (Turkish, Fïrat), the principal geographical landmark of mountainous Turkey east of the plateau. The Euphrates system with its many tributaries roughly bisects the entire mountainous eastern region in a generally southwestern tending direction, but though this river system and its adjacent mountain ranges, as one ascends towards the head waters, are an increasingly difficult impediment to travel, still they can scarcely be regarded as a very well-defined natural frontier. Indeed, if the traveler here is able to get his overall bearings and to disregard the immediate local complexities of mountain and stream which distract and even imperil him as he proceeds, he is now in a uniquely favorable situation to assimilate one geographical fact which has had decisive effect upon Anatolian history throughout all ages, namely, that the peninsula of Anatolia has no feasible natural frontier on the east at all.

Southeast from the plateau a series of mountain formations which has been well-called the "Anatolian sieve" gives easy access to the northern and northwestern fringes of the "Fertile Crescent," the cities of Urfa (Edessa) and Diyarbakïr. East and northeast from that same plateau's saucer rim, one continues by ever more strenuous (but "passable in summer") mountain routes either directly east to Lake Van and so on to Iran, or else north of Mount Ararat and so northeast into the Caucasus. Go where you will—and where you can—you will note many strong points which, when defended, can effectively close one or another route, but you will nowhere find any tenable true natural frontier.

This basic fact, the absence of a natural frontier to the east or northeast of Turkey, has doubtless already caused the reader to review and perhaps dismiss some of the original doubts which he felt as we first surveyed Turkey's present political frontiers on the east and northeast. The point is not that these present frontiers are not "good," but rather that Turkey is distinctly fortunate that they are as good as they now are. Viewed in this light and with the strategist's eye, the Turkish Republic's long-held policy of firm and absolute non-irredentism (the Hatay alone excepted) emerges here not as a matter of admirable self-abnegation but rather as a question of well-calculated self-interest, and doubtless many responsible Turks so regard it today. Here, therefore, we have another important factor in that steadiness in international dealings which we have already noted as an outstanding characteristic of modern Turkey.

Although we now have a clear idea of the essential geographical structure of the country of Turkey, detailed descriptions of its several main regions are necessary to round out our picture. For practical purposes, the Turks themselves recognize seven main regions, as follows:

(1) The Black Sea region, that is, the Black Sea coastal plain, narrow for the most part but extremely well watered, fertile, and populous, plus the mountains which rise from this plain, some of them quite heavily forested and liberally furnished with isolated but productive valleys and small plateaus. This general region in classical times roughly corresponded to Paphlagonia and Pontus.

(2) The Marmara region, that is, the entire Marmara basin, European as well as Asiatic, including the whole of Turkey in Europe, the broken country and fertile valleys of northwestern Anatolia eastward to region (1) and southward beyond Uludağ (Bithynian Olympus, the seat of Homer's gods) to the neighborhood of Kütahya. This region (classical Bithynia, the Troad, Mysia, and eastern Thrace) is for the most part fertile and relatively adequately watered. Through it run the main easy ascents from the Straits area to the central plateau.

(3) The Aegean region, that is, the broad, rich Aegean coastal plains, the fertile and beautiful valleys of the many rivers (especially the Menderes-Maeander and the Gediz-Hermus) which flow west into those plains, and the extensive mountain belt which intervenes between these Aegean lowlands and the Anatolian plateau to the east. This general region, classical Lydia, Caria, and Phrygia, abounds in classical and New Testament sites, among them Ephesus, Miletus, Halicarnassus, Sardis, Smyrna, Laodicea, and Philadelphia. In climate and in general aspect it is a Mediterranean land at its incomparable best, and its charms have been famous for millennia.

(4) The Central Anatolian region, that is, the great saucer-shaped plateau and its perimeter of mountains, classical Cappadocia, Lycaonia, and Galatia. This high, clear-aired country is fertile but arid.

Potentially one of the great wheat areas of the world, its productivity is at the mercy of its capricious yearly rainfall. The edges of the saucer, ascending towards the outer rim, are almost always sufficiently watered to produce a fair crop, but the vast floor of the plateau, which should be the principal wheat area of the country, may in one year be almost a true desert and then, in the next year, with good rains be a wheat field stretching as far as the eye can see. Central Anatolia's climate is continental in temperature, with cold and severe winters in the sharpest contrast to blazing summers. It is in this region that one can best understand Turkey's rainfall problem and the factors which impose it. Annual precipitation here may average as little as ten inches. Wheat is sown by hand, ordinarily in the fall, and rains in October (sometimes also in September) usually give it a good enough start to carry it through the winter. Then, in the spring, melting snows and spring rains must be depended upon to carry the crop on to maturity. Often, however, the total moisture available in the spring is insufficient and the grain dies. During the six months from October to March, almost two-thirds of the total annual precipitation is to be expected. Of the remaining six months, July and August bring practically no moisture, September is quite likely to be as dry as was August, while April, May, and June, as we have seen, are so uncertain that they pose the final problem to the farmer and his crops. The same annual pattern of wet winters, dry summers, fairly wet autumns, and uncertain springs also characterizes the Aegean and Marmara regions, but here the rainfall averages are sufficiently modified, and above all the spring rains are relatively more certain, so that serious crop failures are less of a threat. Even so, spring and summer may produce a succession of rainless months in these regions until all vegetation but the hardiest evergreen is reduced to a melancholy burnt brown.

In contrast to the plateau, Aegean, and Marmara regions, the Black Sea littoral, especially towards its eastern extremity, is quite abundantly watered, even in midsummer, the annual precipitation here reaching almost 100 inches (ten times what may be available on the central plateau), and helping to produce conditions which are at least reminiscent of the famous Crimea.

(5) The fifth general region into which Turkey is divided is that of southern Anatolia, that is, beginning from a point west of the plain of Antalya and continuing eastward to the Hatay; also, to the north,

including the Taurus system which looms over this entire Mediterranean coast. In classical geography, this region comprised Lycia, Pamphylia, and Pisidia, and the two Cilicias, Tracheia and Campestris. The Taurus barrier effectively cuts this region off from the rest of Turkey. Its two fertile Mediterranean plain districts, those of Adana and Antalya, are garden spots fairly to be termed semitropical although here, too, the precipitation pattern of wet winters and dry summers plus the intense heat of the Mediterranean summer certainly does not afford the inhabitants a year-round paradise.

(6) Of the remaining regions of Turkey, the sixth, southeast Anatolia, comprises the northern fringes of the Fertile Crescent (Gaziantap, Urfa, Diyarbakïr) and the mountains which rise to the north of those several plains (ranges of Malatya, Bitlis, and Hakâri), that is, for the most part this region is old Kurdistan. It, too, is generally characterized by hot and dry summers and by cool to bitter-cold winters with skimpily adequate rainfall.

(7) The remaining region, Eastern Anatolia (classical Armenia), is physically the most rugged and forbidding division of the entire country, but its climate, although especially severe in winter, does at least include a more balanced precipitation pattern so that a severe dry season is not ordinarily a conspicuous feature of the year.

3. NATURAL RESOURCES: AGRICULTURE

This survey of Turkey's component sectors, together with our earlier bird's-eye inspection of her long frontiers, will already have disclosed to the reader that Turkey's principal natural resource is the fertility of her soil and that the main factor which limits agriculture in Turkey is lack of water, and he probably has inferred that Turkey's major, and indeed only important, industry is farming. We now proceed to examine Turkey's natural resources in more detail, ever pursuing the answer to our question: What does Turkey amount to today? And we shall, of course, begin with the soil.

Of Turkey's total land surface, some 16 per cent is wholly unproductive, according to the latest (1944) and admittedly incomplete estimate. Another 50 per cent of the total area is called "grazing and pasture land," none of which is farmed and much of which obviously is so little used that it, too, can sensibly be tagged "unproductive." The total area under cultivation appears to be under one-fifth of Turkey's total surface, with the principal factor responsible being aridity and not infertility. Much of the "grazing area" is potential crop land, excellent farm land, given only water.

Most of the land now under cultivation should be ranked as "normal farm land," land cultivated according to ordinary Anatolian methods. These entail, among other things, leaving a plot fallow at least one year in three, so the total area under the plow in any one year is even further lessened. It approaches roughly 13 or 14 per cent of the total land surface. Two per cent more of the total surface is reckoned as cultivated land other than normal farms—market gardens, truck gardens, orchards, vineyards, olive groves, and so on. Hence the grand total of land cultivated in a given year exceeds slightly 15 per cent of the total land surface.

This cultivation accounts for the direct employment of 75 or 80 per cent of Turkey's total population, a statistic which prepares the reader for two further points: (1) Turkey's present agriculture is wasteful of human energy, and (2) Turkey's population is, in terms of the country's total area and potential, small.

The agricultural produce suffices to feed and also, for the most part, to clothe the entire population. No items of food, and not a great deal of cloth, *must* be imported in an ordinary year, and what is imported for the most part comes properly under the heading "luxury goods." Thus Turkey's agriculture suffices to maintain the national life. It, practically alone, obviously ultimately governs the national standard of living and, in a real sense, simply "is" the national economy. On the one hand, the agricultural population—the peasants—are the government's one indispensable financial support: the peasant is the taxpayer. And on the other hand, it is the peasant who produces the bulk of the country's cash-exports. Each of the agricultural exports is a valuable product, but a listing of the most important of them, namely: (1) tobacco, about 20–25 per cent of Turkey's *total* annual exports; (2) hazelnuts, raisins, and figs, together accounting for another 20–25 per cent of Turkey's total annual exports; and (3) such comparatively minor items as wool and mohair-wool, raw cotton, oilcake, licorice, and the like, will remind the reader that most of Turkey's exportable agricultural products are, in the eyes of the international buyer, nonessential or at least low-priority items. This puts Turkey at a distinct disadvantage when international trade conditions are poor, and the disadvantage is doubled when we also recall that Turkey needs her vital imports, which, in distinction to her unprocessed or semi-processed nonessential export items, are almost entirely manufactured goods and machines, just as much when international trade is bad as she does when it is good. This complex situation goes a long way to account for the conviction of many Turkish merchants that the international market is hopelessly manic-depressive.

The main category for Turkey's plant-crops is grain, "cereals and legumes." Usually she has available for export a small surplus of breadstuffs, but this is always at the mercy of Anatolia's capricious rainfall, and also limited by the country's exceedingly inadequate means for storing and transporting agricultural produce. Hence it is not infrequent to find a year when it is more likely that parts of Turkey will go hungry than that she will have breadstuffs which she can export in any quantity. Her major export items, for example tobacco, are less vulnerable but by no means wholly invulnerable on these counts, for they are predominantly non-plateau crops and it is, of course, the plateau which is most likely to have drought. In sum, the overall picture of Turkey's agricultural exports is not enviable: those items which most easily find a market under almost any conditions—breadstuffs—are the very items which are also most at the mercy of her own uncertain climate, while the exportable agricultural products which she consistently produces with the least fluctuations are, by and large, themselves particularly at the mercy of the shifting climate of international trade.

The obviously best corner at which the Turks can attempt to catch hold of this set of problems is to try to step up cereal production, rainfall or no rainfall, by irrigation and by improved methods of farming.

Such methods do not, for the individual peasant, mean immediate, large-scale mechanization, although the government, on its part, beginning in 1942 did resort to a bold venture in the large-scale mechanized farming of sizable plateau areas which had hitherto lain unexploited. These government farms, or farm-camps, have seemed to some observers as if they might as well be in North Dakota for all the direct effect they are having upon Turkey's traditional farming methods. In other words, they grow wheat, but they do not seem to contribute to a solution in the near future of Turkey's basic farm problem, which is simply to change the peasant's agricultural techniques. Such government farms, moreover, do not always successfully grow wheat, for their location inevitably leaves them helpless against an overly dry season, as was for example the case in the summer of 1949.

Rather than immediate large-scale mechanization, the improvements which can most persuasively be urged are less spectacular than that Ankara-inspired program which, beginning in 1942, brought some 750,000 hitherto unused acres under the multiple disk plow. They consist in encouraging the peasant, the real Anatolian-style farmer, to adopt a safe minimum of new methods and to make available to him, and to persuade him to use, a minimum of efficient machines. Here, for the first time in our survey of Turkey, we encounter head-on Turkey's basic problem: how to get the peasant— some 75–80 per cent of the total population—to do anything in any way except exactly the one way he "always" has done it.

"Always" here is no exaggeration. The last important innovation in the Anatolian farmer's methods and equipment practically dates back to the introduction of the use of iron in the region. The peasant's ordinary plow today, as in ancient times, is of wood, iron-tipped, and does not cut deeply into the soil. It is pulled by the same ox who pulls his primitive, solid-wheeled cart, ox and cart alike identical descendants of Anatolia's earliest. As one hears these carts screech their way from village to field, all over Anatolia, in the dawn's early light, one can indeed reflect that a thousand years are as but a single day.

The Anatolian farmer today still sows his seed broadcast, by hand, plows it under (so that some is far too deep and some left on the surface), and reaps and threshes his grain by hand. He almost never uses any fertilizer. He cannot buy any, for there is none to be had, and in much of the country all animal dung must be carefully preserved, for it is the indispensable fuel for winter. From this it is obvious that what could most help the Anatolian farmer, and with him the entire nation and economy which he so largely sustains, would be the use of simple but effective tools and methods: a cheap seed-drill, access to a power-thresher, the use of some fertilizers. Why it is that these things are not yet in his hands will become more evident as our account proceeds.

Irrigation is used in widely scattered regions of Anatolia—rice is even grown in well-watered valleys on the plateau—but it is almost everywhere carried out in the most simple fashion, the works being no more than can be constructed by a pair of hands and a wooden shovel, or than can be operated by an animal turning a water wheel. Large irrigation projects, obviously, are beyond the peasant's province. In today's Anatolian phrase they are *devlet ishi,* the job of the central government. At present, too, cheap easily-cared-for power sources, gasoline or diesel-powered, which could pump water for his fields are also largely beyond the peasant, nor does he ordinarily even conceive that such appliances could possibly come within his grasp.

In addition to Turkey's main plant-crops which, as we have seen, ordinarily suffice to feed the country and to provide a fairly sizable surplus for cash-export of certain nonessential items as well as sometimes an exportable surplus of breadstuffs, Turkey's animal crops also deserve attention. The important domestic animals are sheep, goats (including the famous mohair-wool Angora goat of the Anatolian plateau), oxen, water-buffalo, cattle, and of course poultry, and donkeys. In so far as the Turks can afford to eat much meat, mutton is their staple article of flesh diet, but the peasants, the majority of the country, are likely to enjoy this food only on more special occasions, and sheep are primarily raised for their wool rather than for food. The cattle characteristic of most of Turkey's ranges are not good beef animals, although efforts to develop a better strain are meeting some success, and beef is not a very common or popular item of food. Dairy products are available to the peasant almost everywhere, and his basic diet consists of milk-products, cereals, and vegetables. Excellent fruit abounds in Turkey, but facilities for preparing, preserving, or shipping it are lacking and so it is ordinarily no more than a welcome seasonal supplement to the food locally available. Inadequate facilities for the preservation of meat also mean that it, too, for the most part must be consumed where and when it is killed. In short, though much of Turkey is good grazing country, and although herding is characteristic of the peasant almost everywhere, still the total animal crop of Turkey each year figures as a just adequate contribution to sustain the national life but only incidentally as contributing to the national economy, domestic or export, beyond meeting local consumption needs.

4. MINERALS

Turkey's soil not only sustains plant and animal life essential to the nation, but also produces mineral wealth which materially contributes to the national well-being. One must take care not to exaggerate here. It is true that in the view of an American mining engineer much of the country is "unprospected and unsurveyed," but this does not mean that vast wealth is probably to be discovered. In ancient times, the country was carefully searched for metals, and of those metals which were valuable in preindustrial economy the major deposits were not only long ago discovered, but also well-worked, some of them having been entirely worked out.

In Turkey's production of minerals today, coal heads the list. Even so, it fails to satisfy local demands, and an effort to fill the gap by the production of lignite, in which Turkey is very well off, is under way. A well-conceived large-scale program, already well begun, to develop Turkey's coal industry should eventually not only meet domestic needs quite adequately but also provide a valuable surplus for export. Other important minerals, important in terms of Turkey's present economy, are iron ore, chrome, copper, antimony, lead, and zinc. The iron ore is used domestically, principally at the Karabük Iron and Steel Plant which we shall describe later. The chrome, on the other hand, is produced for export only. Turkey's other mineral production currently gives her little advantage in international trade because costs are so high, but her copper reserves may eventually become a significant factor in the available world total.

Although Turkey's frontiers from the northeast to the southeast are adjacent to major oil areas, until recently she had no proved reserves of her own. Recently, however, what is described as a substantial deposit of oil was confirmed at Ramandağ in southeastern Turkey, not far south of the railway which is being extended from Diyarbakïr on east to Bitlis. A small amount of oil is currently being produced at this place, but as yet no large-scale plans for development have been announced. The oil available here is said to resemble Mosul grade in its high asphalt content.

From all of this it appears that Turkey's mineral resources, although substantial, still give no basis for fanciful exaggerations of untold hidden mineral wealth, or any great encouragement to those who would argue that her best possibility would be to try to convert herself into a preponderantly industrial rather than an agricultural land.

5. INHABITANTS

The population which Turkey's predominantly agricultural economy supports numbers almost 20,000,000, the last census figures (of 1945) being 18,790,174 and the latest estimate (1948) 19,500,000.

The rate of annual increase has been calculated as high as 2 per cent. By and large, Turkey's population picture is thus encouraging. It is strong in that it is a comparatively young population. There are no important harmful imbalances between the sexes or the various age groups. Outward population pressure is not a problem and since, as we have seen, the country contains large areas of now empty but potentially productive dry-farming and grazing land, it is difficult to conceive of a time in the near future when Turkey's people, even should the present rate of population growth continue unchecked, will have a serious need for "living space" beyond their present frontiers. The demographer need not fear that population pressure will soon compel Turkey to falter in her present policy of irredentism.

No adequate overall study of the physical anthropology of today's Turks is yet available. The study of history, however, assures us that the basic population of Anatolia has "always" been what it impresses one as being today—a very complicated mixture. "Predominantly a combination of Alpine and Mediterranean" will do for a "racial" definition, if such definition is really needed at all. The Turks are definitely "white," although this has never seemed very important to them, and still does not except in the case of those few Turks who have lived abroad long enough to become aware that the folklore of western civilization holds the Turk to be a man of color. The Turks certainly are physically of most varied types. It is not very unusual to find light blonds as well as dark brunets, and even flaming red-heads, represented in a single family group, and eye color, too, has a comparable range. Most Turks are villagers whose mode of life forces them to acquire a heavy sun-tan, although even the most primitive peasants take quite complete precautionary measures against the sun's rays. A fair consensus of the opinion of Americans who have observed many Turks in many parts of the country would be that the people as a whole give the impression of being distinctly stocky—short and heavy set. This has been ascribed to diet, but from this one should not also infer that the traditional recent European concept of the Turk as "lazy" has any real foundation. Given the conditions of their climate and life, the Turks by and large are an impressively tough and vigorous people. Public health, urban and rural alike, is deplorable, and this despite the undoubted improvements which the Republic has made in this field. The most prevalent diseases include tuberculosis and rheumatic complaints, both of them abetted by the ordinary peasant practice of sleeping on the earth floor of the house, venereal disease, and also—as in St. Paul's time—malaria. Malaria, indeed, has practically depopulated parts of the country, and an adequate program of mosquito control is as essential as it is difficult to put into practice.

If we recall our characterization of the seven main regions of Turkey, we shall not be surprised that there are sharp differences in the sizes of the several regional populations. The Central Anatolian region exceeds 4,000,000. Behind it come the Black Sea, the Marmara, and the Aegean regions, each with a population in excess of 3,000,000. And finally the Mediterranean region, under 2,000,000; Eastern Anatolia, perhaps 2,500,000; and Southeast Anatolia, less than 1,000,000. Within each of these general regions, again, population distribution is most uneven, always clustering in the few relatively most fertile regions, coastal plains, river valleys, and well-watered plateau regions.

No single city reaches 1,000,000 (although "greater Istanbul" would almost top that figure, were all the suburban regions included), and only four cities are large enough to be called important metropolitan centers. They are: Istanbul, about 900,000; Ankara, about 250,000; Izmir, over 200,000; Adana, over 100,000.

Over three-fourths of Turkey's total population of course lives in truly rural areas, this term including towns up to 2000 population, nothing more than good-sized villages.

Traveler after traveler in Turkey, century after century, has been impressed with one feature of the country which is a constant almost wherever one goes, wasteland regions excepted, and that is that the landscape before him is a checkerboard of well-tended fields but that there is almost nowhere a trace of a human abode. This, of course, is because the rural population follows immemorably ancient practice in living almost exclusively in villages, while these villages are seldom on the main roads and not infrequently are entirely hidden from any road whatsoever. Village location is determined by a number of factors, one of the principal ones being the availability of water, a consideration which often places the town-site in a deep and hidden stream valley, a veritable canyon. To the western mind, building a village as far as possible away from the main route in a spot connected with trunk communications only by a miserable dirt-track which may leave the village mud-bound for half the year seems a flat negation of elementary considerations of convenience, particularly when it is realized that most of the village's cash-income for the year must derive from those surplus agricultural products which it can get to the main roads and thence to some larger market center. Equally likely to give the westerner a sense that inefficiency and inconvenience are being systematically courted and planned is the circumstance that these village farmers of Anatolia must daily, over their poor roads and with their primitive carts, make the roundtrip from dwelling to fields to dwelling, except for some short seasons of the year when the farm labor force (the farm family) may camp out, sleeping in the fields.

One's dismay at such arrangements, in reality, simply betrays how ignorant, as a non-Anatolian, one is of the pervading realities of the land. If we put ourselves as far as we can into the peasants' places, what seemed inconvenient becomes in fact the most convenient solution to an urgent and compelling problem, a solution which ages of pooled experience have taught the Anatolian folk. Admittedly, it is tiresome to live so far from the fields, but what does this amount to when compared with the benefits of mutual security and defense which village life gives, or to the peril from robbers which would haunt the peasant's nights if he and his family were in a remote farmhouse far from neighbors? Admittedly, too, it is inconvenient to live hours of slow and hard travel away from the main road, but what does this inconvenience signify when contrasted with the dangers to which a situation on the main road would have exposed the village during century after century while armies marched and foraged along that trunk route, and taxgatherers and king's messengers bearing authority to take all they wanted, and press-gangs for the army all passed ceaselessly back and forth? Another way to say this is simply that main-road conditions, over the centuries of Anatolian history, have usually tended to exterminate agricultural villages which were too close to the trunk routes. As for the consideration that the peasant cannot get his cash-crops to the main road easily, *we* may assume, but this does not mean that the peasant also assumes, that he labors primarily in order to produce a cash crop. In fact, he labors to feed and clothe himself and his family. Most of what his own toil does not produce, village industry makes for him. From that outside world whose representatives pass along the main road, he wants only such things as salt and sugar and coffee, and in these latter days gunpowder, a looking glass, and perhaps a pocket comb. More than a little extra cash may mean literally nothing to him, for he has developed few needs which cash purchases are necessary to satisfy.

Now it is absolutely true that the peasant's adjustment in all these points represents the most efficient and the most convenient adaptation possible, full allowance made for the pervasive degree of insecurity which for thousands of years has represented the all-pervasive norm shaping Anatolian farm life. It is also absolutely true that under the Turkish Republic this question of the norm of basic insecurity of the peasant's life has altered out of all recognition. Robbers no longer threaten him. Today's armies and taxgatherers are not even a pale reflection of what they used almost always to be. Individual security in rural Turkey compares favorably with that of the individual in Indiana or Montana today. But, and this is the catch, the peasant does not yet recognize this change. When will he recognize it? Once again, we collide head-on with Anatolian rural mentality, and are left with the question: How can the peasant be aroused from his traditional ways of life and thought? Or, as the western go-getter would phrase it, How can you wake him up?

Our insights into the peasant's ways of life and thought have equipped us also to make a fairer appraisal of the total physical plant, the equipment built by man's hands, which exists in Turkey today. The peasant's tools are, as we have seen, poor and primitive, with few exceptions. The same is true of his housing, perhaps of 80 per cent or more of the total dwellings which Turkey possesses today. Peasant dwelling styles vary sharply from locality to locality, the style depending principally on the type of construction material most easily available locally, but no matter what the style, most Anatolian peasant dwellings would be characterized by Americans as entirely subhuman. In the larger towns and cities, too, the overall situation is little better except on the very highest economic levels. Fully 90 per cent of Turkey's people today are dreadfully housed, by ordinary American standards.

6. TRANSPORTATION AND COMMUNICATIONS

In matters of transportation and of the system of communications, Turkey is at least better off than in housing, but here too much is to be desired. The peasants depend mostly upon carts and oxen or donkeys, a horse in the rural regions being a distinct luxury, principally because of the problem of feeding and sheltering horses during the winter. Turkey's roads have been a widely advertised bane of existence for generations, and although today the main roads are seldom impassable in good weather, and although some of these principal arteries are rapidly becoming used as all-weather highways, still no one can assert that Turkey's road system yet begins to approach minimum adequacy. Until the end of World War II, government policy under the Republic, largely based upon already outmoded European views, practically ignored road transportation in order to concentrate upon railroads. The goal has been twofold: first, to bring under government ownership and operation those several scattered and uncoördinated lines, foreign-built and foreign-owned, which were inherited from the Empire, and second, to build the minimum new lines necessary for a unified railroad system. Success has been problematical. At present there exist less than 8000 miles of railroad, all but a fraction of which is state-owned. All are single-track lines and almost all are standard gauge. Turkish Republican construction has been considerable, but is still far from having produced an adequate rail network, or indeed a true network or a real system in any recognized sense of these words. State-operation of the railroads also has not in practice proven to be the blessing which those who instituted it hoped it would be. The transportation picture thus is darkened by excessive freight costs and by poor service as well as by the fact that the construction and maintenance of roads—main highways and local feeder-roads alike—have been foregone in order to finance an inefficient and uneconomic railroad system.

Coastal shipping as well as some few overseas lines is in Turkish hands, almost entirely under state control and largely state-owned. Transportation by sea is perhaps more satisfactory and more efficiently conducted than that by land, but it still falls far short of a reasonable standard of minimum efficiency. Air communications are satisfactory. Radio is a government monopoly conducted in a fashion which provokes only a minimum of justified criticism. Telegraph service is fair. Telephone service is sparse and generally poor. The mail service is generally fair. Like transportation, and to even a greater degree than transportation, communications are an activity of the government.

When one considers communications and transportation as parts of the total functioning Turkish industrial plant of which they are integral parts, and then compares that plant with Turkey's agriculture and agricultural plant, the dual nature of Turkey today at once emerges. Agriculture, apart from those state farms which we have seen are practically meaningless in the sense that they have so little

influence upon peasant agriculture, is a time-honored primitive economy which carries the investigator in one jump almost to prehistoric
times. Transportation, in so far as it is non-peasant and so not primitive, and communications and industry, in distinction, are modern.
They are, if not up to date, at least of the nineteenth century. And
whether they are nineteenth-century or twentieth-century, they are
of the west—built on western models and employing western techniques. And this western-style plant itself is composed of two layers.
The first is the plant which was installed by imperialist Great Powers
during the latter decades of the Empire, to be taken over by the Republic and maintained in use until today. The second layer is what
the Republic itself has built.

7. ÉTATISM

The Republic's program of installing modern plant is summed up
in the general term "Étatism." It is an ambitious but amorphous program for state-owned and state-operated industrialization, having for
its goal the concept of a Turkey self-contained and self-sufficient in
terms of a twentieth-century industrial state. Progress made towards
this goal has been markedly disappointing, even to its most enthusiastic proponents. Moreover that progress, in so far as it really has been
"progress," has itself retarded or precluded what might have been
other forms of progress along other and more promising lines.
Specifically, Turkey's extremely costly and inefficient industrial plant
has had to be financed at the cost of precluding the improvement of
Turkey's agricultural economy. This, of course, is a circumstance of
which Étatism's critics make maximum capital.

Étatist accomplishments to date may be summarized as follows:
Thanks to efforts exerted by the Republic since the early 1930's, Turkey now has a small heavy industry, poorly designed and poorly operated, plus a relatively small scattering of light industries, most of
which are also poorly operated and designed. All this plant has been
erected and is maintained at an incredibly heavy cost to the ultimate
taxpayer, which is to say the peasant. Those few light industries
which do pay a profit—especially the textile mills—are deliberately
run at an excessive profit in order to help cover the losses of the other
state enterprises of Étatism.

It is easy indeed for the American critic to build up a telling indictment of Étatism and all its works. By attempting at once to produce

the eye-catching, specialized products of the contemporary west without first building up the mundane but indispensable foundations upon which such specialized industries must rest, the Turks have certainly tried to put cart before horse, and in some cases have simply tried to make a horse-cart run as if it were an airplane. Étatism has meant building from the top down a structure which American belief holds can rise only from the foundation up. By financing this venture from the sweat of the taxpayers' and the consumers' defenseless brows, Étatism has had the lion's share in keeping Turkey a consistently expensive country in which to live, and so in helping keep the standard of living of almost all of its inhabitants extremely low. Through Étatism, the Turkish Republic has also given its government bureaucracy optimum opportunity to expand, with unhappy results for all, including the bureaucrats themselves, for their own pay by no means meets the cost of life in Étatist Turkey. These are main headings in the usual indictment of Turkey's two-decade venture into state-constructed, owned, and operated enterprise, and there is no gainsaying any one of them. Not only is there no gainsaying these criticisms: their net result in Turkey has been finally to help oust in a free election the administration which had sponsored Étatism in favor of an administration which promises to change course, to bring government increasingly out of industry and industrialization in favor of private enterprise, domestic and foreign.

But there are still two sides to the Étatist coin. Even its most rabid critics cannot claim that Étatism's accomplishments to date, faulty as they are, would have been duplicated or even faintly approached had the government not taken the initiative in some such fashion as it did. It may very well be that Turkey's present industrial plant—preposterous as its imbalances and its heedlessness of the true needs of the country are—is still the best that Turkey could possibly have hoped to get during the last fifteen or so years; that she therefore is lucky to have at least what she does have, and extremely lucky, because now may come a logical time for private enterprise, local or foreign, at last to plunge into the waters which are open only because Étatism has broken the ice, and to begin to salvage Turkey's installed industrial plant for what may eventually become economically feasible operation.

Turkey's Étatist heavy industry, for example, consists essentially of only one plant, the Karabük steel plant, an installation whose location, design, and operation are all poor and even execrable from the

American economist's or steel man's point of view. To salvage this plant, transforming it into an economically feasible component of the national economy, may entail an expenditure equal to its initial cost. It might even entail transforming it into some other sort of factory, not a steel mill at all, and so be an admission that Turkey is not yet sufficiently evolved, economically and industrially, to need or to support her own steel industry. But even if this should be true, Karabük is not just a white elephant for Turkey today: it is also a direct challenge and an opportunity for tomorrow. By meeting the challenge squarely, Turkey could in one move both recoup her costs up to the present time and also demonstrate that an essential lesson has been profitably learned, and so was worth what it cost. Admittedly, this is a large order. It is entirely possible that Karabük may simply continue to produce small amounts of expensive steel of sorts which Turkey does not vitally need. In that case, the worst forebodings of Étatism's critics will have come true.

Industrialization under state auspices has been the Turkish Republic's nearest approach to failure and even to disaster, at home. But an approach to failure is not failure, any more than an approach to success is success. There is no overriding reason why Turkey's new administration, committed to rethink and reshape Étatism, cannot reshape and redeem Turkey's state-owned industrial plant so that in the long run its contribution to the nation will become a positive value. Granted, Turkey's industrial plant as it stands today is in many respects a woeful spectacle. But if one grants that, he may still also grant that, poor though it be, it is vastly better than nothing. And without Étatism, the most probable alternative would have been, practically speaking, nothing. Turkey at least has a small industrial elephant, white though it is. The sensible thing is neither to kill the beast nor to spend time berating its past keepers, but rather to doctor it into health and the proper elephant color. And this is of interest to us in the United States because Turkey is not only our associate in resistance to Russia, but also because she is more and more calling upon our services to help her doctor her several problems, the Étatist industrial plant included.

Thus it appears that although Turkey strikes the new-come observer as a big, empty, and barren land, he need not stay long to learn that it is not so empty that it does not contain many potentials and many problems. From the narrow standpoint which deals only with America's own interests and how Turkey can best serve them, it would be necessary first to assess those potentials and problems not only in themselves but also in comparison with those of Turkey's neighbors before we could attempt to answer the question "What is in Turkey for us?" Few Americans, however, are content with this supremely cold-blooded approach even in theory. And in practice, among the Americans who deal actively and directly with Turkey, it is almost impossible to find an individual for whom the question does not become "What can Turkey give us *and* what can we give Turkey?" This is certainly the sensible way to ask it, if only because what we can do for Turkey will, if done, thereby increase the value of what it is she can do for us. But there is also the question, What can we *not* do for Turkey, and the answer to this must be sought principally in the past, for we know that we cannot remake Turkey overnight, even if we wished to, and what has made Turkey what she is is her own past.

3. The Legacy of the Past

To say that the "Moslem Turks of Anatolia today are what history has made them" is not even a very helpful truism, and to add that Anatolia's history is uncommonly complex will not enable the reader to cut a Gordian knot. In fact, were we to try to consider the entire span of recorded history in this region, the first thing we should learn is that almost nobody ventures to talk about *all* Anatolian history as one coherent unit. There is entirely too much of it, and to master "the field" would require training and language skills wholly beyond one individual's powers. Such a paragon would have to deal with voluminous original materials from Hittite times, Homeric times, Achaemenid Persian, Hellenistic, Roman, Greek-Christian, and finally Turkish-Moslem times—and that list is still inadequate even to sketch the kaleidoscopic complexity of Anatolia's four thousand and more years of history.

1. THE PEASANT AND HISTORY

There is, however, another approach, for beneath the surface of complexity and discontinuity there is a massive substratum of continuity which we have already glimpsed, but which historians have sometimes missed, and that is the comparative changelessness which has persistently characterized Anatolian peasant life. Now the peasants have ordinarily been an almost entirely "mute mass" whose illiteracy made it impossible for them to leave many records of their own. At the same time their masters—the successive ruling peoples of the land—although they have changed frequently, and although one group has often been radically different from the preceding, have still tended to share at least one trait: they have all of them largely ignored, and even despised, the peasants. And this means that what Anatolian records have to tell us about the peasant majority of the land in the past is all too often only a mention in passing and of a very unsatisfactory nature.

One is not, of course, wholly in the dark. For instance, it is justifiable to assert that a great, and a very great, many of the most fundamental patterns and features of peasant life have tended to persist practically unchanged. Consider the structure and the role of the family-unit in the peasants' life, or the structure and the role of the village-unit. Consider the tools and techniques the peasant uses in agriculture or in village industry, the structure and the equipment of his abode and of the abodes of his animals, the materials and the style of his clothing, the elements of his diet, the remedies which he uses to treat the sick. It would be easy to make this list much longer, and every item on it would not only be important; it would fairly beg aloud for systematic study at the hands of the social scientist who, by recording and analyzing present reality, and thereby fixing a base-line against which historical and archaeological records of the peasant past could be projected, would open up what are now still obscure horizons for the study of Anatolia.

Even without such study we are able to assert that the relative absence of change characteristic of peasant life probably extends even to the question of the Anatolian peasant's basic stock, not to introduce the meaningless term "race," for we know that despite all ravages of man and nature, despite war, misgovernment, invasion, immigration, famine, disease, earthquake, and flood, still Anatolia's peasant population, far from ever having been "exterminated," has likely only seldom really been "decimated." It is certainly true that invasion and immigration have been recurring features in Anatolian history. But it is also true that the ordinary fate of those invaders and immigrants, most of them groups composed predominantly of males, has been assimilation into the peasantry, assimilation almost without trace. And there is to date no evidence leading one to assume that this assimilation, persistent and cumulative though it has been, has ever brought in enough "new blood" to work an overwhelming change in the base-stock of the Anatolian peasant.

Of course it pays to be careful to say that it is a *relative* absence of change, and not a *total* absence, which characterizes the Anatolian peasant in history. Some newly-come invaders or immigrants have managed not only to set up as masters of all or part of Anatolia, and so to become a new ruling group of the land, but have also contributed to its total culture elements from their own non-Anatolian cultures, elements which then gradually worked down through the pyramid of society, from the ruling group apex all the way to the very lowest peasant-stratum base. Perhaps the most important culture elements imported in this way have been language and religion. Meaningful examples of each of these are just under our noses when we compare the peasantry today with that of a thousand years ago. In A.D. 1000, Anatolia was, and had been for almost four hundred years, Christendom's single most effective bulwark against Islam, and at the same time also a bulwark of the Greek language against encroaching Arabic. Today Anatolia's population, more than three-fourths of it peasants, is around 98 per cent Moslem in religion and at least 90 per cent Turkish in mother tongue. These are unquestionably impressive changes, the one—Moslemization—a change in religion and the other—Turkification—a change in language, and there can be no doubt that each change has worked effectively upon the broad peasant-stratum of the population.

The real point is, however, that both these changes together still should not tempt us into speaking of a "transformation" of Anatolia's peasantry.

The language-switch from Greek (or from other languages) to Turkish has seemingly not significantly altered a single one of those basic patterns of peasant life which we enumerated above, and neither has the change from Christianity to Islam, except in certain comparatively secondary details. The plain truth is that Anatolian peasant Christianity in its day was best described as a folk-religion more or less thinly overlaid with a veneer of Christianity, while Anatolian peasant Islam today requires precisely the same sort of definition: a folk-religion more or less thinly overlaid with a veneer of Islam.

Admittedly, such descriptions are offensive, or at least untenable, to many devout and learned followers of either one of the great world-religions involved, but individuals of this type are *not* peasants. And of course once one leaves the peasant-strata and begins to ascend the social scale, then changes of religion (and changes of language) do become extremely significant in larger and larger areas of life. This sort of consideration, however, does not apply to our main point: that the overriding characteristic of the Anatolian peasant throughout history has been the relative changelessness of his total way of life, and that even in those areas of life where change has seemingly been most important, in religion and language, such change has in reality meant much less of a transformation than we, upon the basis of our own values and preconceptions, would tend to assume.

The bearing which this resistance to change characteristic of most of its inhabitants has upon modern Turkey is crystal clear. One may, if one wishes, say that the Turkish peasant today is still in the grip of "the tyranny of history," and so imply that he is virtually helpless to progress, however much progress might aid him. One may equally well take the directly opposite tack and say that the Anatolian peasant's resistance to change simply means that his time-tested way of life is the optimum possible accommodation to those long-term factors which govern human existence in Anatolia, and so imply that any sharp change in peasant life would actually only leave the peasant population less adequately adjusted to the environment in which it must survive. A 100 per cent acceptance of the "tyranny of history" approach is fallacious, for it underestimates the liberating force of the new factors which recent history has already focused upon the peasant, and a 100 per cent acceptance of the "optimum adjustment" approach is also fallacious, because it underestimates the dynamic force of the changes in the Anatolian environment which modern times have already made. The midde ground alone is safe, and even in taking it one is best advised to remember, above all, that this Anatolian peasant still tends to change only slowly, even under strong stimulus, while a deliberate attempt to encourage him to change, let alone to encourage him to change *rapidly,* is likely to produce only a high-point in human frustration in the would-be change-maker himself. To change the Anatolian peasant is as hard as pulling teeth, healthy teeth with solid roots going deep.

Now the fact that the Turkish peasant is distinctly change-resistant is certainly not news, nor does he basically differ in this from other peasants, oriental or not. But the further fact that Turkey's current ruling group has, for the last generation and more, been systematically striving to change that peasant, has been moving heaven and earth to change him, is news, and news which concerns us, the United States, today, for the good reason that we are now underwriting some of those attempts.

2. NON-PEASANT: RULING GROUP

When we Americans, individually or collectively, deal directly with Turks, those Turks are almost without exception *non*-peasants, men and women whose level of life is distinctly "above" the patterns of folk life, thought, religion, education, and manners which the peasant represents. Naturally, no value judgment is involved here. The non-peasant need not intrinsically be "better" than the peasant in any sense. The point is simply that he is *different,* and very different. For convenience, we may attempt to term these non-peasants of modern Turkey the "ruling group" or the "ruling class" or the "dominant minority," but any one of these terms is open to many objections. Each one is colored with some implication that the non-peasant segment of Turkey exploits the peasants, and of course the deliberate exploitation of a large group of comparatively helpless individuals by a smaller dominant group is not part of any generally accepted scheme of things as we wish they were. In point of fact, the non-peasant dominant minority of Turkey most definitely does exploit the peasants.

We already know that Turkey exists by virtue of a largely agricultural economy (the peasantry) which supports the total population (peasants and non-peasants), and supports the non-peasants on a far more comfortable level of life than the peasants themselves enjoy. But to infer from this that the non-peasants are deliberately exploiting the peasants, or are *only* exploiting them, is unjust. It is closer to the fact to say that the ruling group has, since the foundation of the Republic in 1923, been doing two separate things. The first it has done because it had to: it has kept the country going and in this sense has lived, basically, "off the peasant," precisely as earlier ruling groups have done. Obviously, there was no alternative to this. But the second thing which the ruling group has been doing since the foundation of the Republic it has done not because it had to but because it has chosen to, and that is to try to improve the status of the peasant, to educate him, modernize him, and even westernize him, to arouse him from his "lethargy," transform him from a member of a mute oriental peasant mass into a participating full citizen of a republic. We already know enough about what this entails to be surprised not at the fact that this modern Turkish effort to transform the peasant has, as yet, enjoyed only a modest measure of grass-roots success, but rather at the fact that it is being made at all.

Plain though the general difference between peasant and non-peasant in today's Turkey is, it is still impossible to draw any single line making a clear-cut differentiation between the two groups. Certain generalizations at least help. For example, ordinarily the non-peasant does not do heavy manual labor. Even in the most urbanized areas, this falls to men—and especially to women—whose life remains largely on the peasant level. Hence the paradox that the lower classes in the larger cities have still to be regarded basically as peasants. It is true that they also constitute a nascent proletariat, an emerging laboring class almost wholly peasant-derived, but that development is as yet so modest, not only in numbers but also in other aspects, that it is still best to say that the urban lowest class is, for most practical purposes, living a peasant-level life in urban surroundings, and remains relatively uninfluenced by those surroundings.

At any rate, the assertion that the non-peasant, the member of the dominant minority, ordinarily does no heavy manual labor, stands. In addition, he usually is literate, to a degree at least, although his womenfolk may be illiterate. Here again, the assumption which follows is that the peasant then is illiterate. This, however, is also no longer strictly true, although it again is generally true for most practical purposes, while those relatively few peasant-level individuals to whom the Republic's efforts have brought true literacy are thereby signalized as being either on their way out of the peasant strata to full status in a lower stratum of the ruling group, or else as being potential pioneers of still unforeseeable changes in peasant life.

The non-peasant ordinarily does not live in a farming community. If he does, he is there not as a farmer but as a trader or an entrepreneur or an official, in short, as an on-the-spot agent through whom the ruling class exploits the peasant. The chances are good indeed that such a non-peasant holds some sort of official job, some position which puts him under direct orders from Ankara, however modest the job itself may be, and so represents in Turkish terms the rough equivalent of a federal job in the United States. That so many of Turkey's dominant minority should be government employees is largely a heritage from the past. For centuries the Ottoman bureaucracy grew unpruned, ordinarily creating a new agency and a new cadre of personnel to meet a new need, and only seldom at the same time abolishing already extant and now obsolete government services and posts. This trend towards "big government" accelerated in the nineteenth century with Turkey's increasing endeavors to reshape herself somewhat along the lines of a European centralized state. With the end of the Empire, the Republic then literally inherited, and had to provide for, almost the entire rank and file of state employees from under the Sultan. In addition, the Republic's program of Étatism, which is to say its attempt to attain a measure of economic-nationalist self-sufficiency, had for one of its principal results a still further expansion of government with a consequent increase in the total number of state employees, so that in the end the typical ambition of a lycée (junior college) graduate in the Turkish Republic to date has been to land some sort of government job. It goes without saying that the total situation which accounts for the size and importance of Turkey's *memur* (official) class is far more complicated than any short sketch can indicate. But the essential fact remains: an astonishingly large number of Turkey's dominant minority is directly employed by the central government today.

If the chances are still high that a member of the ruling group is in government employ, they are higher yet that his father and his grandfathers before him were also, in their time, members of the same group. There is considerable mobility, upwards and downwards, *within* the ruling group. For individuals to qualify for status in it, whether by rising from the peasant strata or by coming into the Turkish fold from some non-Turkish group, is by no means uncommon, although such "naturalization" today is of course not to be compared with the centuries when an expanding Ottoman world-state was recruiting its ruling strata from sizable parts of three continents. But Turkey's ruling classes today are basically self-recruited, self-perpetuating.

Thus we can so far conclude that the dominant minority who have created the Turkish Republic, who in effect in many ways simply "are" Turkey today, and who certainly are the Turks with whom Americans and other foreigners have direct contact, are a class non-peasant, largely urban, largely literate, further distinguished by their practical monopoly of governmental jobs (of which there are a great many) and of the professions, a class by and large comprising the direct descendants of the entire ruling class of the later Ottoman state.

One obvious characteristic of the members in full standing of this group is that they are Turkish, and a second is that they are Moslems. Simple as these assertions sound, they too require amplification if we are really to understand Turkey today. For example, the scientific meaning of "Turk" is solely linguistic. It refers only to the Turkish languages, a relatively clear-cut, easily recognizable family of human speech. Therefore, whatever claims to the contrary enthusiasts may make, a "Turk" in the broadest sense, and in the only scientific sense, is simply a man whose native or preferred speech is Turkish. Turkish peoples are known to us through their own records from at least the seventh century A.D. on, and through records of their neighbors we know of Turkish peoples from much earlier than that. They have lived in many parts of central and northern Asia, and have migrated thence to widely remote regions. Different groups of them have lived, and still do live, on extremely disparate cultural levels, all the way from reindeer or horse nomads to settled farmers and then on to the potentates of Ottoman history and the dignitaries of Republican Ankara. Although we, with our western tradition, tend always to think of a Turk as a Moslem, and so by implication also give a religious qualification to the term "Turk," this is by no means accurate even today, and has been far less accurate in the past. To date sober study has failed to isolate one single trait, ethnic, cultural, or otherwise, which is essentially "Turkish" in the sense that it has been shared by *all* of the Turks of history, or even by a great many of those Turks, and has at the same time not also characterized demonstrably non-Turkish peoples living under comparable conditions—language alone excepted. Hence to say that the ruling group of Turkey today is "Turkish" means, most strictly speaking, nothing more than that their language is a Turkish speech, a trait which they share not only with the peasants of their own country but also with numerous groups in several other countries, notably in Iran, in Afghanistan, and in many regions of Russian Asia.

It is something relatively new in the world for the members of this Turkish ruling group in Anatolia to think of themselves as "Turkish." The process of Turkification, which is to say a compound of (1) the immigration of Turkish speakers into the country plus (2) the spread of the language among the existing population of the country, the role of point (1) having been numerically far less important than that of point (2), has been under way in Anatolia since at least the eleventh century A.D., and today has created a total population which we already know is about 90 per cent Turkish by mother tongue. It was, however, only in the last quarter of the nineteenth century that the Turkish-speaking ruling group of Anatolia came to contain any number of men who self-consciously thought of themselves as "Turks," and only in the twentieth century that this upper class has come to think of itself primarily as "Turkish." The explanation of that mystifying state of affairs—a state of affairs almost wholly veiled from us by the fact that our European ancestors for centuries blithely referred to "Turkey," "The Turkish Empire," and "The Turks" when the people of Anatolia themselves entertained no such concepts and used no such words—must be sought primarily in the classical Moslem tradition which entered Anatolia with the Turks and which dominated there until only yesterday.

The Ottoman Empire was the last great Moslem world-state and the last great Near Eastern dynastic state produced by history. Like its many and ancient predecessors, it was a congeries of peoples, religions, and tongues, and in each of these phenomena it exhibited a range of variety which is almost incredible to the modern western mind. The prime factor which governed an individual's status in the system was not his language, not his social level (provided only that he was a non-peasant), and certainly not his "nationality" in our sense of that term, but was rather his *religion*, or more accurately—his sect. Each officially recognized sect had its own organization (*millet*). Every millet antedated the Ottoman dynasty. The individual's basic personal loyalties remained largely centered in his own millet. Especially among the large subjected (non-Moslem) millets, loyalty to the Sultan and his state was primarily corporate rather than personal and was ordinarily expressed by and through the millet-unit. No feature of the entire system seems more odd today than the degree to which these millets, spread thin as each one was over practically the whole Empire, still remained virtually so many closed corporations, closed socially and closed intellectually as well.

Ultimate power resided, of course, only in the Sultan's own people, "the people of Mohammad," the Moslem millet. But this millet never, in practice, included the entire, Empire-wide Moslem community. Moslem peasants were denied full status in it by the very fact of their being peasants. As for the total of its non-peasant Moslem subjects, the Ottoman Empire came no closer to realizing the ideal universal brotherhood of all Moslems than had earlier Moslem world-states. There were further qualifications. For full status as a first-class Ottoman, a member of the true Ottoman ruling group, one had not only to meet the religious qualification—Orthodox Islam—one had also to be a true Ottoman culturally. And the hard and fast qualifications for full status, culturally speaking, were two: (1) to use *Ottoman* Turkish speech, and (2) publicly to conform to the conventional manners and customs of which that speech was the vehicle.

We have already seen how simply to be a Turkish-speaking Moslem was not enough, for it was only with the tardy emergence of

Turkish nationalism in the late nineteenth century that *any* true Ottomans began to think of themselves as Turks, a term which they hitherto had restricted to the contemned Moslem Turkish peasant. The true Ottomans were not simply Turks and not simply Moslems: they were an exclusive group set apart from all the rest of mankind by a complex of factors. Orthodox Moslems and subjects of the Sultan, they also both spoke Ottoman Turkish and shared, on some level above that of folk culture, in the late sub-variety of High Moslem civilization properly termed Ottoman Civilization.

Free entry into this true Ottoman group was always open to any individual who would establish conformity on all counts—religious, linguistic, and cultural. The Ottomans had their own formulation for this, recognizing as their fellow first-class citizens only those who (1) "served Faith and State" and who (2) also "knew the Ottoman way." These together were the only key to full naturalization into the true Ottoman group. And once one had gained that status one was in for life, for the true Ottomans were also a closed corporation in the sense that there was no exit. Once an Ottoman, always an Ottoman.

When we consider the nature of this Ottoman "layered" society and realize that the true Ottomans were the one group in the Empire who had the greatest vested interest in maintaining the *nonnational* status quo, we begin also to understand why it was that they for so long opposed nationalism in any form, not only the nationalisms of their various subject millets which eventually contributed so largely to the fragmentation of the Ottoman state, but also that very Turkish nationalism to which they themselves finally yielded. The ruling group of Turkey today is the direct and recent offspring of the late Ottoman ruling group, but it has repudiated its ancestor's state *in toto,* and has also repudiated much of its ancestor's Faith and Way. This repudiation, however, did not come about until that Faith, State, and Way, in their Ottoman synthesis, had proven completely bankrupt. When it did come about it consisted essentially of a jettisoning of what were now inadequate elements, techniques, concepts, and traditions, and of replacing them with elements, techniques, and concepts borrowed from the west.

3. WESTERNIZATION·

The first period of the history of the Turks in Asia Minor is called, after the most prominent dynasty of the time, that of the Seljuks of

Rūm (of "Rome," which was to say of "the Byzantine land"). During this time, from about 1071 to about 1300, Turkish invaders entered, bringing with them elements of Moslem culture, and the two vital processes of Turkification and Moslemization began to work, at first in only a portion of Anatolia but eventually throughout the entire country. Local frontiersmen elements were then to be found furthering these developments everywhere. Although these frontiersmen were Moslem and Turkish, they were not therefore also on the best of terms with the Seljuk central government, for that government by and large embodied the administrative and fiscal principles of High Islam, with tolerance of non-Moslem millets and also with a highly Persianized court and high society, all things for which the frontiersmen had little use. The Anatolian Seljuk dynasty eventually dwindled into helplessness while a collection of local rulers, most of them of the Moslem Turkish frontiersmen-type, speedily carved out for themselves small principalities, or *beyliks* (from the Turkish *bey,* "prince," or "chief"), of which the most important was destined to be that of Osman Bey, eponymous founder of the Ottoman (Turkish, *Osmanlī*) dynasty. The first ten members of Osman's line were, without serious exception, men of unusual force and ability. Under them the state grew from an insignificant principality, whose capital was located first at Bursa in northwestern Asia Minor and then as the center of gravity shifted with ever-increasing conquests at Edirne (Adrianople) in Thrace, to become finally an Empire with its capital at Constantinople, which the Turks called by its ordinary Greek name, Istanbul, an Empire which included (in addition to its heartland, Asia Minor) the Balkans, territory to the north of the Danube, most of the Black Sea hinterland, almost all of the Arab world, and the islands of the Eastern Mediterranean as well. This state was, beyond question, the last great champion of Islam against Christendom, and its successes in gaining Christian territories for the Moslem world are self-evident.

For almost four hundred years, from about 1300 to 1683, in its many dealings with European powers, the Ottoman state enjoyed remarkable and sustained success. It was frequently stopped by Europe; it suffered many temporary setbacks at European hands; but once it had formally consolidated an important European territory into its system, it was almost never obliged to relinquish it. During these four hundred years this state naturally underwent great changes internally. From its period of greatest vigor (under the seventh Sultan, Mehmed II, 1452–1481, the conqueror of Constantinople) it progressed to its period of greatest grandeur (under the tenth Sultan, Suleiman the Magnificent, 1520–1566) and then, although still expanding territorially, moved into a time of weak and bad government from which it was only temporarily lifted by the Köprülü family of Grand Vizirs (second half of the seventeenth century). The crowning result of the Köprülü restoration was that it enabled the Ottoman Empire once more, in 1683, to undertake a full-scale siege of the city of Vienna, its major European enemy's principal stronghold. That siege failed, and its date, as we have noted, became a high-water mark in Ottoman history. After 1683 the Ottomans' position against their European foes was completely reversed. Henceforth, despite gallant and stubborn resistance and despite many temporary successes, the Ottomans' fate in the long run was always to be forced to yield territory to one or another European foe. As we look back from our chronological vantage point, we can now safely say that with 1683 the Ottomans' traditional methods and techniques, the total Ottoman synthesis of Faith, State, and Way, had become no longer good to hold its own against its foes. It was not so much that the Ottomans had slipped back, but rather that Europe was changing, was rapidly becoming that new world which, strengthened by a profoundly effective industrial and economic revolution and increasingly motivated by such concepts of human destiny as liberty, fraternity, and equality, was eventually to confront the Ottomans with a foe who differed from them not only in *degree* of power, but also in *kind* of power, a Europe able to deliver its new power on schedule to even the most remote fields of war.

The Ottomans' fatal tardiness in gaining an adequate awareness of these changes in Europe is wholly understandable. They were totally imprisoned within the limitations of their own Faith, State, and Way, purblind within the total horizons of Islam—Islam the religion, Islam the state system, and Islam the civilization. They did not attribute the fact that Europe consistently was outclassing them to new developments in Europe, but rather to the deviations from their own ideal norm, the deviations from their romanticized concept of what Faith, State, and Way had been in the "good old days" of Sultan Suleiman, of which they themselves knew they were guilty. Hence they tried to defeat the European new by a return to the Ottoman old, with foreordained results. From being the terror of Europe, their state rapidly became its "Sick Man," although the phrase was not coined until later. Even so, the size and the deep roots of their system meant that the task of wearing it down was both costly and lengthy, another way of saying that the "Sick Man" was practically never *that* sick.

One reliable source of strength they found in the ceaseless rivalries of those imperialist European Great Powers who were competing for the booty to be had from the Ottoman state, for it frequently happened that some of the Great Powers were so opposed to another one of their number's gaining a particular share of the spoils that they resolved to leave a territory (at least nominally) in the Sultan's control "until circumstances should be more propitious." In addition, the question of who was to get what from the Sultan's domains, and this is an inelegant but accurate capsule-formulation of the nineteenth and early twentieth centuries' "Eastern Question," was infinitely complicated by the fact that the Ottomans' subjected millet-peoples had been able sooner to appreciate the advantages offered by many aspects of modern Europe than could the Ottomans, and even to attempt to avail themselves of those advantages.

At the top of the list of ideas borrowed from Europe by the Ottomans' Christian subjects was nationalism, the modern concept of a nation-state whose population would be homogeneous in language and in national feeling, and which would be independent and sovereign within its own frontiers: a concept as far removed as possible from the basic theory of the Ottoman state. As vociferous young Balkan would-be nation-states struggled to break away from the Sultan, they had no difficulty in gaining the support and "protection" of one or another Great Power sponsor, and so the "Eastern Question" became vastly complicated as the nineteenth century wore on. More and more, the Great Powers were obliged to content themselves with imperialist gains disguised as the "protection" of some small, young state, a state whose subsequent gratitude towards its "protector" was problematical, to say the least.

The true Ottomans, for their part, had finally had the new European reality thrust squarely and unmistakably under their noses with Napoleon's occupation of Egypt (1798–99), and had responded to it by at last beginning themselves to attempt to borrow from Europe in their turn. They were practically in the position of suddenly encountering, head-on and for the first time, a complicated and highly efficient machine of which they knew nothing but which they must rapidly make their own if they were to survive. And their first re-

action was, in effect, to attempt to take over themselves and use *only*
the cutting edge of the machine. This was not only due to an initial
failure to appreciate that one had to have the whole contraption, and
plus that also the training to operate it and service it and even to
construct a new and better machine, if one were to succeed in using
it at all; it was also due to the fact that only a small minority of the
true Ottomans was even now sufficiently aware of the nature of
modern Europe to concede that their own traditional system had been
hopelessly outclassed, and to take measures accordingly.

Those few true Ottomans who saw the position as it was had no
option except to become westernizers. The successive attempts which
they now began to make to introduce western techniques and concepts
into their world should be termed "westernization," and nothing else.
Our usual term for them is still "reforms," but that choice of label
simply reflects our own forefathers' placid conviction that their own
way (there is really no good reason why we should not say "their
own Faith, State, and Way") was morally superior to any other, a
conviction which the first half of the twentieth century has at least
shaken.

This is not, of course, to say that many of the Ottoman attempts
at westernization were not praiseworthy by our own usual standards.
They were. These men attempted to restyle the armed forces adequately, to provide the rudiments of a European-style education
where they would do the state the most good, to recast the entire
state more along the lines of a centralized European government, to
assure all its citizens at least a minimum of basic human rights, and
they finally reached the point of attempting to set up a limited constitutional monarchy with a parliamentary government.

Needless to say, most true Ottomans remained opposed to such
innovations, and abhorred the inroads upon the traditional system
which they involved. Needless to say, too, many of this type of
"reforms" were made, at least in part, with tongue in cheek and
often really only at the behest of one or another similarly insincere
European Great Power. Those of the Empire's peoples whose cultural level would have permitted such measures to be realized among
them were, by that very token, already themselves infected with new
nationalisms of their own, with ideas which were utterly incompatible
with Turkish rule in no matter what guise. And as for the rest of the
Sultan's subjects, they, as we know, were still living at a cultural
level which made the rapid application of such measures to them

little more than an unrealistic dream. Hence it was not in results achieved immediately that the nineteenth-century Ottoman westernizers found their final success. Their importance is, rather, that in their efforts they unconsciously prepared the way for twentieth-century Turkish nationalism's triumph.

We have already noted that the true Ottoman westernizers had a compelling interest vested in an essentially anti-nationalist system and were hence themselves perforce anti-nationalist. For a long time they tried to elaborate a nebulous concept which one might call simply "Ottomanism"—the idea that all of the Sultan's subjects should somehow be equal together (the subjected millets of course being supposed to forget their own inconvenient new nationalisms) and so dwell in one state happily ever afterward. But certain young Ottomans eventually espoused other and more "radical" ideas. One of these, Pan-Islam (its significance: Moslems of the world, unite!), could be of particular use to the Sultan in his role of self-proclaimed Caliph of the Moslem World, a role which he had seriously tried to exploit only when weakness as against Europe had overtaken the state; wherefore it had become diplomatically useful to contend that the Sultan had a "moral leadership" over, and certain rights to intervene on the behalf of, Moslem subjects of Christian rulers in somewhat the same way that the Pope or Christian rulers could "rightfully" speak in behalf of the Sultan's Christian subjects. In point of fact, these Pan-Islamic claims rested on little real or important foundation, for the total orthodox Moslem world at this time was never able in any telling respect either to react or to move as one coherent unit. Pan-Islam, despite grandiose claims made in its name, was really at base largely a diplomatic fiction. And the claims and implications of Pan-Islam were certainly hard indeed to reconcile with that other new idea of the common Ottomanism of all the Sultan's subjects, regardless of their religions.

Meantime, European studies of the Turks of central Asia and of allied subjects had provided facts which could serve as fuel for yet another new concept which was beginning to gain headway among some true Ottoman intellectuals during the last quarter of the nineteenth century and which increasingly flourished in the earlier twentieth century. This was the idea of Turkism. In its fullest or extremist form, Pan-Turkism, it held, as we have seen, that all the Turks of the world ought of right to form one sovereign people (naturally under the rule of the Ottomans). Obviously such doctrine was political dynamite on the international scene, if only because so many Turkish-speaking peoples were (and are) subjects of Russia in her Asiatic empire. Sultan Abdul-Hamid II (1876–1909), a ruler irrevocably opposed to most forms of westernization and who in effect did succeed by repression in holding back the hands of the clock for an appreciable time, was fully aware that Turkism of this sort could cause him only trouble, nor could he, as a good Ottoman, approve either of a more restricted form of Turkism which would have been content to regard all of his own Turkish-speaking subjects as themselves constituting a sovereign and exclusive nation, for such ideas were diametrically opposed to the whole system of government which he upheld.

Abdul-Hamid's methods were simply to repress and if possible to liquidate any and all westernizing elements upon which he could get his hands. These elements notoriously included the Armenians, an unfortunate people who, unlike other nascent nationalist groups of the Ottoman state, had available no Balkan territory which could serve as a geographical nucleus for their own state-to-be, but who instead dwelt largely in Anatolia and so were at the Sultan's and the anti-westernizing true Ottomans'—and the peasants'—mercy. One westernizing element which even the Sultan could not, however, seal off from disturbingly dynamic contact with the west was the officer corps of his own armed forces. This corps, since the beginnings of the westernization of the Ottoman army in the early nineteenth century, had evolved and maintained an admirable spirit. Its more able younger members had been given access to what was certainly the most realistically westernizing education available to any part of the true Ottoman group, and the preoccupations of an active military career naturally involved other illuminating, and even sustained, first-hand contacts with the west.

When younger officers of this type decided to join forces with westernizing true Ottoman civilian intellectuals and with certain "minority" (millet) leaders of a like mind, Abdul-Hamid's day was done. Consequent to the Young Turk Revolution (1908), the Sultan was thus obliged to reinstate the Constitution which he had proclaimed and then promptly suspended early in his reign, and the Ottoman state set out to become once more a limited, parliamentary monarchy. Within the year Abdul-Hamid and a collection of Ottoman reactionaries tried again to dam the stream of westernization, but it had grown to dimensions beyond the control of any power to stop, and the Sultan was deposed.

The Young Turk government then speedily disappointed almost all concerned. Ideologically, the incoherence of its program reflected the imperfect and shallow-rooted nature of westernization as it had so far worked among the ordinary westernizing true Ottomans of the day. That program contained elements of Ottomanism, but added to them the incompatible idea of Pan-Islam, a measure of Pan-Turkism, plus a historical residue of the idea of "Turkish" (Ottoman) superiority within the Empire. In international affairs, too, the Young Turks were unfortunate, the empire becoming the object of almost continual aggression on the part of several European states. All things considered, it is not surprising that the Young Turks' government quickly degenerated into a virtual party-dictatorship whose methods alienated many of their former supporters. Nor, since a dominant element in this dictatorship's mentality was the conviction that the Ottoman Empire should demean itself as a Great Power—which it still was in size but no longer was in developed power-resources—is it surprising that under this government the Ottoman Empire hastily and even precipitately entered the first World War on the side of the Central Powers.

Probably the decisive factor in this development was Turkey's attitude towards Russia, a consideration which was and is so important that it merits separate treatment. During earlier Ottoman history, relations with Moscow had tended to flow through the intermediary of the Ottomans' vassal Tatar Khan of the Crimea. This circumstance, plus the preoccupation of the Ottomans with their time-honored foes in western Europe, in part explains why it was that they so long remained unaware of Russia's own program of westernization and even of her general growth in strength. The Great Power contenders in the Eastern Question upon whom Ottoman eyes were principally fixed had been (1) Austria-Hungary which, like Russia, was principally involved in that question "by land" and therefore looked forward to out-and-out territorial annexations, (2) France, whose interests included a sharp awareness of her own cultural prestige in the Middle East, and (3) Great Britain, while Russia did not figure prominently upon that list. Nevertheless, as time went on it became clear to the Ottomans that the principal Great Power beneficiary of their weakness was none other than Russia, not only in her direct gains but also in the indirect gains which accrued to her as sponsor of Balkan would-be nations. To this we should add the long list of Russian wars with the Ottomans, each one of which Constantinople regarded as an unprovoked aggression, and also the fact that much of this fighting, especially on the Caucasus frontier where the Russians sometimes also appeared as pro tempore champions of Armenian nationalism, was of an exceptionally fierce and cruel nature, including much needless suffering imposed upon the civilian populations. Russia's posture as the successor to Byzantium in leadership of the Orthodox world also greatly irritated the Ottomans, and served to call forth the ultimate in Christian-Moslem hatred.

The sum total of this is that a deep hatred of Russia has been growing among the Moslem population of Anatolia not only for decades, but even for centuries, and for many years has been one of the few deeply felt and constant attitudes shared implicitly by *all* normal Turks, from the lowest peasant-level on up to the chief of state himself. Turkish anti-Russianism is not in the first instance a rational attitude: it is an ingrained prejudice, fierce, blind, and proud. Turkish governments have frequently adopted an officially friendly attitude towards Russia, but this has, so to speak, never fooled the Turks themselves: instead, they have gone right on considering Russia their sworn enemy number one, and frightening their naughty children not with threats of the hobgoblin but with the admonition that "The Russians will get you." The Russians, for their part, certainly cannot be portrayed as anything but anti-Turk, and indeed feel real contempt and hatred for the Turks. But the centuries during which Turkey's anti-Russian prejudice waxed stronger and stronger, although they were centuries of almost uninterrupted disaster for Turkey, were a period of expansion and success for Russia, broadly speaking. In consequence, Russia's anti-Turkism, although strong, is not to be compared in its intensity with the Turks' anti-Russianism, for the latter has been a thorn driven ever deeper by recurring defeats.

It is unquestionable that this hatred of Russia—and one must say that the record goes far to justify the Turks in their attitude—contributed largely to the Turks' hasty entry into World War I on the side against Russia. Of course, more was involved than prejudice. The Turks, like everyone else who had been sufficiently concerned to follow affairs, had fully realized that the late nineteenth-century entry of Germany as a full-scale competitor into the Eastern Question

had so disturbed the principal western Great Powers previously concerned, England and France, that in the long run they were being
obliged to concede to Russia her minimum price, Constantinople
and the Straits, in order to keep her on their side as a make-weight
against Germany. This calculation, naturally, had wholly upset the
earlier nineteenth-century balance of interests under which the Turks
had been able to rest sure that England (and France) would never
willingly allow Russia to reach the Mediterranean under any circumstances.

Prejudice against Russia and all things Russian—communism included—is a major heritage of the past to Turkey today, and a heritage to all Turks, whatever their social level. We shall have reason to
return to this in more detail when we come to consider Turkey's
world-view today. For the present, however, we know—certainly not
"enough," but at least enough to permit us to proceed. We now have
some clear idea of what the older Ottoman past had contributed to
the true Ottoman of later times, and we also know in broad outline
how those later times had forced the then true Ottomans, with reluctance it is true, to attempt at least hesitant steps towards westernization, steps which at last created "the makings" of a viable Turkish
naionalism. But if the Turks of the later Ottoman Empire were to
make a real break with their past, were to embark upon wholehearted
westernization (whose concomitant was practically bound also to be
thorough-going nationalism), it would take a stimulus of the dimensions of an imperial disaster to set the process going and to overcome
the opposition which most true Ottomans still felt for large segments of what thorough-going westernization would imply. That imperial disaster materialized with the end of the first World War. The
Ottoman Empire had borne a heavy share in the hostilities, and particularly in the Gallipoli campaign had turned in an admirable account of itself, but at the end was left prostrate. Partial westernization had proven wholly inadequate. Means of transportation had
collapsed. Physical plant was exhausted and it was not in Ottoman
power to replace it. In terms of twentieth-century *power*, the Empire
had demonstrated that it was completely outclassed.

The Empire was at an end, vast territories were lost. Only a fraction of Anatolia and the Straits Area was to be left to the Sultan,
and that under foreign occupation and tutelage. The Young Turks
had failed and their leaders had fled. Europe now concluded that the
Sick Man had at last been put out of his misery, that the Turk had

been "driven from Europe," and that the Turk was in general done for. In this, however, Europe was only partly correct. What was dead was only the Ottoman Empire. The Turks remained. Turkish nationalism, in fact, was only now coming to birth, for it was only now freed of those Ottoman-style imperial responsibilities which had hitherto encased it.

From the Ottoman debris, the surviving ruling group was soon to make "Turkey for the Turks" a reality in the modern nation-state sense, and then having done this was also to embark upon the even more formidable task of creating enough truly *new* Turks to insure the future existence of this New Turkey. To the story of these events and of the remarkable man who led in them we now shall turn.

4. Atatürk's Turkey

1. TURKEY FOR THE TURKS

The months immediately following the armistice of Mudros (October 30, 1918), when the Ottoman government had acknowledged total defeat and withdrawn from the war, were a time of chaos unusual even in the Middle East. Divers Ottoman territories were occupied by the victorious Allied Powers, which even included a token detachment of United States forces, although we had not ourselves ever formally been at war with Turkey. Everywhere the recently subject peoples of the Sultan had high hopes, each believing that its particular would-be nationalism was now to be realized quickly. Responsible Turks, for their part, fully understood that the Empire was at last a thing of the past, or that at the very least the Sultan would now lose so much territory that his remaining "Turkey" would approach the size it actually now is; some responsible Ottomans also felt and said that this would be a blessing in disguise, for they argued that relief from the burdens of a moribund Empire would more than make up for its loss. On the other hand, scarcely any Turks—or, for that matter, anyone anywhere—also realized how nebulous and chaotic the Allies' plans for dealing with Turkey were. One tangible fact soon emerged from the welter: the Turks, in contrast to almost any other people of the Middle East and of the Balkans, now had practically no friends at all. Even so, Turkey remained passive, passive not only under occupation but also under the realization that the old Empire's own heart-land, Anatolia and the Straits Area, would be not only under Allied occupation (which of course was only to be expected) but would also be so parceled out into new states or zones of influence and protection that the Sultan's government would, in the end, retain only a token sovereignty over one small section of

Anatolia. Here was truly a bitter potion, but it came at the hands of victorious Great Powers, and it was to be swallowed.

There was still one thing the Allies could do to set passive Turkey aflame. That one thing they finally did. They sponsored a Greek invasion of western Anatolia. On May 14, 1919 Allied ships landed a Greek occupying force at Izmir (Smyrna). In so doing, the Allied Powers fully betrayed their basic ignorance of the foundation realities of the situation and of the area. What they were acting upon was the old, soft-headed philo-Hellene assumption that the Greeks were a "superior" and "European" people who could bring law, order, and light to the "barbarian Turk" and who could at the same time "redeem" at least those sections of western Anatolia which contained sizable Greek populations. Every item in that assumption was proven false in the next four years.

To the Turks, from the most humble peasant to the top of the upper class, this Greek invasion was the final straw. We have already glimpsed some of the factors which made this so. One increasingly clear-cut consequence of the impact of westernization upon Anatolia, since the earlier nineteenth century, had been that the hitherto largely voluntary and peaceful processes of Turkification and Moslemization had come to be imposed by force. The nineteenth century had riddled Anatolia with Armenian nationalism and Greek nationalism, two forces which were not only mutually irreconcilable but were also both flatly opposed to Turkish rule in any form. One sharp distinction can be drawn between the national aspirations of these two groups in Anatolia. Early in the nineteenth century, nationalist Greeks with much help from Europe had managed to set up, on ex-Ottoman soil, a sovereign nation-state. Thereafter Greek nationalism within the Ottoman Empire tended to take the form of underground support of the modern Greek "Great Idea," the idea of expanding that Greek State into a modern Byzantine Empire whose capital was to be at Constantinople and whose territory was to include, at the least, western Anatolia and Greece plus as much as possible of the rest of the Balkans and of Anatolia. Many responsible Ottoman Greeks had serious misgivings as to the wisdom of this idea. Many Anatolian peasant Greeks were living on so low a cultural level that they were comparatively immune to its blandishments. In consequence, during most of the nineteenth century at any rate, the Ottoman government was generally prone to regard Greek nationalism principally as a foreign foe, and only secondarily as a domestic peril.

With Armenian nationalism the case was quite the opposite. Nineteenth-century Armenian nationalism produced supporters as fanatic as did Greek, but they never were able to achieve any comparable success, any sovereign Armenian nation-state which, however small for the time being, still could give them status among the nations of the world for today and tangible hopes for tomorrow. Instead, this unfortunate people dwelt either under the Sultan or under the Tsar, neither of which powers was in any sense willing to give the least real satisfaction to Armenian claims, although the Armenians' and Russians' common Christianity (albeit of hostile sects) did sometimes enable the Tsar to appear in the guise of the Armenians' protector.

Much of American missionary activity in the Ottoman world, a movement which began in the earlier nineteenth century and thereafter expanded with great rapidity and success, was directed to the Armenians. One of its major results—perhaps one should instead say "major by-products," for it was certainly not an intentional result and it horrified those keen-sighted missionaries who understood the ultimate implications of what was going on—was to strengthen Armenian nationalist hopes, or (to put it from the point of view of the Turks) to help transform young Armenians into potential revolutionaries against the Ottoman state. As the years went past, more and more of Anatolia's still large non-Moslem population thus became at least potential rebels while the impact of westernization and especially of western nationalism worked relentlessly upon them. And it was the Anatolian Armenians who, beyond all others, came to be regarded as *the* revolutionaries *par excellence*. Only some of them merited this title, but events were moving too rapidly, and the region concerned was in every respect too backward, for careful distinctions of dispassionate judgment to be expected on the spot. History had transformed Anatolia into a tragic cockpit, a land inhabited by three mutually hostile parties, by three parties each of whom sensed that its eventual security could only be assured by obliterating the other two. No one has yet suggested any *practicable* way by which the forces leading to struggle could have been curbed, and few western critics have yet realized that those forces were, at base, themselves preponderantly *western* derived rather than local.

In this struggle, the Turks naturally held and eventually always maintained the upper hand. We ordinarily call the long series of events which by 1918 had resulted in the almost total excision of the Armenians from Anatolia "the Armenian massacres" and "the

Armenian· deportations." These terms are fully justified as they evoke a realization of the unrelieved tragedy which the Armenian Christian population of Turkey suffered under Abdul-Hamid II and the Young Turks. By nineteen-eighteen, this population had been almost totally liquidated: slain on the spot, or converted to the Moslem faith and assimilated (many Anatolian Armenians had already long been wholly Turkified in language), or expelled beyond the frontiers. At the time, the western world professed to be, and in many cases unfeignedly was, deeply shocked at these events. They retain the power to shock us even today, although they dwindle into a sort of melancholy insignificance when compared with more recent happenings among the "thoroughly civilized" peoples of Europe. At least one may recall that the excision of Anatolia's Armenians occurred in a milieu where the masses of people on both sides still lived on a low, frequently even on a primitive, cultural level.

Recounting this grim story simply as a series of "massacres" and "deportations" would, however, tell only part of the tale. What the Ottomans had to deal with was unquestionably a slow-burning rebellion. The Armenians' sufferings do not cancel out the facts that many of them were potential rebels against the state and that final disaster did not overtake them until when, during the first World War and with a Russian army deep within Turkey, many Moslem Turks finally became convinced that their Armenian "fellow-citizens" were serving as an active fifth column delivering them over to their greatest and most merciless foe. That conviction was doubtless greatly exaggerated, but it had enough basis in fact that one can only dismiss it if one is willing to argue that the Turks should not have moved to save themselves.

By 1918, with the definitive excision of the total Armenian Christian population from Anatolia and the Straits Area, except for a small and wholly insignificant enclave in Istanbul city, the hitherto largely peaceful processes of Turkification and Moslemization had been advanced in one great surge by the use of force. How else can one assess the final blame except to say that this was a tragic consequence of the impact of western European nationalism upon Anatolia? Had Turkification and Moslemization not been accelerated there by the use of force, there certainly would not today exist a Turkish Republic, a Republic owing its strength and stability in no small measure to the homogeneity of its population, a state which is now a valued associate of the United States.

What had happened to the Armenians enables us better to understand what was now to happen to the Greeks, and why it was "bound to happen," for it reminds us that this struggle for Anatolia had become a fight which could have only one winner. It was to be take all or lose all. From this point of view—a point of view which is no more hard-bitten than the facts of the case were themselves hard facts—the Greeks, by invading Anatolia on May 14, 1919, certainly "asked" for all they eventually got.

Word that the despised Greek millet had set hostile foot upon Anatolian soil swept through the population with a message which spoke clearly to every Moslem Turkish ear. Here at last was the ultimate, clear-cut challenge. By failure to respond to this challenge in any constructive or firm fashion, the Ottoman Sultanate and court sealed their final doom. The Turkish people, in contrast, responded as best they could. But their army was in the process of being disarmed and disbanded, the Allied sponsors of the Greek invasion were themselves in occupation of key areas and military installations throughout the country, the ruling group—although totally repudiating the leadership of the Young Turks—had as yet produced no effective leadership to face this new challenge, and the peasantry was helpless without leadership. The outlook for the Turkish people was not bright.

Local resistance materialized as the Greeks started inland. It was at once strengthened by the fact that the Greeks' conduct towards the Turks was marked by exactly the same sort of "atrocities" which had marked the Turks' conduct when the shoe was on the other foot. One should also add the same sort of atrocities which had marked the Armenians' conduct on those relatively few occasions when they, too, had enjoyed a free field. But the Turks still had a surprise in store for the world, for it was now their rare good fortune to produce, just when he was needed most, a man who, despite all his faults, proved himself a gifted, courageous leader and a leader as indomitable in peace as in war: a leader who was to lead his people not only to victory over the Greeks, but on into true nationhood, into national sovereignty over a real Turkey, "Turkey for the Turks," and then well along even more surprising roads. His name was Mustafa Kemal Pasha (eventually to be called Atatürk), and he was 38 years old when on May 19, 1919, five days after the Greek landing at Smyrna, he himself landed from an Istanbul ship at the Black Sea port of

Samsun and set about helping the Turks of Anatolia to help themselves.

Mustafa Kemal was born at Selanik (Salonica) in 1881, and so grew up in the very nerve-center of the perplexing Macedonian problem of the late-nineteenth-century Eastern Question. His father was a man of the lowest stratum of the "true Ottoman" group, a petty official who eventually lost his post and was reduced to entering trade. His mother was a peasant woman. When he was still a small boy, his father died. This meant not only that Mustafa's education was interrupted, but that he actually risked slipping down into the peasant class. His mother's determination, however, sent him back to Selanik where his father's family saw to it that his education continued. By passing a required examination he was able to enter the government's military secondary school (at the age of 12), and thenceforth his future was assured, if only he would do his work well, for it was a pillar of the later Ottoman system, as of the earlier, that the state should support and train able true Ottoman youths up to the level of their abilities—and in the military career this remained true even in the reign of Abdul-Hamid II.

Mustafa Kemal's school career was marked by his excellence (whence his by-name Kemal, "excellent") in his studies, and also by the fact that through his education he was fully exposed to the underground western ideas which young true Ottoman intellectuals of the time were constantly agitating. Possessed of great physical vigor, when he entered active duty he bestirred himself to exertions not overly common among Turkish officers of the time, and speedily made something of a name for himself among his professional peers. His "radical ideas," which is simply to say that he actively worked against Abdul-Hamid's reactionary repression, for a time threatened his career, but an "arrangement" was found which got him around these obstacles, and his professional future appeared bright. His role in the Young Turk revolution was active but relatively modest; he never figured prominently in the inner councils of the party. On the contrary, his relations with the party's leaders were poor, a fact which accounts for his having been eased into the Sofia military attaché's office at the close of the Balkan Wars. During the first World War, however, his ability was too great for professional jealousies to keep him down, and particularly at Gallipoli he shone with greater distinction than any other Turkish commander in the field. By the time World War I had ended, he had behind him a record of service on all of Turkey's fighting fronts, he had visited France (before the war) and Germany, and he had had wide experience of men and affairs. More important still, he was almost the only well-known Turkish military figure who had emerged from the war without having responsibility for serious military disaster coupled with his name.

Personally, he was in many senses a typical westernized true Ottoman figure. His westernization was perhaps more thoroughgoing than that of many of his contemporaries, although this is debatable. In fact, when one gets men of Kemal Pasha's generation, or younger men of this description, to talk confidentially about each other, a frequent charge is that "so-and-so really *knew* almost nothing about the west, whereas I . . ."—a line of argument in itself an illuminating side light upon the realities of the western impact upon the individual. However well-grounded Mustafa Kemal's conception of the west may or may not have been by 1919, there is no doubt that he was far more cynically disillusioned with the current version of the Ottoman Faith, State, and Way than was common among his fellows. Much of this is to be attributed to his own personality, which had a distinctly sardonic side, and also to his health. In his personal life he in no sense typified what well-bred people of his class regarded, and regard, as the best. He frequently typified the worst. His rudeness, the hectic and even libertine character of his life, and his incessant drinking, which contributed to the cause of his death, are all proverbial in Turkey, and are also matters of unquestioned fact. But to write about these things with any frankness, and indeed even to mention them publicly at all, is simply not done in Turkey today. Instead, this intensely human man, whose achievements are so truly all the greater for his failings, who was never so colorful and never more the leader than when taking his almost diabolical pleasure in flouting conventions which he despised, has been reduced from a full-sized human figure to the status of a myth—the farsighted, infallible stereotyped leader, as spotless and as lifeless as a marble bust.

Mustafa Kemal, then, was not so much a well-rounded epitome as an exaggerated embodiment of certain westernized true Ottoman characteristics of his day. Like that entire class he was a palimpsest on which the writing of the west might be large and clear but still was by no means so fully writ as to blot out the other writing of the inherited Ottoman past. And just as he was, he was ideally endowed to carve out a future and a destiny for himself and for his people. When ruthlessness was required, he was ruthless indeed. When circumstances required him to be politic or to dissemble, he excelled at these. His immediate goal when he landed at Samsun in 1919 was to rally the army officers' corps (many of whose numbers had already purposely been transferred to Anatolia) and through them to try and bring some measure of order to those local and diffuse resistance groups which were springing up in various regions. There was trouble everywhere: trouble in the east, where an autonomous Armenia, and a Georgia as well, were in somewhat tenuous existence; trouble in the southeast with the British in Iraq; in the south with the French and, further west, with the Italians; trouble on the Black Sea coast where a Greek "Pontic" state was aspired to, and so on—throughout the country.

The officers' corps did for the most part respond, and even responded with some alacrity, the principal difficulties here being with individuals who themselves aspired to leadership or at least to high commands in the nascent nationalist movement. Response from the civilian true Ottoman authorities scattered through Anatolia was less wholehearted and less ready, and the same was generally true of the professional men and the intellectuals, who were almost entirely centered in Allied-occupied Istanbul. It is no injustice to say that *widespread* support of the nationalist cause came from those people only after it began to show at least some prospects of success. And that, in view of the difficulties involved, naturally took time.

Mustafa Kemal Pasha presented himself as the would-be liberator of the Sultan, whom he portrayed (not entirely sincerely) as well-intentioned but deceived and helpless in the hands of a few traitorous advisers, all of them wholly under foreign control. Throughout these earlier stages of the nationalist movement, all of its leaders always took care to speak in terms of the ultimate good of Faith and State. Mustafa Kemal perforce tried to alienate no single important section of the true Ottoman group, but in so far as possible to combine its total force with that of the Moslem peasantry, the "whole people" to be under his personal leadership, a point which was made extremely plain from the very start. The movement soon took the formalized shape of a National Pact, uniting resistance groups in Thrace with those in Anatolia. Despite all the opposition which Istanbul authorities could offer to it, whether the Sultan's government or the Allied authorities, it quickly gained strength. It was armed and supplied by

the "confiscation" of all Ottoman war material upon which the nationalists could lay hands, and it eventually received a substantial
and even essential measure of aid from the Soviets, with whom the
nationalists gladly entered into treaty relations. The European powers who were committed to back the Greeks against this Turkish
nationalist movement now began to realize that they had bitten off
more than they could chew, at least more than they were willing to
try to chew in view of their perplexing preoccupations at home and
in other areas more vital to them than Turkey. Italy made a graceful
and rapid exit from the fray. France and England remained, but on
terms of mutual distrust, and in this case it was the British who
eventually accused the French of perfidy deeply dyed, for the French
finally came to an understanding with Mustafa Kemal Pasha's government while the British still favored support of the Greeks.

An effective nationalist provisional government was installed at
Ankara, then the railhead of the line from Istanbul, on April 23,
1920, just less than one year after Mustafa Kemal had landed at
Samsun. Its several attempts to capture a measure of control over
the Istanbul Ottoman government, and its participation in the elections for a parliament which was to sit in Istanbul were all unsatisfactory. It is fair to conclude these moves were actually more in the
nature of token attempts than otherwise, for the major effort of the
nationalists throughout these months was basically military: the ordering and the equipping of armed force sufficient to deal with the
non-Turkish armies then on Anatolian soil. In the east, the Armenian
situation was eventually resolved, in part by military action and in
part by treaty with the Soviets, who were busy making their own
arrangements on what became their side of the frontier. The main
foe was always the Greeks in the west. They had advanced to occupy
not only the Aegean coastal plains and the Marmara region, but also
up to and over the western lip of the Anatolian plateau where they
even threatened Ankara itself. Their advance, however, was really
less impressive than it seemed. In the essentials, in military action
and in civilian government, the Greeks were proving themselves ultimately incompetent, while the political situation in Greece, unstable
as ever, further crippled the efforts of their leaders and administrators
in Anatolia.

Mustafa Kemal's provisional parliamentary government in Ankara
meantime not only grew in military strength: as its relationship with
the Istanbul government steadily worsened, it also made it ever more

clear that Ankara regarded itself not as trustee even for the Ottoman dynasty, let alone the then "reigning" Sultan, but rather was speaking for the Turkish people, peasant and non-peasant, the Moslem Turks of Anatolia and Thrace. Ankara's power of course rested directly upon those peasants. They fed it and they bore arms for it, gladly active in a cause which they fully understood—namely, to get rid of the Greek invader of the homeland. Full-scale military operations, beginning with the summer of 1921 and ending with the capture of Izmir, September 9–11, 1922, gave the Turks uncontested control of almost all the territory which they were claiming for their state. The Greeks from Greece were literally driven into the sea, and a large number of the Ottoman Greeks of Anatolia shared their fate, this sad cavalcade of disillusioned humanity being ferried to Greece within the space of a few days. There they were eventually joined by the rest of the Greek Orthodox population of Turkey, the Greeks of Istanbul alone excepted, through the agency of the "exchange of populations" which figured in the final settlement made at the conclusion of the war.

It had been a vicious fight, a fight to the death in which whole populations were ultimately involved. Its outcome is symbolized not by the burning of Izmir, a final atrocity of which each party still accuses the other, but by the fact that the Greek population of Anatolia and Thrace was now, in its turn, as effectively excised therefrom as the Armenians had been in theirs. Once again, by force the Moslemization and Turkification of Anatolia had made a fundamental advance.

The best term for this Turkish-Greek war is not the Turkish Revolution, although this is often used; it is the Turkish War for Independence or, better still, the Turkish War for Sovereignty. Full sovereignty in a nation-state was exactly what the Turks gained, Turkey for the Turks at last, and a Turkey in which almost everyone now really was Turkish, in religion and in language: hence, if only the peasant–non-peasant gap could be closed, this now was a prospectively coherent nation-state which had already asserted self-determination of peoples within its own frontiers in a fashion President Wilson's fourteen points had not precisely foreseen. The question of what the *government* of new Turkey would be was something else. The answer which Mustafa Kemal and his aides gave to this question is what merits the term "The Turkish Revolution," not the preliminary war for sovereignty.

In that war, from almost the very start of the national resistance movement, Mustafa Kemal's chief military collaborator had been Ismet Pasha (later Inönü), a fellow-officer and associate from World War I days and a true Ottoman who, in his own way, had perhaps become as westernized as had Mustafa Kemal, but who had made that transition without suffering the almost total disillusionment with old values which overtook the other. Mustafa Kemal now deputized Ismet Pasha to head the nationalist delegation to the peace conference, this being in those now-distant days when peace conferences inevitably followed wars. Ismet most successfully acquitted himself of his charge. In the long-argued Treaty of Lausanne, he finally got recognition in substantially the form Turkey wanted it (July 24, 1923), and thereafter he served as Mustafa Kemal's right-hand man in the government of the state, being Prime Minister from 1925 to 1937, when he temporarily retired, and then returning as President of Turkey from Mustafa Kemal Atatürk's death in 1938 until he was dismissed from that office by the electorate in the elections of 1950.

Ismet Pasha's treaty of Lausanne was, generally speaking, satisfactory to all concerned, even to the Great Powers who had supported the Greeks against the Turks. Those Great Powers were now accustoming themselves to the fact that the Turks were not, as they had so generally supposed, oriental natives fit only to live on the colonial level under the higher cynicism of the mandate system, but were instead a nation which had risen from defeat to assert its identity and its right to a place in the sun against all comers. This is the sort of hard fact which spoke most eloquently on the international scene in the 1920's and which still does today. Since 1923 no responsible statesman anywhere has ventured far on the assumption that Turkey is not a sovereign state, or would not actively defend her sovereignty if attacked.

At Lausanne, Turkey on her part accepted boundaries about as they are today (the Sanjak of Alexandretta excepted), and relinquished all claims to the empire which she had lost. The Capitulations, a system of extraterritorial rights for European powers which had plagued the Ottoman Empire during its later centuries and whose abolition had been an ultimate ambition of every Ottoman reformer and patriot since the early nineteenth century, now went into the discard heap of imperialist measures which would no longer work. Henceforth foreigners living in Turkey were under Turkish law as Turks abroad were under foreign law. Turkish law, moreover, was itself to be "reformed," in some measure westernized. It was already clear, however, that the decision as to how it would be westernized now rested solely with the sovereign Turks themselves. Turkey's remaining minorities, the Greeks and Armenians of Istanbul and the Jews of Istanbul and Izmir, were to be guaranteed basic civic rights. The Straits Question, greatly simplified since the Imperial Russian government to which England and France had finally conceded Constantinople was no longer alive to attempt to collect on that promise, was amicably dealt with by the device of declaring the area a demilitarized zone under international supervision but Turkish sovereignty, passage to be open to ships of all nations in time of peace and also in time of war so long as Turkey remained neutral. Should Turkey become a belligerent, she was to close the straits only to her foes and not to neutral shipping. This arrangement was scarcely ideal from the Turks' point of view, but it was as good as they could get and it had the advantage of being workable. They kept it faithfully until 1936 when Italy's policy in the eastern Mediterranean, and especially the Ethiopian crisis, had not only brought the Turks to begin serious armament preparations, but had also led other signatories of the Lausanne treaty to the conviction that the demilitarized Straits regime should be altered. Accordingly on April 11, 1936 the Lausanne signatories were petitioned to consider a revision, and on July 20 of that year, in the Montreux Convention, this request was approved, with Italy abstaining from the vote. The Straits then reverted to full Turkish control and were fortified. This entire Montreux chapter deserves citation as another example of the Turks' astuteness and steadiness in internal affairs and perhaps also as proof that in such matters virtue can sometimes be more than its own reward.

In addition to the Treaty of Lausanne, there had also been signed a separate Greek-Turkish agreement providing for the compulsory exchange of populations. The system devised was eventually extended to include more than Greece. For Turkey, it meant that her territory was finally cleared of inhabitants whose language or religion had become gauges of at least potential loyalty to some other nation-state, the Greek and Armenian populations of Istanbul alone excepted, for the people of this sort now all left. They were only partly replaced by Moslem Turks who had hitherto been subjects of Greece, Bulgaria, and so on. To the American reader, comfortably unaware of the pitch to which nationalist tensions rise in this region, the spectacle of large numbers of people painfully being sorted out and relocated in this way, in a sort of hectic international game of musical chairs, is most dismaying, especially as one appreciates the human suffering and sadness involved in plucking simple people from their traditional homes and possessions, and plumping them down in what is still a strange land, for all that it also "should be" their "own land," in habitations and at work unfamiliar and uncongenial to them. Yet, in a broader view it may be that these Draconian measures save much more misery in the long run than they cause at the time. The exchange of populations marked a near-final stage in the forcible execution in Turkey of the centuries-old, and formerly largely voluntary, processes of Turkification and Moslemization; it marked an acknowledgment that the old Moslem millet system of a layered society had become unworkable; and it represented a tenable solution for problems which this had caused. Turkey emerged from this long ordeal, through which she had attained a homogeneous population, on many counts poorer. For one thing, she had suffered a sizable net loss of population—how large it is impossible to say, for it occurred before even approximately accurate statistics were available for this area, but certainly a loss to be reckoned in millions. More important, what she lost was largely a class of relatively skilled farmers (compared with the peasants she received in exchange) plus almost the whole of Anatolia's small-town artisans and craftsmen and tradesmen. Her loss was thus a severe economic and social setback in many respects. There are Turks aware of this, but they can still contend that nevertheless the net gain represented in getting the population-uniformity essential for a viable nation-state overweighs all other considerations. As for the western observer, he may properly regret that the trend of history should be such as to make such an assertion true, but he can scarcely hold that it is not true, unless for some reason he opts to argue that the Turks should not have tried to survive as a nation.

So, by 1923, the result of the first World War and of the action-packed years which followed it was, for the Ottoman Empire, death, and for the Turks, life in a new, comparatively small nation-state which they had themselves erected, by force and by diplomatic skill, in the face of heavy odds and with little sympathy or help from any effective non-Turkish power aside from such aid as was given them by Soviet Russia. *Turkey for the Turks* was a reality. The war for national sovereignty was at an astonishingly successful end.

It is at this point that the real measure of Turkey's great good fortune in possessing the leaders she did begins to emerge. Her leaders now had the energy and the vision not to relax, not to regard their success as an end in itself, but only as an essential step towards the real end. *Turkey for the Turks* as it now stood would have poor chances of survival in the turbulent twentieth century, and they knew that. What was needed was nothing less than a truly *new* Turkey, new because its inhabitants would be new-style Turks. July 24, 1923, the date of the Treaty of Lausanne, marked the attainment only of the goal *Turkey for the Turks*. Three months later, with the proclamation of the Turkish Republic, October 29, 1923, came a more important date, for this date, Turkey's independence day, marked the formal starting point of the real Turkish Revolution; the systematic attempt quickly to evoke enough New Turks to ensure New Turkey's continuing survival.

2. NEW TURKS FOR A NEW TURKEY

Mustafa Kemal's raw material as of October 29, 1923 is familiar to us in general outline. It included the remaining "true Ottoman" class, perhaps 15 per cent or a bit more of the total population, and the peasants. Non-Moslem minorities were of trivial significance, numerically and otherwise. Westernization had made only the most tenuous and tentative progress among the peasants. During the nineteenth century they had made general acquaintance with the coal-oil lamp, and quite ordinarily used it in their houses; some of the more prosperous of them had western style heating-stoves, but this was relatively rare; and the western-produced looking glass was in nation-wide use. These, however, were mere trinkets when compared with what a total direct impact of the west upon the peasant might produce. And to date, little more than trinkets were evident. The growth of an effective self-conscious Turkish nationalism among illiterate people at this cultural level was clearly almost impossible. If such a development was to come, it could not be expected to come from the grassroots up, but would have to be evoked and imposed from the top down.

The ruling group, in contrast, was already quite extensively westernized, but a great deal of that westernization was also made up of fundamentally trivial details and trinkets. It was often more in the nature of a thin veneer laid over the living heritage from the past than it was a vigorous, self-perpetuating organism. In area after area of life, those individuals who were approaching the west were still obliged to deal only or largely with the *letter* of the west, while the *spirit* behind that letter still largely eluded them. Differences between one westernized individual and the next were exceedingly great. Each such man, it is true, was a sort of cultural palimpsest, but there the likenesses between them were likely to end. In the case of some men, of whom Mustafa Kemal Pasha may serve as the type, contact with the new and partial adoption of it had involved disillusionment with and finally contempt for most of the old. In the case of others, admiration for and adoption of the new had not also impaired respect for older values, and this type of westernized Turk sought in life a satisfactory synthesis of what he could consider the best of two worlds. Neither of these types, however, could fairly be held to represent majority opinion among the ruling group of 1923. They were leading that opinion, but personally they were far in advance of it. That opinion was to be found rather in individuals whose westernization was not only more tentative but also far more unwilling, a westernization which was in many cases and in many respects in fact *most* unwillingly accepted, and accepted at all only because the traditional patterns and concepts of the older Faith, State, and Way offered no possible alternatives which could seriously be regarded as feasible.

Thus the attempt to evoke and raise up enough truly new style Turks, enough thoroughly westernized Turks, to make a truly New Turkey viable had to begin with the ruling group itself rather than with the peasants. It was not only that large-scale and deep-seated changes in the peasants were practically impossible. Quite beyond that there was the consideration that only an upper class itself united in effective westernization and determined eventually to bridge the gap with the peasantry could hope for success in what would be a nationwide Operation Bootstraps.

So, to begin, Mustafa Kemal aimed his Operation Bootstraps principally at the partially westernized ruling group inherited from the Empire, for it was the only ready material with which he had to work. His program is best described as wholesale, forced-draft, compulsory westernization-plus-nationalism, aimed in the first instance at the upper class and secondarily at the peasant, and designed to produce as quickly as possible a Turkish state and nation which would have not only the several kinds of strength necessary to survive, but which would also have the blessings of western civilization, such as this new Turkey's young leaders conceived those blessings to be.

Step one concerned the form of government. As successes had enabled the leaders of the nationalist cause more and more to forsake sophistry in favor of open propaganda for the future which they ever more clearly discerned, it had become increasingly plain that victory for the Ankara regime might well entail the end of the Ottoman dynasty. The point was not pressed. Despite all his ruthlessness, Mustafa Kemal seldom ventured to rouse serious opposition until the need for action was fully at hand, and then he regularly took care to see one major move through to success before opening another one. And in 1923 there is no doubt that the majority of the ruling class—but not its nationalist leaders—was still generally loyal to the dynasty. A show-down came on the 14th of October, 1923 when Kemal Pasha, with his indomitable personal methods, forced through the reluctant provisional assembly the measure which made Ankara the permanent capital of the Turkish state. This was a move full of implications. Ankara had been well enough for wartime headquarters, but it was nothing but a miserable Anatolian provincial town, devoid of almost all comforts of life, scorched in the summers and frozen in the winters of the plateau's severe climate, treeless, sewerless, without modern buildings, and all the rest. To stay there, deliberately forsaking the inviting comforts of metropolitan and Levantine (that is to say, non-national) Constantinople with its palaces and mosques and countless Ottoman monuments and associations, and also with its capitulations-geared economy and its millet-system geared society, this was really to burn one's bridges with a public declaration that the nationalists' reiterated claim to stand for the Turkish people, for the nation in whom alone sovereignty and government should rest, was not a mere slogan but was the principle upon which the government now would act in most un-Ottoman fashion. And Mustafa Kemal Pasha had his way. Ankara remained the capital. Before the month was out, the sequel came. On October 29, 1923 the Turkish state was proclaimed a Republic whose power and sovereignty were theoretically vested in the entire citizenry, to be exercised by means of a unicameral legislature, the Grand National Assembly, which was to be responsible only to the electorate. From its own membership the legislature was to choose a President to serve as Chief of State for a four-year term, this being the life of the Assembly as well. The President was then to designate a member of the Assembly as Prime Minister, and the

Prime Minister to choose his Cabinet from among the Deputies, the Cabinet and Prime Minister serving only as long as they commanded majority support in the Assembly. In addition, the Assembly was to elect its own presiding officers. Special provision was to be made for an independent judiciary. This system, whose several European inspirations are obvious even from a short sketch, has remained largely unaltered until the date of this writing, although changes in it are currently being proposed.

Why was it that Mustafa Kemal and his associates chose a republican form of government? The assertion that they simply and more or less slavishly imitated western models, in so far as they understood them, is a facile and unjust oversimplification. Any attempt to treat any phase of westernization in any area of the Orient simply as a slavish imitation of the west is bound to produce only a lifeless caricature of reality. Of course, the factor of imitation is always present in the westernizing individual's mind, but it is seldom itself dominant. Instead the real and complex motivation is frequently so preponderantly patriotic or idealistic or crusading that the western ideas which the westernizer strives to introduce into his own milieu thereby become important to him simply as "his own," and certainly are his own in fundamental senses. So, in the cases of Turkish nationalism and of Turkey's westernization, the western critic whose principal goal is to tabulate specific western origins and specific paths of entrance of western influence, as important in themselves, is really going down a blind alley. That elements in Turkish nationalism derive from late-nineteenth-century French fiction, as has been argued, may very well be true, but it is not very important. Turkish nationalism is important in direct ratio to two sums: (1) the sum of the people who embrace it, and (2) the sum total intensity with which they embrace it. And these things depend not upon the pedigree of that nationalism, but upon living Turks themselves.

Turkey's republican form of government, despite vicissitudes, has enjoyed ever-increasing popular support. This is one of the most important points there is to make. There were many imperfections in the republican machinery at the start, and not all of them have been worked out to date; but the idea of a republic and the active participation of the citizenry in the conduct of the Republic have increased in esteem, in esteem-put-into-action, almost steadily since 1923.

At the start, the Republic's constitution was still a compromise with the Ottoman past. It provided for the abolition of the Sultanate,

but not that of the Caliphate, and hence for only a partial dethrone-
ment of the dynasty. Thus it left the old "Faith" partly intact, not
the *faith* of Islam in the sense of a personal religion, for of course
every citizen was legally at liberty privately to profess or abstain
from professing any religion he chose, although social pressure still
required him to be nominally a Moslem if he were to enjoy real, as
contrasted to technical and legal, status as a full citizen of the state:
the old Faith which was left partially intact was a remnant of the
Ottomans' Moslem ruling institution—the Caliph in his somewhat
nebulous role as titular head of the Moslem world, the surviving
machinery of religio-legal courts administering traditional Koranic
jurisprudence, the religio-educational system with its large plant and
possessions and the entire system of Pious Endowments which had
been erected by devout true Ottomans over the centuries and which
ranged all the way from soup kitchens to the establishments of the
still relatively numerous and influential religious brotherhoods—the
dervish orders.

It was a step radical enough to abolish only the Sultanate, at first,
and to leave a member of the dynasty the shallow consolation of being
a Moslem Republic's Caliph; the constitution now stated that the
official religion of the state was Islam, but conditioned this with pro-
visos safeguarding the status of non-Moslem citizens, on paper. Such
a theocratic-republican compromise could not be anything except
short-lived. The potentially effective ruling-class opposition to
Mustafa Kemal, and the effective leadership which that opposition
might give the peasantry, were concentrated precisely in those High
Moslem vestigial institutions which clustered about the Caliphate
and the brotherhoods. These latter also, in their secret-society character, provided an ideal focus and opportunity for antirevolutionary
intrigue. Memories of how the Masonic order had been of use, in
just this way, to the Young Turks before 1908 were fresh in many
minds. Eventually, this entire High Moslem apparatus went by the
board. But not too soon. Mustafa Kemal knew how to time his
moves.

When he moved, the Caliphate was abolished and the Ottoman
dynasty exiled from the country, root, stock, and branch (1924).
The article naming Islam the state religion was eventually deleted
from the Constitution (1928), and the concept of *layikçilik,* laicism,
was henceforth a basic and a widely advertised principle of the state.
Henceforth there was legally no religious qualification for citizenship

or for the holding of office. On paper, discrimination against non-Moslems no longer existed in any form. Such a change as this could naturally not become effective overnight, nor is there any reason to suppose that the men who put it through also assumed that there would be a rapid change in fact. Here we have a good example of what was a basic technique. Mustafa Kemal would set up a western concept or a western-style institution as new Turkey's legal norm, and then encourage emergent new Turks to evolve in the direction of that paper norm, to "grow into their new shoes."

At the start, the total eligible electorate was by no means ready to exercise the franchise. Let alone the peasants, not even the ruling group had traditions wholly fitting them for this; but forms of an election were carried out. Mustafa Kemal organized his own party, ran it, picked its candidates, had them campaign (on a one-party ticket, for they ordinarily ran unopposed), and was unquestioned party-boss after his candidates were in. Certainly this made him a "dictator." But in the first half of the twentieth century, there were dictators *and* dictators. Once you grant that Mustafa Kemal and his associates had the long-term idealism to see in Turkey of 1923 the makings of what could eventually be a functioning republic, what other course was open? And is there any serious question but that they did have that vision? Atatürk himself worked to undermine his own "dictatorship." He died a relatively poor man, poverty-stricken for a chief of state in the eastern Mediterranean. İnönü, in his turn, then proceeded (or, as the cynical may say, was obliged) to make "democracy work" and did so well that he was voted out of office. These men and their associates truly indeed broke with their tradition as Ottomans. They speedily discarded all that they regarded as currently untenable in their own distinguished heritage. They did not set up a military state, although many of them were military men by profession.

This was long-term idealism hard to match anywhere, any time. But they also knew the present state of their people's affairs perfectly well, and they did not let short-range idealism emperil their long-range hopes. Attempts at a political opposition leading towards a multiparty system proved premature and were speedily forsaken. Vindictiveness on the personal level frequently marked Mustafa Kemal's decisions. But the long-range aim was true. Mustafa Kemal's legislature might be hand-picked and might serve as a rubber stamp, voting "unanimously" with monotonous regularity, but the total composition of that legislature probably was a more balanced representation of all possible vocal and responsible elements in the land than any conceivable system of truly free elections could possibly have achieved at the time. The last word in these matters is still to be said, but no one can blink the fact that in 1950 the electorate of the Turkish Republic, exercising a direct and (in so far as literacy permitted) a secret ballot, went to the polls in a strength of 87 per cent of the total voters registered and there in a landslide returned a new government. This was a bona fide democratic home-owned-and-operated election whose result included the unseating of a popular military figure from the presidency, whereupon the defeated party cheerfully yielded power and the new government at once took office and control. This is admittedly not the millennium, but it is certainly a closer approach to it than one finds elsewhere in the twentieth-century Middle East and Balkans. And it shows to what extent the 1923 hopes that Turkey could develop and grow until it could fill its new governmental form with solid fact were justified.

On the older people, the Operation Bootstraps program of forced-draft, wholesale, compulsory westernization-plus-nationalism could of course be only partially effective. Not so the younger generation. It was on them that the program concentrated, for them that the new forms were set forth as challenges to be met. Not that life was lived only on a plane of heady idealism. There was also the consideration that the mere possession of the forms itself dulled foreign criticism, and the final, seldom-expressed fact that the whole program was being accepted in no small measure because, distasteful though many of its measures were, no one could suggest a convincing alternative as a means to survive, while to go back to the old promised nothing but extinction.

The Turks are fond of saying that they chose the revolutionary rather than the evolutionary way. So they did, although the choice was exercised and imposed by a relatively few men of long-range idealism plus short-range resolution to succeed by whatever means were necessary.

This revolutionary way said a firm good-bye to the old dream of Pan-Islam. It discarded the whole apparatus of High Moslem rule. It junked the established law of the land in one clean sweep, introducing the Swiss Civil, Italian Penal, and German Commercial codes in one day, February 1, 1926—another set of forms into which the New Turks would have to grow. Polygamy was abolished. Divorce became a civil action, marriage a civil contract. Women exercised the franchise, at first in local, then in national elections. Women sat in the assembly. The fez was forcibly discarded, and the head which was eventually to "think Western" began now at least to think under the shade of a western-style hat. Religious garb was not to be worn in public. Religious leaders were plunged to the depths of disesteem from the pinnacle of social esteem which they had so long, and in the opinion of Operation Bootstraps, so sterilely enjoyed. The dervish orders were extirpated. Women were discouraged, but not forbidden, to wear the veil. Most of these measures, and they are no more than a sampling of how life was, so to speak, remade overnight from the top down, had taken place before the first four-year elections in September 1927. Needless to say, the sole party, the People's Party, triumphed, and Mustafa Kemal was reëlected President. Shortly thereafter, to the party, in a speech lasting from the 15th to the 20th of October, he gave a public accounting of his stewardship of affairs, from 1919 on, in what was not only one of the longest but also one of the more remarkable orations of modern times. Along with every-thing else, this man was also an orator.

During the Republic's first four years, it had been forced to come to grips with what might become a major problem, its Kurdish citi-zens. Of the some 8 per cent of Turkey's citizens who are Moslem in religion but non-Turkish in speech, almost all are Kurds, something less than 2,000,000 in all. The Kurds are a rude and rugged mountain people, seminomadic, mostly living in forbidding and inaccessible country athwart Turkey's frontiers with the Arab states and with Persia. They have been a problem for every central government which has had to deal with them for thousands of years. Their level of cultural life and the nature of their tribal structure have largely insulated them from the blandishments of nationalism. Statements, and they are frequent, which imply the existence of an all-embracing, coherent Kurdish nationalism operating in Turkey as well as in Iraq and Iran, should be largely discounted as either propaganda or irre-sponsible journalism. In so far as Kurdish nationalism is a genuine threat to existing Middle Eastern states, it is Persia and Iraq (and not Turkey) which are vitally concerned. The Turkish Republic's first major Kurdish troubles came in the spring of 1925. There were further troubles, especially along the Persian frontier, in 1930, and in general it is fair to say that for years the Turkish army was on the alert against the Kurds. It is not accurate, however, to speak of wars or even of many large-scale punitive campaigns. Here again, one must discount journalistic exaggeration, exaggeration all the greater because the general policy of the Turkish army, which shares the typical Balkan spy-sensitivity and proclivity for closed military zones (all of these matters on which this region has of course by no means a monopoly), has managed almost entirely to close off the Kurdish regions from any general travel on the part of even those few westerners who are interested.

Turkey's Kurdish policy has worked in this way: once a particular disturbance has been mastered, the usual sequel has been not to deport, and certainly not to exterminate, the Kurdish community or tribe involved, but rather to remove only the local leaders, *aghas*, to enforced residence in non-Kurdish parts of Turkey. An immediate consequence of this is to relieve the Kurds of the exactions of their own aristocracy, exactions beside which the demands of the Turkish government are sometimes comparatively small. Beyond this, Kurdish males are generally held to the regular term of compulsory military service in the Turkish army, under conditions which may seem impossible to the western eye and at least onerous to many more urban Turks, but which by and large represent a level of easier existence for the Kurd than what he has known before. He sees parts of non-Kurdish Turkey. He goes home with money in his pocket. Above all, he learns the Turkish language. Already it is rare in much of "Kurdistan" in Turkey to meet any but an old male who does not know quite a little Turkish. Females adopt the new speech less readily, for obvious reasons. And the spread of Turkish speech among these Kurds means, of course, that they at once qualify for generally full status as Turkish citizens, for they are Moslems to begin with, folk-Moslems it is true, but with a folk-Islam not seriously hostile to that of the Anatolian Turk himself. Already the government feels able to allow Kurdish aghas to return from exile to their own regions. To this extent, the Kurdish question has lost its thorns. In short, it is not premature to conclude that already the Turkification of Turkey's Kurds is so well advanced that it points to a relatively sure solution of what might otherwise have serious results: the full acceptance of this people as assimilated, and so naturalized, Turks of Turkey. Kurdish "blood" is reckoned no particular handicap or disgrace. Indeed, no "blood" is "bad" in Turkey. It would certainly be misleading to portray the lot of the Kurds in the Turkish Republic as particularly fortunate. Their traditional society and their traditional raid-

ing economy have been disrupted by force and against their own desires. Even so, when one comes to formulate a balanced view of
events, he can only conclude that the impact of the Turkish Republic
upon the Kurds must go down as preponderately a labor of "civilization" which is to be regretted sincerely only by those who regret to
see a Turkish problem solved, and which is to be criticized severely
only by those who hate to see still another anachronistic exhibit in the
Middle East's living-museum dwindle away.

A bright spot not only for the Kurds but for all citizens of the
Republic is that it now is much easier to become literate, to read and
write the Turkish language, than it was twenty-five years ago.

On the 9th of August, 1928, Mustafa Kemal Pasha Atatürk ("Preceptor of Turks": this name for him is not technically correct until
1935, when he put through the "last names revolution") addressed a
public meeting in an Istanbul park, announcing to it a forthcoming
reform which has ever since been as intriguing to non-Turks as it
has been effective upon the Turks themselves. This was the measure
which required that beginning within one month, the Turks were
gradually to forsake the Arabic letters in which they had written
their language since Turks first became Moslems in any numbers, and
were to replace that script with an especially adapted version of the
Latin alphabet. This *was* revolution. The suggestion for some such
change had been made before, even in Ottoman times, and so was
not "brand new," but it had never before received really serious
official consideration. The idea that it was now actually to be put into
effect, and that in short order, was new enough for all.

To understand some of the countless ramifications involved here
requires much background knowledge. Classical Ottoman speech, of
which Atatürk himself was a master and which he was now deliberately repudiating, bore in itself eloquent testimony of how the Turks
of Rūm had come into the Moslem world through its Persian sectors,
for this language was not only laden with Arabic words and phrases,
but also abounded in Persianisms. High Ottoman literature, the
formal literature of the true Ottoman class, had for centuries been so
heavily Arabized and Persianized that without exaggeration a knowledge of those two languages is equally necessary with a knowledge
of Turkish if one is to understand many Ottoman works, above all if
one is to understand the large body of Ottoman classical poetry. It is
true that the nineteenth-century western impact upon the true Ottomans had been particularly effective in the changes which it had

worked in the form and the content of their literature, both of which largely had espoused French models, and also in the vocabulary and even in the (Arabic and Persian elements) syntax of Ottoman. Many French words and phrases had been incorporated *in toto*. Even so, much of the old remained, and the tradition that a classical education should include both Arabic and Persian was by no means dead, although it was slipping from general favor. In the case of Arabic, moreover, cherished matters of religion were included in the considerations involved. That the Moslem scriptures, the Koran, were technically supposed not to be translated from the original Arabic, although of course they had been translated, and that mosque services, funeral services, the recitation of various standard prayers, and much more were supposed to be conducted only in Arabic—even on the peasant religious level, all of these were matters deeply rooted and deeply felt.

This is still largely true. One of the first acts of the Democrat government of President Bayar was to lift those restrictions upon the use of the Arabic language in religious ceremonies and in the muezzin's calls to prayers which the Atatürk regime had imposed and the İnönü regime had retained. At the same time there came an appreciable relaxation in official insistence upon the use of the somewhat artificial "New Turkish," radically purified of Arabisms and Persianisms, which Ankara had previously sponsored. Both of these moves were extremely popular, and each represents a partial official reacceptance of elements of Ottoman culture which many Turks obviously still prize. But their importance should not be exaggerated. Re-legalization of the use of Arabic for religious purposes does not also necessarily imply a large-scale swing back to traditional Islam but is simply an official recognition of the persistence of certain elements of that tradition. It certainly has no important pro-Arab or pan-Moslem overtones. There is no serious agitation for a return to the general use of the Arabic alphabet nor is such a movement conceivable. The alphabet reform is not only basic; it also is wholly and unreservedly established.

Even the more conservative in 1928 had to concede that much was to be said for a change of alphabet. The Arabic characters are ideally adapted to their original purpose, for the fact that they most efficiently record a wide variety of consonantal sounds but are poor in vowel symbols coincides exactly with the nature of the language which produced them. Turkish, however, is altogether different.

Arabic gave it far more consonant symbols than it needed, although still several common Turkish consonants had no adequate representation in Arabic letters, but the Arabic vowel symbols were totally inadequate to represent the Turkish constellation of vowel sounds. In consequence, Turkish in Arabic letters was so complicated a system of writing and of spelling that it consumed years of a student's energies really to master it, a contributing cause to Turkey's overwhelming illiteracy rate. The proposed version of the Latin alphabet, on the other hand, would have one symbol for each sound, no more and no less, could be learned in a few weeks or days or even hours, with no exceptions in spelling at all. Also, its users would write from left to right as Europeans do. They could use ordinary typewriters. Europeans traveling in the country could at once read the name on the signboard at every railroad station (but likely not pronounce it, for some of the sounds assigned were far removed from what those letters ordinarily conveyed in Europe). The new letters would be a westernizing device *in excelsis*. If the hat had made the new Turk outwardly western to the top of his head, the alphabet now would make him outwardly western to the tips of his fingers. And it has. No single measure has done so much to break the tie of outward resemblance to the rest of the Moslem world.

No Turk under thirty-six or thirty-seven years old is now ordinarily able to use the old letters with any facility. And since the old letters were in themselves also a shorthand system for the pen of a skilled writer, something has been lost here too. More than that, no Turk under thirty-six or thirty-seven can ordinarily read anything published in his own language before 1928. Very few older works have been transliterated into the new letters. To teach or use the old letters is (or was) technically illegal. Actually they are still widely used by the older generation, but the younger generation has had its principal bridge to its own cultural past burnt for it. Even when transliterated, the older literature is still almost incomprehensible in the new letters, and though much lip-service is given to the Ottoman classics in class work, to try to teach them today is, as one able teacher in the field has said, like moving a dead elephant. Atatürk would have rejoiced at this, for he was out to kill the past. When it came to literature, even he doubtless regretted that many things he himself prized would have to perish in this process, but he believed that nothing less than one clean stroke would suffice, and he dealt the stroke. It is impressive testimony to the force of, and the power wielded by, this one man to think that he thus "abolished history" and sent a nation back to school. The end result to date is not only a people increasingly de-Moslemized in outward marks—other objects of Atatürk's reforms included the Moslem calendar, the observance of Friday as the weekly day of rest, the Moslem system of telling time, and the Moslem systems of weights and measures—but also a people among whom basic literacy is an increasingly common phenomenon, although even yet the rate does not approach 50 per cent. Time, however, is now strongly on literacy's side.

Education was a constant preoccupation of the Turkish Republic under Atatürk, and remains so today. The problem was no less than to design from the ground up a modern educational system where comparatively little that was modern, although that little was in some cases also comparatively good, had existed before. The state had to find hitherto nonexistant personnel for this hitherto nonexistant system, to extend the system until it would make education compulsory on the nationwide scale, to produce texts from which to teach (and those now in the new alphabet), and buildings and teachers: in short, to build almost everything. To date, success has been only qualified. By copying the French system with its absolute centralization of all authority in a Ministry of Education, the Turks have overladen their educational structure with bureaucracy and politics, and shackled it with red tape. Textbooks still largely tend to range only from mediocre to poor. All facilities remain in sadly short supply, the worst deficiency still in the supply of reasonably qualified teachers. But progress does continue.

Two extremist contentions of Turkish nationalists have entered deeply into the texture of Turkey's teaching, with largely unfortunate results. Both of these are intellectual overtones of the older Pan-Turkism, the one a theory of language which, on unscientific grounds, sees in Turkish speech the original language of primordial mankind (the Sun-Language Theory), and the second a theory of history built upon that assumption and holding (1) that all human achievement is basically Turkish (since all humans began as Turks), and (2) that there is an unbroken thread of purposeful development from the earliest known Turks straight to modern Ankara, a thread moreover in which is to be found the central meaning of World History (the National Historical Thesis). When these "theories" began to be propounded seriously on the official level (1931), they were smilingly rejected by those individuals whose personal knowledge allowed them to see the absurdities involved. But that so few Turks then did, or could, see those absurdities is itself a fair measure of how newly and tentatively the westernized Turk had as yet emerged from the intellectual limits of his old Faith, State, and Way, and of how unsophisticated and naive he was sometimes likely to be, by certain modern (contemporary European) standards. Theories of this sort, however, also had their real uses. They helped to short-circuit pride in the Ottoman past, and this was of positive value in Atatürk's eyes. By claiming the Hittites as Turks and portraying them as Anatolia's base stock, they "legalized" the historical part of "self-determination" as they "proved" that Anatolia had "always" been Turkish. By expanding Pan-Turkism to include humanity entire, they most skillfully drew those of its fangs which, had the idea been left specific, would certainly have aroused other Turk-ruling states, and in particular Soviet Russia.

On quite another level, they gave their sardonic proponent in chief, Atatürk, the diversion of watching certain intellectuals, Turkish and European, gyrate as they labored to produce short-order "evidence" to corroborate newly announced "fact." This entire chapter reflects glory upon no one except those few Turkish professors who preferred to lose their jobs rather than to teach this sort of thing. Soon enough, the Sun-Language Theory and the Historical Thesis were allowed practically to lapse on the higher level, but they remain written into the elementary textbooks and so still color the views of most literate Turks, although not those of the better educated. To that degree they are, if not harmful, at least misleading. On the other hand, as examples of chauvinism in national education, these aberrations are not to be compared to the ordinary practice in several of Turkey's neighboring lands where elementary education too often includes heavy doses of drawing from memory the maps of "my country as it is" and "my country as its frontiers should be of right." How light a dose of overt chauvinism nationalist Turkey has had, and how speedily she has shaken most of it off, can be measured by a foreigner who has lived observantly in other Balkan or Middle Eastern states as well as in Turkey. He certainly will find the Turks no less self-centered than are the people of other small nations, but once he conquers the language barrier, he will also find that their traditional hospitality is unforced and that their quite admirable self-assurance has in it little of the dog-in-the-manger quality which characterizes chauvinism in its more malignant forms. The Turks do want

to be left alone, but in so far as this attitude is tinctured with chauvinism, it seems to be the sort of chauvinism that time is curing.

Nor is anything permanently wrong with Turkish education, anything that common sense, an increasing sense of at home-ness in the
new world Turkey has recently entered, and more money for teachers
will not cure. Turkey has excellent prospects for realizing all of these.
One often hears it said that the Turks made their contribution to
Moslem culture, and now are voluntary apprentices to western culture. Any new contributions on their part must wait till that apprenticeship is over. One could argue many details of this proposition at
length: but the overall assertion does largely hold. The only man
who will doubt it is the man who, after comparing the Turkey of
1900 with the Turkey of 1950, still claims that there is nothing new
in the world.

Even before 1929, Turkey had raised her tariffs and set out along
a road towards economic-nationalist self-sufficiency which is called,
in Turkish itself, *Étatism.* We have already seen that Étatism became, in essence, a collection of temporary expedients eventually
canonized for lack of better, and that it is now under heavy fire.
Étatism's roots came in part from the deeply felt reaction to the old
capitulations system with its concomitants of foreign debt, foreign
dependence, and foreign interference. Turkish nationalism had, and
has, in this respect an understandably xenophobic streak. There was
also the feeling that without industry Turkey was not "modern."
Considerations of the national defense then played an increasingly
large role as Étatism evolved. No one yet has found a satisfactory
answer to the contention that if the Turkish government had not
taken the initiative, no one else would have: from this it follows that
Turkey has largely to thank the state for what industry she has. Better an imperfect and an unbalanced plant than none at all? Étatism
has many obvious weaknesses. It was with the large-scale entry of
government into business administration that the bureaucratic patterns embodied in the Ottoman legacy were able to work perhaps the
most harm in the Ankara regime. The traditional idea, still tacitly
held by many of those out of government as well as by many of
those in, that government exists not to serve the people, but to be
supported by them, and as a convenience of the ruling group and
for the purpose of employing, if necessary, the total manpower of
that group, alters only slowly. In many aspects the republican regime
still remains a collection of forms into which the new Turks *may*

grow. The basic question even today is often not "When will they grow into them?" but "Are they growing in that direction at all?" In economic policy and practice, more than in any other one field, the foreign critic still finds his best reasons for continuing to suspend favorable judgment. But even the most jaundiced critic cannot find conclusive evidence on which to base a thoroughly unfavorable judgment. The Turks of the Republic unquestionably become newer with every year. Even by the time of Atatürk's death (1938), many a high-school child could not remember any life but that of the Republic. Here was a measure of real change. As for their elders, who could remember the old, there was little doubt that most of them, too, whatever particular reservations they might make, agreed that on balance the new was better. Their country was doing well, well at home and well abroad.

In 1932 Turkey had been admitted to the League, and had begun to take what was, for a small state, even a leading role. In the formation of the Balkan entente she stood out. In the pact which in 1937 linked her with Iraq, Persia, and Afghanistan she again led. Her relations with Germany were more than correct, they were cordial and, economically speaking, almost vital. But even so, it was resolved that she would try to keep to the democratic side in the impending struggle, and her weight in the international scales was certainly for peace. Relations with Russia remained correct, although it had long since been made clear, officially as well as unofficially, that the Republic's gratitude for Soviet aid in the War for Sovereignty did not extend to permitting the least communist activity in Turkey, while genuine *popular* gratitude towards Russia was, as we know, practically nil. Russia was still Russia as far as the Turk was concerned, and nothing more need be said.

International affairs naturally occupied an ever larger share of Turkey's attention as the world moved towards war. Her policy of (1) surviving and (2) prospering, if possible, allowed no room for costly idealism, and her leaders' poise and realism became more and more evident. At the same time, Atatürk's health began to fail seriously. Personal relationships with him became more hectic, and reverberations of this were widely felt in the government. Every further relaxation of his hand upon the throttle could mean a corresponding slowing in the westernization drive. Unsympathetic observers began to hint that New Turkey was largely façade, unsubstantial, meaningless façade behind which the reality was little more than the persisting true Ottoman mentality. The fact that so little tangible change had been made in the highly change-resistant peasant seemed to confirm these gloomy opinions. And then, Atatürk sickened and died, November 10, 1938, only a few days after the celebration of the new Republic's fifteenth independence day, and less than a year before World War II began.

The question was obvious: had Mustafa Kemal Atatürk, after getting Turkey for the Turks, also been able to get the necessary minimum of New Turks to enable his New Turkey to survive? During the rule of Atatürk's successor, a term of office which began as a "rule" but which has ended as a "chief magistry" in similar circumstances to those with which Winston S. Churchill's term of office also ended, events were gradually answering this fundamental question with a strong "yes."

5. Inönü's Turkey

Atatürk's fatal illness had not been sudden, but worked slowly and so gave ample warning to all that a change in leadership was approaching. On the surface, that change could not have proceeded more smoothly than it did. The day after the President's death, the Grand National Assembly met and elected as his successor Ismet Inönü, the same Ismet Pasha who had been Atatürk's principal military assistant during the struggle for Turkish sovereignty and then his principal civilian assistant during most of the subsequent Operation Bootstraps of the Republic's development.

Their close association had not, however, lasted until Atatürk's death. Inönü had left the Premiership, in September 1937, after holding it for so long, and since then had been living quietly in Ankara, at one time reportedly under police surveillance. It is idle to speculate in detail upon what it was that caused the estrangement between these partners of such long standing, for the story has never been made public and likely never will be. In the view of many, the diametrically opposed standards of personal conduct characteristic of the two men were in themselves sufficient not only to account for a final break, but even to make it remarkable that the break had not come sooner than it did. And there were, of course, many points of difference, quite apart from personal grounds. That Atatürk died cherishing no malice towards Ismet Pasha seemingly follows from the fact that his will provided bequests to the Inönü children, but there are at least a few presumably well-informed individuals who claim to see even in this an indication that Atatürk believed that Inönü had preceded him to the grave.

However the value of such rumors may have been, it is unquestionable that in the months of Atatürk's increasing physical helplessness, behind-the-scenes politics in Ankara had unrolled so rapidly and so effectively that decision was entirely ready for the event, and Inönü captured the presidency without overt opposition or disturbance. Those who had claimed that power could not be transferred peacefully in the pseudo-Republic, but "real dictatorship," of modern Turkey were now confounded by the fact, and those who had held that Atatürk's arbitrary methods had alienated his people were silenced by the impressive and unrestrained manifestations of genuine national grief which marked his funeral, at Istanbul, at Ankara, and throughout the land.

The funeral ceremonies were doubly impressive, thanks to the foreign participants who, many of them with special naval detachments and detachments of armed forces, both at Istanbul and at Ankara, seized the opportunity to display the military might which they could bring into an eventual war. And among the Turks, for their part, few responsible leaders in 1938 seemed to doubt that war was near.

We have seen how Atatürk exploited France's weakness in the eastern Mediterranean in order to obtain the Sanjak of Alexandretta for Turkey. One of Inönü's earlier accomplishments as President was to carry through to the final annexation of that territory. Atatürk had also done what he could to prepare Turkey for the sad day when general hostilities would break out, and had striven hard to postpone that day. His purported final political testimony, as reported on the lips of the people, had been to be as ready as possible and then, come what might, to stay on England's side, because that side was certain to win in the long run.

Whatever of truth there may have been in this report, such was in the event Turkey's actual course. There can be little doubt that she now followed that course with a cooler eye and judgment under President Inönü than would likely have been the case had his more impetuous predecessor been still in power. But that Inönü was Atatürk's equal as a leader, few Turks have ever contended.

At home, Inönü attained not only the presidency but also permanent leadership of Atatürk's single party, the People's Republican. Thus the new leader's machinery for governing was essentially the same as that of Atatürk. It remained to be seen what his methods would be. For Prime Minister, Inönü at first retained Jelal Bayar, who had assumed that office under Atatürk at the time of Inönü's dismissal into private life, and who now remained in it until January of 1939. Obviously there were differences between the new President and the Prime Minister—one should note that this is the same Bayar who eventually defeated Inönü for President in the elections of 1950 —and indeed many differences now began to come to the surface everywhere once Atatürk's hand had finally disappeared. It was, however, equally obvious that 1939 was a year too full of possible peril abroad for the Turks to risk the upsets of any widespread housecleaning at home. A number of somewhat unsavory individuals who had been personal hangers-on, official or unofficial, under the former regime soon disappeared from the public eye, but apart from this there were relatively few changes of importance.

In fact Inönü's regime, from the beginning until it at last became reasonably clear that Turkey could emerge unscathed from World War II is best described as a period of largely voluntary moratorium upon overt political agitation or unnecessary change within the country. This moratorium was in all truth largely voluntary: it was almost instinctively adopted. Few people of the country rejoiced in it, but only the clearly irresponsible failed to perceive that these were no years in which to risk willfully rocking the boat. Under the surface of events, political agitation and political evolution continued. Party caucuses were now far stormier than had been the usual case in Atatürk's day, but such differences were not officially publicized, while the Assembly in official sessions continued to vote unanimously with such regularity that *oy birliğile* ("by a unanimous vote") was the first Turkish phrase a foreigner was likely to learn. When the times were again propitious, political development reëmerged, and reemerged with a vengeance. But between 1939 and 1945 the overriding preoccupation of sincere Turks was not to attain democracy, or a free press, or free trade, or any other goal in one bound; the objective, purely and simply, was (a) to keep sovereign and (b) also, if possible, to keep uninvaded. That Turkey alone of *all* the nations in her entire area realized this objective was certainly in considerable part due to her consistent good luck, but luck alone is by no means an adequate explanation. Turkey was ready to capitalize on luck, and also ready to make her own luck. Her successfully maintained neutrality was chiefly due to the cool, farsighted, uncompromising policy of enlightened national self-interest which the government followed, and which it could follow thanks to the national instinct for not rocking the boat needlessly.

To say that Inönü kept Turkey out of the war is doubtless an oversimplification, but it is an admissible oversimplification. Thanks to his continuation of Atatürk's policy between the latter's death and the outbreak of hostilities, September 1939 found Turkey definitely aligned with England and France, and eventually allied to them through a pact (signed in October 1939) which distinctly stipulated that in *no* case would Turkey become a belligerent *against* the Soviet Union. Similar reservations—reservations in fact if not always reservations on paper—operated in all of Turkey's alliances, those with most of her Balkan neighbors and those with Iran and Afghanistan. Never was Turkey committed to take action on the side against Russia. This did not mean that she was a satellite of Russia. Far from it. Nor did it mean genuine friendship for, or gratitude towards, Russia on Turkey's part, in return for the assistance which the Soviets had rendered Turkey in the 1920's and again in the 1930's. On the contrary, while Atatürk was still in his full prime it had been made repeatedly and unmistakably clear that Turkey would have no room for communism or for pro-Russian groups of any kind, official or unofficial, that although Turkish-Russian relations would always remain as correct and cordial as Turkey could keep them, the deepseated and almost universally cherished Turkish popular dislike of Russia and all her works had not abated one particle. Now, with the outbreak of hostilities, that national, unofficial bias against Russia flamed up. Russia's actions did nothing to allay Turkish feeling. Instead, early in the war the visit of Shükrü Sarajoğlu, then Foreign Minister and subsequently (July 1942) Prime Minister, to Moscow where he was given diplomatically the complete brush-off, substantially confirmed popular suspicions of Russia's intentions. It was naive indeed to suppose that Turkey's responsible authorities did not, in fact, fully understand that the eventual fate of their country formed one of the principal points then at issue between the members of the Nazi-Soviet alliance. No Turk ever allowed himself to refer to Stalin as "Yusuf Amja" (Uncle Joe).

As for Germany, Turkey was keeping on strictly last-name terms with Herr Hitler, too. There was a Turco-German neutrality pact, and there was some reservoir of pronounced pro-German feeling in Turkey, but no important fraction of responsible Turks had ever been strongly for Hitler. Many influential Turks retained vivid memories of what collaboration with Germany and service under German command had meant for them in World War I. German prestige in Turkey was high, no more. In addition, the Nazi foreign-trade policy had made German trade predominant in Turkey's overseas economy.

Even pro-German Turks, however, frequently suspected that a German victory might, at best, be vastly more difficult to adjust to, and quite possibly also far more of a threat to Turkish independence, than an Anglo-French victory could possibly be, and it definitely was not until after Germany had attacked Russia that sizable support for Germany appeared in Turkish public opinion.

We already know that Turkish hatred and fear of Russia are at base irrational factors, and so of an entirely different order from whatever emotions Turks felt as far as England, France, or Germany were concerned. Hence one is not surprised that Germany's victories against Russia aroused real enthusiasm in Turkey. The surprising thing, instead, is that throughout everything, even up to the highest tide of German success in the Caucasus and in Egypt, Turkey still restrained herself to remain faithful to her anti-Axis ties. She did not, it is true, ever actively implement her engagements to aid England and France, any more than she actually went to the aid of her several smaller allies when they were attacked. In fact, hostilities had soon reached a scope and a size where no one seriously expected the Turks to enter in, unless they themselves were directly attacked. Henceforth, in Anglo-American thinking, when military counsel was uppermost it was generally argued that a neutral Turkey was far more of a help and far less of a burden than Turkey as an active belligerent on our side would be, and it was rather at those junctures when nonmilitary considerations were temporarily prevailing that serious attempts were made to encourage or compel Turkey to enter hostilities.

Russia, now in her extremity, naturally took towards Turkey a far different tone than she had taken during the time of the Nazi-Soviet alliance. Apart from the level of official amenities, this change in tone had little effect upon Turkey. And Russia's eventual successes were received by the Turks with unofficial but unfeigned dismay.

In reality, once the crises of 1942 were passed, Turkey became a relative backwater in so far as the main course of events was concerned. This development was largely agreeable to Turkey. Not that the war did not hit the Turks hard. They continued to navigate their Black Sea and Aegean coastal waters, dangerous though they were, but international trade was of course terminated. The widespread use of air power meant a sharp change in the role of Turkey's Straits Area in wartime. Now the "narrow seas" were effectively closed to international traffic by foreign aircraft based at some distance. Ground-control of the Straits Area itself, and close-in naval blockade, were no longer the vital considerations they had formerly been. In consequence, although the control of what little shipping passed the Straits was still an embarrassment, Turkey no longer had to fear a direct attack as much as she had had to in previous wars.

On the economic front there was increasing unrest. Essential imports ceased, and for want of them essential services at home slowly dwindled. Relatively serious shortages appeared. Both sides were active in Turkey at preëmptive buying. This Turkey turned to her own advantage without paying much heed to its possible long-term effect upon prices, or to the inflation which had already begun to appear. It is only fair to add that in so far as she judged she dared, Turkey gradually moved to deny the Axis powers access to vital materials. In this, as in other respects, she did not seriously falter in her passive adherence to the anti-Axis cause. And by her continuing full mobilization, which was maintained at great and increasing cost to her economy, she consistently rendered the Allies an important positive service.

All the belligerents exerted themselves to conduct propaganda in Turkey, generally with far less effect than individual propagandists permitted themselves to realize. Throughout the war Turkey was too hard-pressed to permit herself the luxury of paying more heed to words than to deeds. Turkey also served as a marvelous field of action for numerous spies from both sides, amateur and professional. Istanbul city in particular enjoyed a period of cloak and dagger prosperity which its polyglot quarter of Beyoğlu (formerly Pera) will not soon forget.

The German attack on Russia, as we have noted, meant a lessening of pressure on Turkey. When that attack began, Turkey at once proclaimed her neutrality, and followed this with a reaffirmation of her neutrality pact with Germany. In August 1941 came an Anglo-Soviet guarantee of aid to Turkey in the event of Axis attack, soon followed by a Turkish-German trade pact. Turkey's neutrality had in a sense become valuable to both sides, or at least each side had decided that Turkey would likely not be of immediate aid to it as a belligerent. The British, under the standing Anglo-Turkish alliance, were giving increasing aid to the Turks—planes, special training and equipment, and funds, and were also in a position to grant or deny to Turkey vital imports. The entire situation in which the Allied

Powers strove to strengthen Turkey and enable her to maintain her position of armed neutrality plus sympathy towards, and aid for, the anti-Axis countries was regularized and formalized on December 3, 1941—just before Pearl Harbor—when President Roosevelt declared the defense of Turkey vital to the security of the United States and thereby extended lend-lease aid to cover Turkey's needs. Thenceforth Ankara set itself to press as strong a case as possible for aid in large amounts, always asserting its readiness to enter active hostilities just as soon as its minimum needs in equipment and supplies had been met. And the actual condition of the Turkish army, an excellent pre-mechanization land army, when compared with the forces fighting in World War II, effectively meant that to bring the Turks up to the minimum standard necessary for successful open belligerency would be a greater drain upon Anglo-American resources than the probable gain would justify. Thus, Turkey kept out.

In January 1942 the Soviet Government professed itself satisfied with Turkey's attitude, an attitude which it regarded as meriting reward. The twin prospect of Soviet approval and lend-lease support could not, however, conceal from the Turks that the anti-Axis forces were now in grave difficulties both in the Caucasus and in Egypt. The summer of 1942 was perhaps the war's most tense period, as seen from Ankara, for the prospect of German forces standing on Turkey's Caucasus frontier as well as on her Greek and Bulgarian and Aegean frontiers was not remote, and neither was the prospect of German forces crossing east of Suez, with the central Arab world then falling under Axis control of some sort, and Persia as well.

The situation at home was equally disturbing. Living costs continued to mount. Replacements for overstrained machines, which one by one wore out, were almost unobtainable from abroad and could not be produced at home—not a single spark plug or light bulb or tire, to mention only simple and obvious needs of every day. Étatism of course had been obliged to stop all planned expansion long before this, and the problem now was how to keep the industrial machine functioning at all. Each expedient that was adopted tended to have little tangible result except to send costs higher. Shortages extended to the food supply and were worsened by the effects of 1941's poor crops. Food rationing was introduced. Eventually rationing included many, if not most, of the staples of life. Rationing restrictions, however, and indeed all attempted controls, were consistently avoided and circumvented by the public. The black market and black bourse became accepted features of normal life. In consequence, the gap between rich and not-rich was further widened, while many previously quite prosperous people were reduced to real misery, especially in the cities. Concurrently the class of newly and flashily rich war-profiteers stirred up general resentment by its blatant conduct. Government employees' salaries by now had become ridiculously low in terms of living costs, and it was at least understandable that overt corruption should become more widespread. The simplest transactions, even the purchase of fuel or of food in any quantity, had ordinarily to be furthered by illicit payments. Each week saw new restrictions and controls attempted, but each attempt was promptly perverted so that in the end it frequently actually worked against the interests of those whom it had originally been designed to protect. Along with these practices something of the atmosphere of late Ottoman rule inevitably returned. That atmosphere was particularly evoked by a political misstep with far-reaching results, an attempt at a capital-levy which so misfired that it eventually figured as one of the underlying causes of the election upset in 1950.

President Inönü's administration has certainly to bear the responsibility for the *Varlik Vergisi* (Capital Tax) of 1942–43. Rightly or wrongly, it was especially attributed to the then Prime Minister, Shükrü Sarajoğlu, who had assumed office in July 1942 upon the death of Dr. Refik Saydam, and who since the end of the war has faded into obscurity in private life. In general design the Varlik Vergisi was entirely defensible, quite comparable to measures resorted to in other war-distracted countries. The ordinary tax-collection machinery, always poor at best and now more widely evaded than ever before, was entirely unable to reach the war profiteers. Hence, extraordinary machinery was to be set up. But the method by which these extraordinary assessments were to be made proved to be open to the gravest abuse.

In each community or administrative subdivision of a community, a local committee was chosen. Sitting *in camera* this levy-board was to consider the available tax lists and other pertinent information, and on the basis thereof to levy an assessment upon each man's wealth, the tax to be paid in cash within a relatively short period and under heavy penalty.

Even this arrangement might have been workable in wartime Great Britain, say, but not in Turkey. Among its basic flaws were these: (1) no limit was fixed upon the assessment which could be levied on any single individual; (2) there was no genuine legal appeal from the decision of the local tax boards; (3) only Moslem Turks sat on those tax boards, although this of course was not stipulated in the law. The results were outrageous and disturbing.

It is true that for the majority of the population, the peasantry, the Varlïk Vergisi meant nothing. For most non-peasant Moslems, likewise, the levy meant at most a small cash payment, entirely justifiable and easily borne. But for non-Moslem Turkish citizens, and for some non-Turkish Levantines resident in the country, the tax became a small-scale bloodless financial massacre.

While the economy had been going from bad to worse under the war's impact, older Moslem Turkish concepts of full and second-class citizenship, inherited from the Ottoman Empire, and only nominally superseded by the Republic's principle of laïcism, had reëmerged more and more clearly, and public opinion among the ruling group had fixed upon "the minorities" as its all-sufficient scapegoat. Especially the Turkish-citizen Greek, Armenian, and Jewish communities of Istanbul were held responsible for all of Turkey's domestic wartime economic ills, and it was upon them that the full brunt of the Varlïk tax now fell.

Almost *all* of these minority citizens, right down to street-bootblacks, old ragmen, and beggars (three categories of enterprise which the state licensed and for which lists of personnel were accordingly available), were assessed sums far beyond their powers to pay. Small businessmen and large, provided they were not Moslem, fared similarly. A few outstanding minority individuals were assessed astronomical figures. Practically no Moslems suffered anything comparable, and those who did were almost exclusively members of the *Dönme* community, a group of oriental Jews who in the seventeenth century had been led to embrace Islam and become technically Turkified, but who since have remained aloof, usually marrying only within their own group and reportedly maintaining secret vestiges of Jewish religious observance in their homes. The Dönme group has made a distinct contribution to later Ottoman and to Republican Turkish intellectual and professional life, and includes enough wealth to make a good target for the Varlïk Vergisi. And certain members of it, too, were now victimized in this highly discriminatory capital levy.

With the final posting of the Varlïk Vergisi lists in Istanbul, pandemonium broke out. The tax had been imposed by old and supposedly discarded methods: it could be evaded by recourse to the techniques of the past. Many persons made a partial payment, and then sat tight to await developments. Non-Moslems who on one ground or another could claim the "protection" of some influential foreign embassy did so, usually with satisfactory results. Newspaper opposition to the measure was feeble, in part because of repressive measures against those journalists who wanted to speak out, but principally because most newspapers, however reluctantly, still basically approved. Those members of the ruling group whose devotion to ethics and to the often expressed ideals of the Republic was real enough to keep them from sharing in the general return to Ottoman mentality which was one of the characteristics of the Varlĭk episode were utterly dismayed. When the entire situation had at length become plain and when it was common knowledge, for example, that an Istanbul Greek who could claim only the protection of the then feeble Greek Embassy would have either to pay his full assessment or else stand prosecution while another, and entirely comparable, Istanbul Greek who could claim, say, English protection, could get his assessment "forgiven" or at least greatly reduced, one eloquent and resolute Turk put that entire situation into a nutshell with the remark, "By God, *they* have revived the capitulations!" and this was no more than the truth.

Foreigners long-resident in Turkey were exercised and disillusioned. Overnight, Atatürk's attempts to incorporate the minorities into Turkey, in so far as those attempts had had some measure of success, were undone. Greek, Armenian, and French (the street language of most of Turkey's educated Jews) were suddenly to be heard on lips which had previously spoken only Turkish in public. Resentment and discrimination welled up everywhere. Republican Istanbul was lapsing into Ottoman Constantinople.

Injustice is certainly always serious, but even injustices may be only relative. This was, sadly but undeniably, the case in 1942–43. The Varlĭk was a disaster in Istanbul terms, but it was scarcely a fleabite in world-wide terms. The Great Powers—an appropriate phrase indeed in this context—were obliged to think in world-wide terms. England and the United States were frying fish too important for them to risk the loss of Ankara's good will for what was then a basically trivial matter, and the news of the Varlĭk was hushed up in the Anglo-American press. In Istanbul, only a few of the heavily taxed individuals refused to pay at least something. These were solemnly prosecuted and convicted of unwillingness to support their "country" in its hour of need, and sentenced to work off impossible sums by hard labor, at so much per hour. One small trainload of such "convicts" was sent to eastern Anatolia, to shovel snow, and there these men remained, pilloried in many newspapers, for some time. Their hard labor was largely for the benefit of press photographers, but their discomfort was real enough. Injustice, discomfort, and humiliation, however, made up the full tale of their woes. The inhuman punishments then being applied in much of the rest of Europe were never resorted to, and eventually the Varlĭk victims were returned home. The last of them were hurriedly fetched to Istanbul just before President Inönü went to Cairo in December 1943, to meet Roosevelt and Churchill.

So ended the infamous Capital Levy in Turkey. It had done comparatively little, in long-range terms, to help meet the country's economic problems. Hushed up though it had been, it eventually advertised some of Turkey's weaknesses to the world. In Turkey it had violently reopened the entire minority question and revealed to all that the true Ottoman concept of what made a first-class citizen was still vigorously alive behind the laic façade of the Republic. Bút it had not done Turkey any vital harm.

It is perhaps credible that many of the men in command, from President Inönü on down, were themselves both distressed and surprised to discover the lengths to which taxboards made up of "average citizens" had been ready to push matters. It is certain that Ankara had resorted to a Capital Levy only in real despair. Turkey's rulers now certainly had to recognize the power of this Ottoman-mentality reaction in the citizenry at large. If that was how a sizable proportion of their fellow citizens felt, 1942–43 were no years in which to have the matter out. No amends could ever be made for injustices done. The only honorable amend for the *Varlĭk Vergisi* would be a future repudiation of its mentality in favor of further strides towards true democracy. And the Capital Levy had shown how far away that goal still was.

The truth is that the task of holding Turkey together on the home front was becoming increasingly difficult and uncongenial. There was the problem of censorship of the local press and of foreign correspondents based on Turkey, a censorship which did not exist in law but which nonetheless functioned in fact. There was the increasing discontent of younger men, and of older liberals, at the endless restrictions which had to be imposed. Allied failures in Aegean warfare brought further uncertainty to the Turkish scene. The necessity for a voluntary moratorium on political agitation could not be denied, but that did not make the situation any more pleasant to bear. There were the shortages. There were ever higher prices. And, above all, there was the cost of continuing mobilization to the economy, plus war-scares and war-nerves on every hand.

Foreign policy now became perhaps less perplexing. Mr. Churchill visited Turkey in February 1943. President Inönü saw Churchill and Roosevelt in Cairo, immediately after the Tehran Conference. It became increasingly clear that Turkey was reluctant to enter the war without promises of impossible amounts of supplies, but that short of war she would be of more help to the Allied cause exactly as that cause prospered. Thus in 1944 Turkey cut chrome shipments to Germany, dismissed her Foreign Minister, Numan Menemenjioğlu, who had become (fairly or not) the symbol of a now-outmoded type of "neutrality," tried to throw a sop to Russia by arresting a few men accused of plotting the "liberation" (with German help) of parts of Russian Turkistan, recognized the French Provisional Government, and on August 2, 1944, finally broke relations with Germany. Each of these moves was welcome and correct in the eyes of at least one of the anti-Nazi powers, but all of them were in fact by far too little and too late to be of any real and decisive effect upon the course of hostilities. Turkey by now was simply a minor power and a back-water, in terms of the world at war.

This was not an entirely happy state of affairs, but worse was to come, for Turkey now quickly became the target of the feigned resentment and the hostile and acquisitive plans of one of the soon-to-be victorious Great Powers—Russia. Turkey's token declaration of war on Germany and Japan (February 23, 1945: to go into force February 28) had been timed to get her under the deadline for a seat at the San Francisco meeting of the United Nations founders. It was followed in less than a month by the first Soviet demands for revision of the Turkish-Russian nonaggression pact and of the Straits regime, and eventually by demands for the "return" to Russia of the northeastern Turkish provinces of Kars and Andahan, which Russia had at one time annexed.

To all Russian demands Turkey said no, and said it with increasingly strong Anglo-American support. Direct negotiations with Russia were finally broken off in consequence of Turkey's flat refusal to en-

tertain two-power discussions of Russia's claims and demands, and
these matters were then taken up "on a higher level." At Potsdam
and at the London meeting of the Foreign Ministers no progress was
made on the Dardanelles issue. The Truman statement of October 12,
1945, supporting a revision of the Montreux convention with the
regulation of the Straits to be put under the United Nations, of course
also failed to satisfy Russian aspirations. Turkey's position became
unenviable indeed. It is very likely that the Russian radio in Turkish,
active since the beginning of Russian pressure upon Turkey until
now, has set an all-time high for sustained and concentrated vilification and abuse.

But even this cloud had its silver lining. When the postwar pattern of southeastern Europe under Russian domination had emerged,
with it and solely thanks to it also came Turkey's opportunity to
serve, if only for want of a better, as the "easternmost bastion of
western democracy." She embraced the chance. On the 5th of April
1946 the U.S.S. *Missouri* anchored in the Bosporus, opposite the
Sultan's Palace of Dolmabache where shuttered windows marked the
room in which Atatürk had died. A new chapter had opened. The
war was over. Turkey had chosen sides for the cold war. At home,
the 1946 election was coming. Turkey was on her way. But, where?

To attempt to answer that question in 1946 required a calm and
a perspective which were hard indeed to attain. It helped if one compared what had happened to Turkey in each of the first two world
wars. Into the first, Ottoman Turkey in its most imperfectly westernized and modernized Young Turkish guise had leaped. Important actions of that war were fought in the Middle East, and Middle Eastern
forces (Turkish Forces) took a sizable role in them. From World
War I the Ottomans emerged defeated, their Empire lost. By great
efforts and under great leadership they then succeeded in at last realizing the goal of a Turkey for the Turks, and with their sovereignty
recognized then set about speedily to develop a modern nation-state
which could hope to survive under twentieth-century conditions. During this interval between the first and second world wars only two
Moslem peoples attained what could reasonably be called unqualified
sovereignty, Turkey and Persia, and of these only Turkey also was
able to amass and support sufficient armed force seriously to deter
aggression from abroad and so to provide that sovereignty with a
genuine foundation. Turkey, again, was the only one of all the Moslem nations to have an appreciable, although qualified, degree of

success in a program of compulsory, forced-draft westernization plus nationalism—in getting enough New Turks to make New Turkey seaworthy for twentieth-century waters.

Important actions of World War II were then also fought in the Middle East, but in this struggle, unlike World War I, no important Middle Eastern forces had themselves been actively engaged. As had so long been true, the area remained a power-vacuum, with neutral, armed Turkey only a partial exception.

When one shifted one's standard of comparison from the Middle East to the Balkans, Turkey still emerged at an advantage. Her prospects as a new nation in the 1920's, when compared with those of most Balkan states, seemed poor enough. But thanks to luck, courage, ruthlessness, leadership, and enlightened self-interest, she largely succeeded where they had largely failed. She did not become involved in World War II. She did not enter that war. She remained at least passively faithful to her English and American associates. She survived intact, unoccupied, and with at least the forms of her Republic unaltered. At home, her uneasy moratorium on political development was at an end, and she now could if she wished resume her ventures in growing into the new structure whose shell had been erected in Atatürk's time. What Balkan country could say as much? True, Turkey once again was under heavy pressure from a Russian government which sought to dominate her and gain the Dardanelles, but she once again could now hope for the support of other powers anxious to contain Russia and, in their own interests, avert a Russian attack on or annexation of Turkey. And those friendly powers now were headed by the United States of America.

Seen in this perspective and calmly, the events of the recent, abnormal war years certainly did not dwindle into insignificance, but they did appear at least less important than those of the Republic's prewar years. The thoughtful observer could not escape the conclusion that the erection of the Republic, marking the beginning of a major swing of the pendulum ahead, was still far more important than the short swing back marked by the years of the Varlïk Vergisi. When the critic measured the Turkey of 1945 against her own past, he still was principally impressed not with the distance she still had to go, but by the distance she had already covered. World War II had not fundamentally altered this. And when the critic then compared Turkey with her post-World War II neighbors, he found little to make him change his view.

Ïnönü's Turkey had not emerged unscathed, but it had emerged
safely. Its policy remained: to survive and to prosper as it could.
The war's end had made long-term survival highly problematical,
while postwar conditions were not making prosperity easy to attain.
The patriotic Turk who himself had the heart and the poise really
to face the problem had to concede that no one could adequately
appraise his country and its chances simply by measuring Turkey
against the yardstick of her own past. There was another measure
which, in the long run, almost certainly would finally prevail, and
that was the yardstick of twentieth-century force. Was Turkey up to
par for the mid-twentieth-century course? However great the advances Turkey had made, what did they amount to in terms of the
realities of today? Was it not true that the Turkish blacksmiths of
1914 had been closer rivals to 1914 Pittsburgh than were the Turkish
steel workers at Karabük to the technicians of Oak Ridge? Was it not
true that all of Turkey's exertions to get enough New Turks to insure New Turkey's survival, that all of Operation Bootstraps, represented in the end really only a net *loss?* In terms of power, in terms
of military power, the answer to these sharp-edged questions was very
probably an unqualified "yes." Turkey of the late 1940's was farther
from world-par than Turkey of the early 1920's had been. In terms
of what Étatism had accomplished, the answer to such questions was
also "yes."

These reflections were melancholy indeed for the well-informed
Turkish patriot. But these were not the only relevant terms. When
it came to internal cohesion, to patriotic and nationalistic coherence,
to national resolve, to all the vital intangibles of true nationhood,
Turkey now was infinitely better off than she had been before. And
she was already demonstrating that this was true. Not the least of
her good fortune was that her citizenry included able and determined
men who were now resolved quickly to take Turkey much further
along the path which could lead to new strength through true democracy in practice.

Most of the men who formed the opposition in Turkey from 1945
onwards had once been loyal and convinced supporters of the official
People's Party and of its Étatist program. The rank and file of this
potential opposition was fairly young, including many citizens whose
entire adult lives and whose earlier formative years had passed wholly
during the Republican period. New times, new ideas. These were the
people who cherished new ideas, and now there was no longer an over-

riding reason of state which could restrain them from putting their ideas to work openly. The leadership of the opposition, creating a new party which chose for itself the name "Democratic," was largely of the Atatürk-Inönü generation, or only slightly younger. The central figure was Jelal Bayar, product of a humble true Ottoman family, civilian trained, a financier, an early nationalist, a one-time exponent of Étatism, Atatürk's last and Inönü's first Prime Minister. His immediate associates included ruling group figures from many walks of life. These men essentially embodied a protest vote, and the limited cohesion which the Democratic Party had at this time did not rest principally in any positive program, but rather in negative criticism of and resentment toward the mentality of the men who had been in power so long. Many individuals embraced the Democratic cause for basically personal reasons. They had been personally offended by President Inönü or by other leaders in the administration, and the Turks have a rigid code of personal honor—*sheref*—somewhat reminiscent of the oriental concept of "face." Insults are swallowed, if need be, and cherished until the opportunity for revenge arrives. In political opposition, that opportunity might now be found.

Other individuals embraced the Democratic cause from more idealistic motives. They believed that one or another, or several, of the Republic's professed ideals-on-paper should now be put into force, either as a matter of principle or else perhaps even as one of expediency, for Turkey was of course now anxious, consciously and unconsciously, further to approximate what she conceived to be the forms of the states who had come to be her only stay against Russia—Great Britain and the United States.

Not all of the Turks who felt that their country's best interests lay in more democratic practice joined the Democratic party. Many preferred to stay in the People's Republican party and try to influence its development in a liberal direction. President Inönü himself perforce acquiesced in the formation of the Democratic party, although it was avowedly out to unseat him, and guaranteed that it should have a free hand in campaigning, save only that nothing should be done to imperil Turkey's international relations, which of course meant nothing to embroil her further with Russia. For that matter, the foreign policy platforms of the true parties were, and still are, almost indistinguishable. Such differences as exist center around the international relations aspects of the question whether Turkey should try to continue some sort of Étatism or should try instead to attract foreign capital to invest in privately conducted enterprise in Turkey. Each party was and is wholly anti-communist and anti-Russian, and even a suspicion of communist sympathies was and is enough to get a man into serious trouble in Turkey. At the end of the war, this atmosphere of an officially unavowed but still active witch-hunt for communism extended to the Turkish press, which now in all other respects was increasingly if not entirely free of restrictions. Only a fraction of that press has ever, by any stretch of imagination, faintly deserved the label pro-communist nor has any pro-Russian paper long endured.

The first national election in which two parties seriously participated on a large scale came in July 1946. It was marked by some terrorism and coercion on the part of the People's Party and then by great and widespread dishonesty in the compilation of returns. Finally the Democrats "obtained" 65 seats as against 396 for the People's Party, and in the end had to be content with a result which by no means reflected the total vote they would have pooled in an honest count.

In this predicament, the Democrats adopted an eminently sensible line. They protested, and they acquiesced: concurrently, they firmly asserted that they never again would acquiesce in a rigged election. And they set to work to organize the entire country for the next national election, due in 1950, meanwhile not wasting time on less important local issues or by-elections. An initial defeat had its uses. There were some defections from the Democrats, and other parties were formed. Only one, the Nation Party (*Millet Partisi*), has shown any appreciable strength, but not enough strength to be a serious factor in any calculations to date. This party can fairly be characterized as a coalition of extremists. It embraces such disparate elements as die-hard supporters of the High Moslem tradition, the strongest chauvinists, and so on, and its strength resides only in a few urban centers.

During the campaign of 1946 the Democrats brought into the open a fundamental question. Atatürk had been concurrently the Chief of State and the Permanent Head of his People's Party. Inönü in his turn had been designated Permanent Party Chief. Obviously, it was easier to translate this title into German than into English. Atatürk's picture and Inönü's picture were hung together, everywhere, in every official building, every classroom, every store. This, too, found its counterpart in non-democratic rather than in democratic countries. (Since the 1950 elections, Inönü's picture, has been removed and Atatürk's hangs alone.) In many ways the tradition of exaggerated deference to the Chief of State as a great man *ipso facto* had continued unbroken from Ottoman times, and some of the extremely exaggerated forms of polite deference which had been used for the Sultan were retained for the President, if not always officially then at least generally in the press and in public life. To most, if not all, of this the Democrats took violent and telling exception. Such remnants of Ottoman mentality were, of course, hard to exorcise, as was the entire Ottoman-like atmosphere which had reappeared during World War II. But the Democrats pressed their attack. Success came slowly. Still, it came.

Not long after the 1946 elections, a number of the principles for which Bayar and his supporters had campaigned were, with reservations, actually made into law by the Grand National Assembly's People's Party majority. In December 1946, the state of siege proclamations, which in some regions had almost suspended civilian in favor of military rule, were at last dropped technically, although this measure was not yet actually put into full operation. In January 1947, it was agreed to guarantee the secret ballot and the public count in future elections, but this was no more than an expressed agreement. It was not yet a bird in the hand. In the same way it was stipulated that henceforth the opposition was to have fair access to the government-controlled—and only—radio stations for campaign use.

More important symptoms ensued: tangible steps were taken away from the "police-state" organization which at least some Cassandra's had claimed to see in Turkey's future. The question of to what degree the Turkish Republic at one or another time has or has not approached a state of affairs which one justifiedly could call a police state is, of course, an essential point in the argument whether Turkey, under Atatürk or under Inönü, ever really deserved to be called a dictatorship with all which that term implies in overtones from Hitler's Germany, Mussolini's Italy, and the lands behind the Iron Curtain. And when the question "was the Turkish Republic ever a police state?" is put in those terms, the answer is an unqualified "no." Turkey is a backward land in which the entire idea of civil liberties, as *we* conceive of them, is still almost brand new. The struggle to realize such civil liberties, then, has been a hard and at times a disheartening fight, and this assertion is made not with reference to the minorities, whose hopes for real civil liberties in Turkey are very frail, or to the peasants, but rather with reference only to the civil liberties which the ruling group hopes to attain for itself. Those rights are far from finally won today. But all this still does not make Turkey a police state.

Her secret police force, for a land of 20,000,000 inhabitants, is minuscule. The Istanbul headquarters, its most important branch, housing files and all for a city of a million inhabitants, is a comparatively small establishment. It is true that foreigners have been regarded with some suspicion in Turkey. It has been supposed that a dossier was kept for each resident foreigner, and until the Democrats changed the law in 1950, foreigners were required to get specific permission for even an overnight trip. One trip meant going to a police station (not the secret police, of course) four times: before departure, upon arrival, before returning, and on return—a system which, if it accomplished nothing else, at least firmly discouraged tourist travel, and which now is being altered principally for that reason. The entire system was basically a late Ottoman bureaucratic heritage. An occasional foreigner may also have had a plain-clothes man set to watch him, but such shadows are largely figments of the Beyoglu minorities' exaggerated imagination and of its impact upon credulous travelers. In Anatolia foreign travelers have frequently had difficulty with military zones, in some of which photography was not allowed and into others of which even entry was forbidden. Many travelers have concluded that such zones were designed not to conceal what was in them, but rather to hide what was *not* in them. And most foreign travelers have needed Turkish companionship because of the language problems and other unfamiliar situations with which Anatolia confronts them. But for the rare foreigner who can find his own way, it has been entirely possible to spend months in Anatolia, let the hotel men deal with the police, civil or military, and in the Turkish phrase "never see a policeman's face" oneself.

Turkish restrictions, then, have made Turkey a distinctly uncomfortable country for non-Turks (and also for Turks) to live in, but restrictions of this sort, however cumbersome they were and however glad one is to see them go, still never made a police state in the twentieth century.

As for the Turkish citizen, he may well have feared to fall into the hands of the police, may have had ample justification for claims that police methods retained all of the arrogance and brutality and arbitrariness, and much of the veniality, characteristic of Ottoman times; but he still was not routed out of his bed at night and wrenched from his family and friends, to disappear forever. He could always listen to any radio station he wished. His problem was not to evade the thought-police, for there were none, but to get money enough to buy a radio, and electricity to run it. False accusation as a communist meant serious danger, as it does in many countries far less backward than Turkey, but by and large the ordinary citizen could hope for justice from the courts, even in the most stringent years. In long-range terms, a steady bettering of the total position in civil liberties since Abdul-Hamid's day to the present is a fair characterization, despite the many falls from grace which have marked the way. But it is a characterization, of course which applies *only* to the Turks, the Moslem Turks—the citizens whom "Turkey for the Turks" is for. At present the drive for a much fuller underwriting of civil liberties is stronger than ever under the new Democrat administration, and will probably result in the incorporation of a thorough-going Bill of Rights into the Constitution. This measure, one should add, would likely have had an equal chance of being passed had Inönü's party won the 1950 election instead of Bayar's. The first tangible advance towards it came in February 1947, with the revocation of "Article 18" which, among other things, denied the right of habeas corpus.

The point we are treating should be probed to its logical conclusion. Turkey has many imperfections, but the Turkish Republic is not and never has been a police-state. Even when one regards only the treatment of minorities, and this is not a matter of basic importance in terms of the entire country, and contrasts the present status and recent history of those unfortunate groups, Varlĭk Vergisi and all, with what has happened to minority groups in the countries right around Turkey's frontiers, Turkey's score is still relatively good. Would you rather be an Armenian in Turkey or a Jew in Romania? A Greek in Turkey, or a Turk in Bulgaria where some 250,000 Turkish citizens are now facing forcible deportation? A Jew in Turkey or a Jew in Syria? Or would you rather be in Russia? These are the meaningful questions in the twentieth-century Eastern Mediterranean. Turkey is no police-state.

Neither is she a paragon of virtues. The claim is sometimes made that the high-leadership of the Republican party was surprised and dismayed at the rawness with which the rank and file of party workers had manipulated the election of 1946. Be that as it may, the continuity, cohesion, and growth of the Democratic Party *in defeat* soon made it clear that Turkey had by now sired enough truly new-style Turks, resolved to have their rights, to make another such election in 1950 unthinkable.

Henceforth, the course of domestic events in Turkey was a duel between the Democrats under Bayar, who were not burdened with the responsibilities of government and so could demand whatever they chose, and the People's Party under Inönü which tried to convince the country that under their leadership there now were being made, effectively and in a reasonable and feasible form, those very reforms for which the opposition was agitating. By December of 1947, President Inönü had relinquished actual leadership in the People's Party, although he remained titular head, and so gave official notice that a two-party system had replaced the former one-party system. The nine-year-old state of siege was finally revoked in fact. In July 1948, the secret ballot and the open count for the 1950 election were made law. Government had succeeded government since the end of the war, each successive Prime Minister striving to capture public confidence and the national imagination, and to assure the people that real progress was being made. In January 1949 came the government of Shemsettin Günaltay, representative of the younger, more liberal elements of the People's Party and obviously the best bid for popular support which the Party could or would allow President Inönü to make. More and more it was becoming clear that the leaders on both sides were actually appealing to the electorate. True, it was an electorate composed of an ill-matched team, the ruling group —old and young, liberal and conservative—on the one hand, and the enfranchised peasant mass, which the ruling group would presumably literally lead to the polls, on the other hand. But it *was* an electorate, and the politicians were seeking to appeal to it and were not dictating to it or coercing it. Many foreigners, many minority Turkish citizens, were highly suspicious. To them, this two-party system *had* to be a put-up job. The Democrats would be allowed to make a "fair showing," Inönü would be reëlected in 1950, and that would be that.

The more one kept away from Istanbul with its minority enclaves and Ankara with its bureaucrats, however, the more specious such doubts became. In June 1949, Bayar stated publicly that if in future elections the Democrats were not granted fair terms in an honest and aboveboard election, they would have no alternative but to take measures to ensure their rights. This declaration set the keynote for the coming campaign. The People's Party screamed "revolution." The Democrats answered, "Nonsense. But what we are doing will *save* the Revolution you profess to uphold, and will save us all the necessity for a shooting revolution later on." The whole of this discussion was carried directly to the villages, by press, radio, and word of mouth. By the summer of 1949, except in the most desolate regions, it was almost impossible to find even a small village which did not have its own Democratic Party headquarters, with a plain sign over the door.

This was a case of the Democrats' first organizing all the members of the ruling group whom they could attract, right down to the lowest, those living on almost the village level and retaining only a feeble grasp on ruling group status, and then using *them* to indoctrinate the peasants. And it was at nationwide, persistent, man-to-man grassroots organization that the Democrats outstripped the party in power. When the Republicans woke up and tried to duplicate this accomplishment, they no longer had enough time.

No feature of the nationwide political agitation was more remarkable to the "old-Turkey-hand" than the total disappearance of hesitancy or fear on the part of common people as they discussed their government. Small townspeople and peasants might be hazy about many of democracy's finer points, might be unable to give much of an answer to your question, "Why?" when they had opened the conversation with the forthright assertion, "I am a Democrat," but there was no blinking the fact that they did not fear their government. This deserves to be regarded as a major accomplishment in the purposive impact upon the peasant of the Turkish Republic. The Anatolian was not, after all, completely resistant to change. A change had been made. The arguments which the Democrats used with most effect, in all regions and at all social levels, were economic. Prices were too high. Government costs too high; taxes too high. These assertions found enthusiastic agreement everywhere, and the best efforts of the party in power could not meet them, for that party had not been able to get prices down.

Immediately at the end of the war, Turkey's financial position had seemed relatively hopeful, despite prices five times what they had been in 1939 (with a far smaller increase in salaries, although the peasants were relatively well off), and the promise of United States aid had been encouraging. In September 1946, the lira was devalued to 2.80 to the dollar,* at which figure it has since been maintained, even after the 1949 devaluation of sterling, and it was hoped that this would greatly facilitate Turkey's participation in international commerce. Devaluation, and even the redemption for a time of Turkish currency in gold, did not prevent, however, the rise of another black market in dollars, with the lira sometimes falling to almost 5.00 to the dollar. A disastrous wheat shortage caused by drought in 1949 further complicated matters, and behind all of course were the chronic difficulties of the Étatist establishment with its costs in foreign exchange, now higher than ever before, and the all-pervasive costliness and inefficiency of the rest of the government machine. In consequence, the general public became more and more alienated from the administration, on which it blamed all of its economic woes. American aid did not come as rapidly as the man in the street had expected, and when it came it was principally aimed at military problems and only incidentally at the economy. Bayar was thus the more able to make a successful plea to the dissatisfied consumer.

That the campaign, bitter though it became, still remained within the bounds of what Anglo-Americans expect a democratic campaign to be, and did not lead to civil strife or to unbridgeable rifts was above all due to the poise and moderation of the leaders. From 1945 on, Bayar himself and his principal lieutenants had been the targets of much vilification and abuse, publicly and behind the hand, principally from the more reactionary elements of the People's Party. As a matter of policy they did not retaliate in kind, but stuck to the defense of principles in their statements and to the organization of their supporters behind them. This self-restraint paid. It was largely reciprocated by the more effective leaders of the People's

---

* The dollar exchange value of the Turkish pound (lira), equal to 100 piastres (kurush) since 1938 has been:

1938: (official)	. . . .	. 126
(black market)	. . . .	
		over 200
1943: (official)	. . . .	. 131
1944: commercial transactions:		
at sale of dollars (40 per cent premium)	. .	. 183
at purchase of dollars (48 per cent premium)	.	. 193
1946, Sept.: (official)	. . . .	. 280
1948: (official)	. . . .	. 280

Since 1948 the black market rate has varied from *ca.* 380 to almost 500.

Consult, Ömer Celâl Sarc, "Economic Policy of the New Turkey," *Middle East Journal,* II-4 (October 1948), pp. 430–446.

Party. As the campaign neared its end, of course, tempers rose, charges flew thick and fast, and "campaign oratory" reached a pitch of frankness utterly unknown in Turkey before. It was everywhere understood, however, that this nationwide calling of spades spades still was only campaign oratory, and no one who was following events doubted that when the ballots were counted all parties would acquiesce in the result, if only there was a fair count.

One factor which most worried sympathetic observers was the record for violence and rioting which Turkey's university students had been accumulating since the lifting of the moratorium on politics at the end of World War II. They had rioted in Ankara to compel the dismissal of teachers accused of communism, and had demonstrated by the thousands for the return of Cyprus to Turkey—that is, against the possibility that Cyprus should be given to Greece. In Istanbul they had rioted and wrecked a Russian-owned book store, the presses of newspapers accused of pro-Russian leanings, and so on.

In May of 1949, when Turkey had lost in the finals of the Mediterranean Friendship Cup (soccer), anti-Turkish manifestations in Athens were followed in Istanbul by the most shameful anti-Greek demonstrations ever known under the Turkish Republic. And just before the elections of 1950, the public funeral of Marshal Fevzi Chakmak, an aged Turkish military head who had lent his name to the extremist Nation Party, was interrupted by student demonstrations. Does this mean that Turkey's university men, the individuals who are receiving the best education the country has to offer, are going to approximate the chauvinist university mobs so characteristic of many countries in Europe in the interval between the first two world wars? It certainly does not mean that all of them are, or that most of them are, and it probably does not even mean that many of them are. But there is no doubt that some of them may be going down that headstrong and disastrous path. Such investigations as have been made seem to indicate that in all these demonstrations only a smallish number of bona fide students was involved, that these students—and all the young demonstrators—were serving, know it or not, as the tools of adults active behind the political scenes. In each case such adult leaders of course represented extremist groups. The students to whom they appealed were, by and large, the poorest, those whose living quarters and recreational opportunities represent a standard of hardship and degradation absolutely incredible to Americans, and those whose future prospects are the most bleak. But the fact remains that their educations to date had still left these youths naive enough and sufficiently open to suggestion to do what they did. Here is a real and present danger for Turkey today, although not yet a major danger. Nothing could be better calculated to lose the country its reputation for stability and reliability in its course than the rise of such a student movement. The people who can do something about this matter fully realize the problem and the risk. Turkey's educational leaders are actively at work to remedy the causes. As always, their main preoccupations are two: where is the money to come from? and where is the necessary personnel? One may at least feel certain that the present administration will exert itself to find an answer to the first question. And the answer to the second can only come from Operation Bootstraps itself. Meantime, Turkey's well-wishers justly find more cause for fear in this problem than in any other single portent in the country today. Some informed readers of this study may feel that it somewhat minimizes the importance, potential if not actual, of extreme Turkists and racists in recent Turkey. But it is the author's best judgment that such individuals constitute no very great problem, provided only that the students keep their heads. Here is the real threat, and many able Turks agree that this is the case.

Election day was May 14, 1950. Of Turkey's registered voters, some 9,000,000 adults, men and women 22 years old and above, more than 85 per cent exercised their franchise. They marked their ballots in secret if they were literate, choosing from three party slates—the People's, the Democratic, and the Nation—with some independent candidates thrown in for good measure. The result was a solid Democratic victory: 50 per cent of the total vote Democratic, 45 per cent for the People's Party, and about 3 per cent for the Nation Party, this latter showing its principal strength in Istanbul. This vote, of course, was for members of the Assembly. By the count of members elected, the Democrats won a landslide. The new Assembly would number 408 Democratic members, 69 from the People's Party, one from the Nation Party, and 9 independents. Voting and counting of the ballots proceeded without incident, and no voice contended that the election was in any important sense unfair.

Inönü's term of office was ended. He had been President for twelve years. Atatürk before him had held the office for fifteen years. Now the new President, Jelal Bayar, whom the new Assembly at once elected, faced a four-year term.

6. Turkey Today

1. TURKEY'S SOCIAL ORDER

Turkey today is a basically healthy country. Not only is she healthier than she used to be, which is to say much improved when measured by her own past; she also, and this is more important, is a healthy society by any reasonable standards. As the social scientist might put it, on every significant level of her fundamental class structure, Turkey's is an essentially open class society in which both upward and downward mobility are common features. There is no important class of people in Turkey to whose able members the society does not give a minimum adequate chance to get ahead, to better themselves and to rise in the world. Conversely, on no level of the Turkish class structure are large numbers of individuals automatically kept up in positions of important prestige and privilege unless they themselves merit those superior positions. There is free mobility, downward as well as upward: together, these go far to guarantee that Turkish society today should not generate significant potentially harmful tensions.

Turkey's non-Moslem minorities are not happy. Only for a few years of the entire span of the Republic's history to date did those minorities need fear active persecution, and even in those years (the season of the Varlĭk Vergisi under the Ottoman-like mentality which prevailed during part of World War II), the worst that they had to fear was financial injustice. But even in the best seasons under the Republic, the minorities were still the objects of continuing discrimination, and they are so in fact today, although the present administration, and the Inönü administration during its last phase, both have done much to give non-Moslem citizens formal protection against overt discrimination. But that the minority citizens are un-happy and discontented is really of importance *only* to those people themselves. It is not important in terms of Turkey's total society for the good reason that the minorities are, and since 1923 have been, negligible factors therein.

Even when the minorities are taken all together—and this is a meaningless approach, for a persisting characteristic of the minorities is that they dislike each other at least as much as they dislike the Moslem Turks—Turkey's total non-Moslem population is insignifi-cant. Numerically it is a small fraction of the total, some 2 per cent, and that fraction shrinks with the continuing emigration of those minority citizens who wish to leave Turkey for good. In political life, the minorities play no important role, although some few usually have seats as deputies. Those minority figures who do consent to sit as members of the Assembly are regarded by their co-minoritarians, as one perspicacious American has put it by an apt translation of Turkey's religion-line into terms of America's color-line, as "white man's niggers." In Turkey's intellectual and artistic life, the non-Moslems are effectively a cipher. The same is true in the sphere of education, except for the minority private schools which are wholly self-contained and inbred, although they function of course under the authority and control of the Ministry of Education. It is in Turkish economic life that one would expect the minority groups to retain their greatest shares of influence and of prestige, but here, too, minority influence has dwindled and been curbed until it is no longer of basic importance. A few outstanding individuals in the professions are non-Moslems, and there the list must end. On Turkish domestic policy, on Turkish international relations, on Turkish financial credit, even on Turkey's reputation abroad, the minorities no longer exercise important influence.

This situation is new. It is in the sharpest contrast to pre-World War I days, when the minorities frequently exerted even a decisive influence upon Ottoman policy. The meaning of the excision of minor-ity groups from any position of influence in new Turkey has not yet been wholly grasped in many foreign studies of, and opinions about, Turkey, but it is fact and it will eventually be universally understood. The foreigner must realize that the clash of nationalisms which re-moved the minorities from the Turkish scene was a clash of mutually *exclusive* nationalisms. Only one could finally win, and its final tri-umph had to include the excision of the others from the land. A foreigner may lament that Greek nationalism or Armenian nationalism did not triumph in Anatolia, but they did not. This chapter of history is closed, unless Russia tries to resurrect it as a pretense for intervention in Turkey, and the non-Moslem minority remnants in Turkey are of no real importance except to their own unfortunate selves. Their presence represents no threat to the health of Turkish society, and the tensions under which they live are foreign to the bulk of today's Turks as well as inoperative upon those Turks.

Hence the covert distinction between the status of Moslem and non-Moslem in Turkey, although real, is not significant in an appraisal of modern Turkey, for it does not impair the health of Turkish society. Any able non-Moslem who is restless under the prevailing restrictions is at liberty either to emigrate, which many do, or else to qualify as a true Turk, in religion and language, whereupon the mobility horizons of Turkish life are at once open to him. This happens. Not often, but sometimes, minority individuals "turn Turk."

In the case of Turkey's *important* minority, the Kurds, Moslem in religion but non-Turkish in language, we have seen that Turkification, which means effective assimilation, is now spreading widely among them. Every formerly Kurdish individual upon whom that process operates also comes thereby into command of the mobility horizons open to whatever class level he enters in the Turkish social structure. As a rule, of course, that level is the peasant level.

The Kurds, in the ordinary European view, are "uncivilized" while Turkey's non-Moslem minorities are "civilized," and there are certainly many senses in which this is true. But it is not important as far as modern Turkey is concerned. What matters is that the Kurds, a minority of large dimensions and hence of potential danger to Turkey, are being peacefully absorbed. What might have been a cancer in the body politic as well as in the body social is instead usefully and healthfully being incorporated into both. Only deliberate foreign interference, and perhaps only foreign invasion, can seriously threaten Turkey with any real Kurdish problem. Here Turkey is making a gain which all well-wishers of peace will hope to see consolidated.

One would expect to find the major tension-producing conflicts in Turkish society in the relationships between the peasant mass and the non-peasant class, rather than in problems of minorities. But investigation will demonstrate that here, too, Turkey's social structure is in a healthy condition.

Each general class, peasant and non-peasant, has within it a wide range of upward and downward social mobility. The fact that there is a great difference in status and prestige between the highest and the most lowly members of the non-peasant class, between the President of the Republic and the man who delivers bread to the President's house, is much more readily apparent to *us* than is the wide range of difference in status which also separates the leading peasant from the most lowly peasant. Because we are ignorant of them, the nuances of peasant life escape us. If we knew enough of peasant standards, however, we would realize that such a range of status in the peasant class does also exist. An ambitious but "low born" young peasant, a peasant whose prestige-rank in his own class is low, has the chance in Turkey to rise to a better level, just as the young non-peasant with a low prestige rank has the chance to improve his position. Social mobility exists to provide each with an available access to satisfaction. This, of course, is not the same thing as a guarantee of success. It is only a guarantee of opportunity to try. But if a man tries and misses, he still sees around him many similar men who succeed. In each class enough men do succeed to prevent the building up of a significantly strong tension within the class.

Prestige, whether in the peasant or the non-peasant groups, is compounded of the social esteem which the individual enjoys because of his wealth, that which he enjoys because of his skills and accomplishments, and that which he enjoys because of his control over the actions of other individuals. Family position counts for comparatively little on the prestige scale. A poor family background, peasant level or non-peasant level, is not a really great handicap. A good family background is, of course, an advantage, but it is no guarantee of success. As for inherited wealth, the problem there is to hang on to what one has. Turkey has never had a system of primogeniture. Large inherited fortunes have always been as atypical as were those few individuals who claimed to be "aristocrats." The pervading atmosphere, a rule proved, of course, by many exceptions, has much in common with our own "shirt-sleeves to shirt-sleeves in three generations" concept of social mobility.

The prestige of women, however, despite their technical emancipation under the Republic, is still almost wholly governed by the prestige-rank of their fathers or of their husbands. It is still possible to count on one's fingers the Turkish women who enjoy a marked degree of social esteem truly thanks to their own exertions and accomplishments. This assertion, of course, is not also a prediction. Doubtless more and more Turkish women will attain rewarding social status on their own accomplishments. Some younger women are seriously devoted to careers, and the important obstacle they must now overcome is simply traditional mistrust of a woman's making her own way in such "un-Moslem," which is to say "untraditional," fashion. Most of the restrictions which Moslem society has put upon women are not inherent in the essential religion of Islam itself, but are nonessential accretions thereto. To disregard those restrictions is not to be a poor Moslem. It is simply to jettison a portion of High Moslem tradition.

Mobility horizons for the woman who seeks to make her own way on her own merits and accomplishments are not as adequate as they are for men. But this constitutes no danger to the Turkish body social. Quite the contrary, for the would-be career woman is still a rare phenomenon. Indeed, it may be argued that the mentality characteristic of the *average* Turkish woman, of the non-peasant and especially of the average peasant woman, is a major brake retarding Turkey's Operation Bootstraps. The society still teaches girls that their status in life should depend upon that of their father or of their husband. Most marriages are still arranged. The couple involved have, of course, each of them a power of veto over the match (although not necessarily so in the case of the peasant girl), and the terms of the marriage include financial aid from both families, and in general are designed to get the couple off to as good a start in life as possible. In defense of this system the least which can be said is that it is realistic, that it is subject to whatever balance mature judgment can bring to the eternal question of who had best marry whom, and that it produces happy marriages. As a rule, the groom is somewhat older than the bride, both are young enough to approximate what is physically probably the optimum age for marriage, and both usually come to marriage with a realistic attitude towards sex, regarding the production of a large family as life's most desirable goal. Children are cherished. Not to have a son is one of fate's worst blows. In most family relationships one often finds a note of normal adjustment which may be called characteristic of Moslem communities. Many individual people are, of course, unhappy, but the fact remains that family life is relatively sound and that suicide is rare in Turkey today. The impact of the west is, unfortunately, altering this in a direction fairly to be described as for the worse. The family-unit is being somewhat reduced in its importance. Divorce is increasing. Hollywood and cheap western fiction combine to hold up before many young Turks a ridiculously distorted and exaggerated concept of what romantic love means in western society, and some of the young Turks try to conform. Westernization is by no means an unmixed blessing. Even so, it would be ridiculous to maintain that the basic stability of Turkish family life has been seriously impaired by westernization or industrialization or urbanization to date. Here, too, one foresees no clear or immediate large-scale threat to the healthfulness of Turkish society.

The basically significant cleavage in Turkish society is that between the peasants and the non-peasants. We are already informed on the major differences involved. The peasants are largely illiterate, highly resistant to change, suspicious of central authority, usually limited in their horizons to their own pocket or "gulf" of landscape, relatively uninterested in rising above the subsistence level economy by which they have so long satisfied their needs. On each of these counts, the members of the non-peasant ruling group are, generally speaking, at the opposite extreme. They are literate. They are, especially under the Republic with the collapse of High Moslem tradition, no longer resistant to change, but frequently active protagonists of change. Their suspicions of central authority have decreased to the point where they have assumed the functions of a genuinely democratic electorate. Although their horizons are still seldom world-wide and their thinking naturally centers on Turkey itself, still they strongly support a policy which makes Turkey a stable and constructive factor for peace in world affairs, and there are almost no valid serious reasons to fear that this will rapidly be changed. In terms of the economy, this non-peasant group has always lived on the peasants, but has also always been actively interested in developing and maintaining for itself a standard of living as far above that of the subsistence level as possible.

In view of these many points of sharp difference, one would tend to assume that the large peasant mass and the smaller ruling group have always lived at sword's points, the one the object of unremitting repression and exploitation; the other constantly on guard against a servile revolt. Nothing could be further from the truth. A genuine, widespread peasant revolt is unknown in the history of the Anatolian Turks. The peasants today are a problem to Turkey's leaders not because they threaten to take the bit in their own teeth but for the opposite reason: it is hard to encourage them to make *any* changes at all in their way of life.

One consequence of this is as welcome to Ankara as it is obvious: the Anatolian peasant is not susceptible to communist propaganda. On the contrary, he would be the final obstacle to an attempt to establish a communistic regime in Anatolia by force. This absence of harmful tensions between the upper class and the peasant-level mass is as yet little understood. It cannot be explained simply by the observation that there is no great problem of landownership in Turkey, although this is true. Part of the explanation appears when one realizes that there is, in the last analysis, no real line of sharp demarcation fixed between the two general groups. Just when an agha (a peasant leader and village landowner who also deals with the non-peasant class's middlemen on almost equal terms) himself becomes a member of the ruling group and so leaves the peasant class is impossible to say. Should he move to a city, he has been technically urbanized, but his new city life will likely be so close to his former life in most essentials that "a town-dwelling peasant" is still the most accurate characterization of him.

Many lower-level members of the ruling group have peasant-level wives. For a family or an individual to slip back from ruling group status, however humble, to peasant status, however high, is regarded as disaster and all possible measures are taken to avoid it. This in part accounts for the great size of the present state payrolls of the Turkish Republic: the state is attempting to provide for all that it can of the families who were the ruling group of the Empire. It accounts for a part of the emphasis upon finishing a *lycée* education, for this certificate ensures that its holder can continue upon the modern ruling group level of life, however humble, in his employment and also, as a reserve officer, in his compulsory military training, while the privates ordinarily came from families without serious pretensions to ruling group status. It accounts for the fact that though many peasants voted in the 1950 elections as members of a free electorate, still they by and large seem to have voted under the guidance of their own local Anatolian pocket's ruling group leadership, and their votes generally reflected that leadership's views. Certainly no candidates were themselves bona fide peasants. Any man able enough to get himself recognized as a possible candidate would, by that same token, already have risen from peasant to full non-peasant status.

Fluid mobility from the peasant group to the non-peasant group is far less common than is a considerable rise in status within the peasant group, but it is by no means uncommon. In Ottoman times the army certainly was a main channel through which a humble peasant boy could rise to the highest posts, provided only that he (1) had the ability and (2) got an early enough start on his military career. This holds true today.

And new factors which further aid in the peasant's rise have been increasingly added to the scheme of life under the Republic.

With the new alphabet and with increasing attempts to make elementary education available on a nationwide scale, the youth—or at least the young males—of the peasant mass are now becoming literate to a degree hitherto unknown and undreamed of. Military service shows the peasant boy many parts of Turkey in addition to his own pocket of Anatolia; gives him a taste perhaps of city life; in all probability puts him into his first effective contact with such machines as trucks, diesel engines, and portable generators; teaches him some reading and perhaps some writing; and then finally sends him home. Back home, since the end of World War II, he has been increasingly likely to find some wealthy peasant agha able and eager to buy a small truck or tractor which the peasant boy can drive and keep in repair. This type of private enterprise has already revolutionized local transportation in Anatolia, and is also revolutionizing the level of technical skill found in the village. It is the young peasant men who are becoming Anatolia's truckers and tractor-drivers, the young village blacksmiths who are rapidly becoming mechanics and turning smithies into garages.

More fortunate peasant young people, male and female, may have an opportunity to attend Village Institutes, one of the most successful and promising ventures yet launched by the ruling group in its attempt to rouse the peasantry to a common sense of purpose as modern Turks and to bring it rapidly up to a minimum level of new technical efficiency. The Village Institutes are trade schools, boarding schools, built in villages by the students themselves and designed to give the able young peasant firsthand participating knowledge in improved methods of farming, housing, cooking, child care, simple medicine and veterinary surgery, and so forth, in surroundings which teach the student these things without at the same time divorcing him from, or spoiling him for, the peasant level of life. Upon leaving such an Institute, the graduate is expected to return to his or her own community, or to a comparable community, there to serve not only as a teacher but also as a living preceptor of the sort of basic, gradual, minimum change whose immediately demonstrated profits will recommend it to all peasants who see it at first hand. Beyond doubt such a program as that of the Village Institutes is of immense potential significance. The limiting factors at present are personnel and equipment, today's 18 or 20 institutes obviously being but a drop in the bucket of what is needed. At present the score is scarcely better than one institute for one million peasants. Certainly if the benign infection from these centers is to spread rapidly among the peasants, many more centers will have to be established.

Not all members of the ruling group would like to see the peasant modernized, which is to say "depeasantized," too rapidly, not even in the most minimum sense. This is wholly understandable. The rapid creation of a literate, vocal, united, and self-conscious Turkish peasantry would, of course, upset many ruling group applecarts. But there is no cause for concern here. Despite all that has been done by the Republic's leaders, and despite the total impact of the west upon the peasant to date (especially since World War II), the peasant's nature is still basically change-resistant. No transformation overnight is at hand. Relations between peasant mass and ruling class continue largely unstrained. The basic cleavage of Turkish society persists, but is no more a threat to the health of that society than formerly.

This assertion can be made with confidence despite the small-scale emergence under the Étatist industrialization program of a nascent industrial proletariat which seemingly is largely of peasant origin. There was always a seasonal force of migrant peasant labor, some of it seminomad, employed in agriculture. The Étatist program of industrialization through state capitalism with its development of state-operated industries has utilized some of this migratory labor. But the labor, despite scattered efforts to raise its standard of living by providing factory housing, factory commissariats, and the like, still remains migratory. The ordinary pattern is to leave one's own "country" (one's own pocket of Anatolia) and work in a factory long enough to accumulate a small sum of money, and then go home to one's family and live that money up. The problems this puts in the way of the plant manager who tries to retain a semiskilled permanent labor force are self-evident. The training and retention of adequate foremen are especially vexing. In so far as a superior stratum of foremen and skilled workers has evolved, there exists a relatively stable nucleus of wage-earners, an emergent professional proletariat. But this class is still so small and·the elements which will make it up as it grows are still so uncertain that no predictions about it can safely be made.

The beginnings of an emergent small capitalist middle class in Anatolia are familiar to us. We have seen that the urban center contains a small and still largely undifferentiated middle class. Peasants aspiring to higher levels of social status may try for a place in any of these classes, but are most likely to find a place in the largely undifferentiated proletariat group. How and whether these several classes will materialize in Turkey is, of course, a fundamental question. One can go no further now towards an answer than to say that their growth has not yet introduced, and does not appear likely to introduce, interclass tensions which will soon be harmful to the state. Moslem Turks of all classes and of all foreseeable classes appear still to share those fundamental patterns of loyalty to the state and of separateness from other states which the Republic has built upon. In addition, they also come more and more to share in some sense of common purpose as citizens of the Turkish Republic, although the penetration of this feeling into the broad base of the peasant mass is of course slow and as yet not fully demonstrated. A strong feeling of Turkish nationalism has not yet reached all citizens on the lowest social levels. But no other feeling hostile to the idea of Turkish nationalism is effectively at work on those, or other, levels, and no such feeling seems to be at hand. Hence one concludes that Turkish society, on all levels of the ruling group and of the peasant class, and even in the emergent middle class and proletariat, is notably free from harmful tensions which would seriously impair the healthy functioning and growth of that society. Many factors work to slow down social evolution and social differentiation. This is exasperating to those who would purposely speed up one or another phase of such development and evolution, but it is not necessarily regretable. On the contrary, since haste is likely to make waste, as the Étatist venture has proved, Turkey's informed well-wisher may be content that her development in basic essentials should be as slow as it seems to date to have been sure.

Perhaps it is not fanciful to argue that the real wisdom in enforcing Operation Bootstraps so rapidly upon the upper levels of Turkey's social structure was that only this degree of urgency "from above" could produce even slow evolution in the lives of the peasant.

2. THE TURKS' VIEW OF THEMSELVES

If we attempt to fathom the real nature of modern Turkey by asking the question, "What is the Turks' own view of themselves?," we at once realize that there is no single answer. The peasant mass, still dominated by loyalty to family and region, to faith and then to a new central government whose nationalism only now begins to seat itself firmly in the peasant mentality, is not sufficiently self-conscious to entertain any coherent overall view of itself. Ask a peasant what he is and he will tell you where he is from, his name, his family. He assumes you know he is a Turk—who isn't? Or ask him why he is a Turk. The answer boils down to this: one is a Turk because one isn't something else, because one isn't a non-Moslem, or a Bulgarian, or an Arab, or a Russian, or something else. Naturally, one is glad one is a Turk: they are a brave and honest people, and why should anyone ask questions about that?

Ascending the social scale, one finds far more eloquence in the answers to "What are you?" and "why?," but not necessarily more ordered ideas. A Turk is a Turkish-speaking Moslem, citizen of the Republic. Period. In their modern literature and art, today's small group of creative Turks are perhaps still generally, or at least too frequently, more concerned to achieve convincing replicas of current western models than to strike out on their own. The assertion that Turkey has made her contribution to Moslem culture and is now a conscious apprentice at western culture holds true to a surprising extent. And the relative absence of "real Turkish" elements in modern Turkish art and literature is enhanced by the fact that creative artists tend to come from those very urban groups who throughout their lives have the least direct contact with the life of the peasant majority of the inhabitants of the country.

A frequent plot in Turkish literature under the Republic treats of the intellectual, ruling group urbanite, thoroughly westernized and idealistic, who goes to serve the peasant in the village and to aid in the peasant's "national regeneration," only to be overwhelmed by the harsh realities of peasant life and by the unresponsive Anatolian mentality, and finally to suffer breakdown of some sort. This plot has even been handled by writers who themselves had had little experience of Anatolia.

The influence of Western European forms upon Turkish art, and especially upon Turkish literature, was one of the earliest manifestations of the western impact upon Ottoman culture. It long antedates the beginnings of Turkish nationalism. By and large, French literature and French art have been *the* models for the Turks. In writing, this has been clear in poetry and prose alike. The classic forms of Ottoman *divan* poetry have disappeared. In their place have come western verse forms and a system of scansion far better suited to Turkish speech than were the artificial "longs and shorts" of the older classics. This system derives from Turkish folk poetry while the content of most modern Turkish verse is western derived or at least much influenced by western ideas. The classical Ottoman music remains alive, as does Ottoman folk music. But these, too, have yielded ground to western music, classical and popular. A new school of Turkish music is evolving in the work of a small group of composers and performers. Its products to date are largely imitative, but the most successful of them have Ottoman as well as western roots. Ordinarily they are designed for western instruments and make use of the western scale, as true *ala Türka*, in distinction to *ala Franka* (western European style), compositions do not.

The Moslem literary tradition gave great importance to the tale, and in this the Ottomans had created much. The modern novel and short story, however, are largely western-inspired in form as well as in content. In both forms, and especially in the short story, the Turks excel. Drama, too, is properly to be described as largely a western-inspired non-Moslem innovation. The Turks are having increasing success in it. In every form of literary creation it now may be maintained that the more gifted writers are making it ever clearer that Turkey's literary apprenticeship to the west is drawing to a close. More and more, writers are treating Turkish materials realistically, without self-conscious considerations of whether some western author or school would or would not approve some particular style or device, and the result is an increasingly vigorous, emergent new Turkish literature.

The press, daily and periodical, grows in strength and in technical competence. Between them, Istanbul and Ankara can boast of several newspapers whose format and contents are truly admirable. At many points, and in none more than advertising, American influence is evident, especially since 1945. The press is of great importance in the formation and diffusion of ideas throughout the entire country, for the larger dailies circulate in all urban communities. It is now an almost completely untrammeled press, and freedom of the press is being increasingly founded in law. All extremes of opinion, except pro-Russian, are represented. Most papers should be called "independent Democrat." The influence of the press was an important factor in the 1950 elections.

One particularly effective facet of the newspapers is their use of photography. Another is the recently revealed Turkish genius for cartoons. Since 1900 the traditional Moslem avoidance of representational art has almost disappeared from Turkey. Scruples about the rightness of portraying the human face and form, in drawings or in photographs, have vanished except in the most conservative quarters. Together with the development of Turkish painting has come sculpture, and to an even greater degree than in the case of literature, Turkish artists and sculptors were dependent upon western models. A prospective end of Turkish subservience to western models is not so clearly in sight for painting and sculpture as for literature, but no one need doubt that it will eventually come. Meantime increasing success in combining old Turkish design and old Turkish miniature painting techniques with western elements marks a partial resurrection of respect for the Ottoman artistic heritage.

A willingness upon the part of creative artists to see values in the Ottoman achievement as well as in the most modern (and all too often the most extreme) western styles is perhaps least evident in modern Turkish architecture. Only a handful of Turkish architects have, since the foundation of the Republic, made any serious attempts to evolve a distinctively Turkish style, and not many of their designs have been built. One consequence is that Ankara, with its block buildings, severely plain and "modern," is a most un-Turkish-looking city (a point entirely welcome to the mentality which wishes to discard the past) and also a city of buildings poorly designed to give comfort in Anatolia's summer weather. But here, too, there are signs that the final product of the western impact upon Turkish art will go far beyond mere imitation of western models and will eventually evolve into a "truly Turkish" synthesis of Ottoman and western heritages. With experience comes self-confidence. When Turkey's apprenticeship to western culture is done, she may again have her own distinctive contribution to make to west as well as to east.

One element characteristic of some modern art and architecture is the artificial introduction of motifs from the ancient Anatolian past, or from those segments of that past which the now largely defunct official theory of history professed to regard as "Turkish." This archaizing chauvinism in art has not been very successful and will probably not long persist. Indeed, as for art, so for chauvinism, one sees that with increasing self-assurance comes a diminution of slavish imitation and an increase in truly independent creative thought whose end product is neither wholly traditional nor wholly anti-traditional, wholly oriental or wholly western, but a self-contained true Anatolian synthesis of all.

There is a school of thought in Turkey which takes Anatolianism for its name (*Anadolujuluk*) and which aims essentially at that very mature self-assurance which will be content to regard all new Turkish achievements as stemming from new Turkey's own Anatolian soil, and which will not attempt to compensate for self-consciousness of supposed shortcomings by slavish imitation of any essentially non-Anatolian factors, whether from the distant days when non-Moslem Turks flourished in central Asia or the more recent times when disillusioned young Ottomans tried to be more French than the French themselves.

It is not the entire population of new Turkey which labors to win through to this balanced view. Most people, non-peasants as well as peasants, by and large have never given such questions a moment's conscious thought. It is only Turkey's few, self-conscious, ruling group intellectuals and artists who are now engaged in this adventure. They have been politically at least less ineffective than comparable intellectuals in most neighboring lands. At the same time they have done well in their apprenticeship to nontraditional culture, less well at not concurrently losing sight of the basic values of their own rich tradition. If world conditions permit Turkey to endure, then as she develops, one can expect her ever-evolving view of herself to be reflected in an increasingly vigorous and distinctive new Turkish art.

3. THE TURKS' VIEW OF THE WORLD

The present-day "Turkish view of the world" is no more capable of simple formulation than is Turkey's current "view of herself," and for much the same causes. The average peasant's horizons scarcely yet embrace the whole of Turkey, let alone the whole content of Turkish nationalism. The non-peasant is not provincial in the peasant's sense, but he is invincibly provincial when it comes to forming a tenable judgment on Turkey's relative importance in the world today. It is not that his education has left him Turkey-centered. Only the exceptional man in any country, large or small, "retarded" or "advanced," does not partake of national egocentricity. It is that the Republic's efforts to enlist education in the service of its program of wholesale nationalism plus westernization have given him an exaggerated idea of what Turkey's accomplishments to date amount to when measured in terms of the current world par. This is neither wholly good nor wholly bad. It is not good if a portion of Turkey's electorate or electorate-to-be demonstrates in the streets of Ankara or Konya for the return of Cyprus to Turkey, for in the long run this can only work to impair Turkey's hitherto well-merited reputation for sober steadiness in international affairs. But if Turkey is a true democracy in which a portion of the population feels Cyprus should be "redeemed," how can the government democratically forbid such demonstrations? Or how long will politicians refrain from campaigning upon such irredentist platforms?

At the same time, it is not wholly bad that Turkey's citizenry does not clearly understand how relatively weak the country is today in comparison with world par, for such understanding could at best only serve somewhat to dampen the national ardor and will to survive, and no well-wisher of Turkey, or of any small sovereign state, could wish to see that country's spirit flag. Without the spirit, life is gone.

Turkey's attitude towards Russia is, as we have seen, shared in its essentials on every social level of Turkish life. It is an antipathy deeply rooted in history and in profound religious differences, and incorporated firmly into folk culture and folklore. It is basically not rational, and the stronger thereby. That anything short of the passing of many years could truly alter it is practically out of the question. To suppose that any Ankara regime could retain popular allegiance while attempting to serve as a Russian puppet is almost beyond imagination. To suppose that the corps of regular army officers would countenance such an attempt is flatly unthinkable. To argue that any regime in any circumstances could restrain the Turkish people from resisting a Russian invasion is to betray ignorance of a deep-seated, nationwide Turkish emotion. These things could only become possible with the maturity of a new generation of Turks whom some catastrophe had wholly separated from the mentality of today's Turkey.

Turkish feeling towards the Balkan nations—and here we are, of course, speaking of the ordinary individual's attitude and not of Ankara's official and diplomatic "sentiments"—can also be characterized fairly as an antipathy, but in no sense comparable in intensity to Turkish antipathy towards Russia. Bulgaria probably shares with Greece the lowest position in Turkey's regard for Balkan nations. These are the two Balkan states with which the Republic has common frontiers. Formal relations, as contrasted to national attitudes, with Greece are far better than with Bulgaria, and were so before World War II. Bulgaria's current maltreatment of her Moslem-Turkish citizens naturally evokes profound Turkish resentment. True sympathy with Greece in her wartime and postwar ordeals was practically nonexistent. A stock question for Americans in Turkey today is "why do you not give us as much aid as you do Greece, especially since we are so much more able to turn it to advantage?" In Turkey's attitudes towards her other Balkan neighbors, too, there is a note of competition and of exasperation. All of them were once her subjects. All became "nationalized" and "westernized," and broke away from the Empire long before the Turks began to strive for status as a sovereign, westernized state. In each case, the break entailed not only fighting and Great Power interference with much wild talk of the "Turkish yoke" and "Moslem barbarism"; it also frequently involved Russian participation and indirect, if not direct, profit to Russia. None of these considerations endear her Balkan neighbors to Turks. They trust none of them. Attitudes toward them, however, are not of a compelling intensity, although they would become so in case of open conflict. Responsible Turkish opinion today would probably like nothing better than to see the Balkans redeemed from the Iron Curtain into full sovereignty and incorporated into a Balkan Alliance in which Turkey would play her full role. Popular feeling is not strong enough to put any obstacle in the way of Turkish official attempts towards such a Balkan future. No sane Turk, however, expects Balkan nationalisms and Balkan tensions quickly to subside, or to see the reign of sweetness and light in that turbulent peninsula in this century.

Towards Iran, the Turkish peasant feels a distant antipathy. The Shiite Moslem Persian he considers contemptible. Neither does his folklore portray the Persian as a good fighter or a formidable foe. Ruling class Turks feel for Persia a general apathy tinged with apprehension. The apprehension is the fear that Persia may eventually be so weak as to let Russia into the Middle East and so leave Turkey more completely surrounded than she now is. Persia's attempts at

westernization during the interlude between the wars are regarded as
a sensible try at imitating what Turkey was doing, but as by and
large a failure. Moslem Persia's cultural prestige in Turkey, maintained for so long, has entirely vanished among the discarded impedimenta of the High Ottoman tradition. In 1900, the study of
Persian was as esteemed as the study of Latin was among us. Today
Turkish interest in Persia might better be compared to American
interest in Sanskrit. Some few Turks are bilingual, knowing Persian
as well as Turkish, but this is no longer a source of any appreciable
social prestige. Trade with Persia and Persian financial interests in
Turkey are not of importance. Outstanding points at issue between
the two countries have for generations tended to dissolve in the face
of the common threat from Russia. In so far as a stable Persia can
contribute to Turkish security, Turkey actively wants a strong Persia.
That a militarily strong Persia, a Persia able of her own resources
seriously to deter foreign aggression, will or can soon exist, Turkey
does not believe. Popular apathy towards Persia in no way handicaps
Ankara in its dealings with that country. No Turks regard the Persians themselves as in any sense a direct threat to Turkey. No serious
agitation for, or hope of, annexing the Azerbaijani Turks of Persia
to the Republic exists, officially or unofficially, nor is there important
Azerbaijani sentiment for incorporation into Turkey. The Turks regard the Persians as somewhat unable to deal with their Kurds and
so as contributing to unrest along the frontier, but do not view this
as a serious problem.

It will be noted that the ordinary Turkish attitude towards Persia
today is the older Ottoman antipathy, dating from the centuries when
Persia was the Empire's one seriously threatening Moslem foe, but
greatly tempered by the later Ottoman apathy towards Persia which
developed when both were the objects of western imperialism but
when Persia especially was passive and helpless.

The Turkish attitude towards the states and people of the Central
Arab World—Egypt, Jordan, the Lebanon, Syria, Iraq, Saudi Arabia,
and the Yemen—is similarly based on a heritage from the Ottoman
past. All of these lands were once Ottoman possessions; most of them
remained so until 1918. The Turks have no particular feeling that
the Arabs waited until the Empire was in difficulties and then stabbed
it in the back. They realize that forces quite beyond the Arabs' control cut the Arab world off from the Ottoman Empire, and they are
fully reconciled to the loss. Indeed, as we have seen, they regard it

not as a loss but as one of the preliminary essentials necessary for the ultimate attainment of full Turkish sovereignty. At the same time, the Turks have little admiration for the Arabs. They regard the Arab world currently as generally benighted, foolishly tardy in trying to follow the path which the Turks have rushed along, inexcusably weak in its inability to cope with Israeli force, and politically immature and unstable to the point of endangering the entire Middle East. The bond of fellowship in Islam, in orthodox Islam, is tenuous. Pan-Islam has always been an idea more effective in western European foreign offices and imaginations than in Moslem lands and hearts. Peasant Turk and non-peasant Turk alike generally dislike the Arab, Mohammed's people though he be, and mistrust him as well. The Arabs reciprocate fully in kind. Formal relations with Arab states are kept as correct as possible. Trans-frontier relations with Iraq and Syria are not a problem, and Ankara doubtless prefers to deal with a sovereign Syria and Iraq instead of with the former Great Power mandatories of those countries. But the general Turkish attitude towards the Arabs is one of centuries-old disillusionment. Many educated Turks know the Arab world quite well, but few expect much from it in the near future.

Political instability in Iraq and Syria and the possible penetration of communism into the Central Arab World preoccupy Ankara at times, but the Arabs no more than the Persians are news in Turkey. By and large, the Turkish press covers the world, but for months at a time one can read far less of Persia and the Arab states in a good Istanbul daily than would appear in a good New York daily, and this was true before the Palestine controversy became news at all. In short, Turkey's face is to the West. She is convinced that not many domestic developments in neighboring Moslem lands are of any vital interest or concern to her, and she ignores them accordingly.

Her attitude towards the problem of Israel and the United Nations is an excellent illustration of this. Originally, Turkey hoped to preserve Moslem and Middle Eastern solidarity, and so opposed the creation of Israel. But when it became clear that the issue involved factors which Turkey regarded as of vital concern to her own interests, when it became clear that the United States supported Zionist claims as an integral part of its own policy, Turkey had no qualms in promptly abandoning her support of the Arabs. This the Arab states bitterly resent, but Turkey does not regard their resentment as a threat to her vital interests. Turkey's concerns are to survive and to prosper. To achieve these she has done all that she has done. Her modern role of the "easternmost bastion of western democracy" not only gives her her best chance to continue towards her goal, but also to develop internally as she wishes. It is fantastic to suppose that the coincidence that Persians and Arabs as well as Turks are Moslems will deeply affect the foreign policy of the Turkish Republic any more than it gives the average Turk any real feeling of sympathy for Arab or Persian as fellows in one faith.

Proposals that Turkey head a Moslem bloc or an Asiatic bloc awaken little response in Turkey. They are even sometimes resented. Turkey would far prefer to belong to a western bloc, and her preference rests upon first-hand awareness of realities in the Moslem world as well as on her desire to be considered "western."

The economies of the lands of the central Moslem world, Egypt partly excepted, do not complement or supplement Turkey's, but are in out-and-out competition with it, and Turkish trade with them is not important. Egypt is an exception only as one of Turkey's best customers for tobacco.

Turkey's other important market in the Middle East is Israel. Turkish recognition of Israel was prompt, and Israel has since been a profitable outlet for Turkish produce. The balance of trade is greatly in Turkey's favor, however, and Israel is taking what measures she can either to adjust that balance or else to cut imports from Turkey. That Israel will remain so important as a market for Turkey seems unlikely.

Israel's existence has had another consequence for Turkey, the emigration to the new Zionist state of something more than half of Turkey's Jewish population. Those who have gone represent no overwhelming loss in the Turkish point of view. By and large they were the very poorest urban class, from Istanbul and from Izmir. With their departure came a final end to the feeling, often proclaimed under Atatürk but flatly contradicted by the Varlĭk Vergisi under Inönü, that Turkey's Jews were on a somewhat different footing from the other minorities, that they had never had national aspirations of their own which had troubled the Empire and hence would be retained as citizens in good, if not quite in full, standing in the Republic. Indeed, the Turkish record for the treatment of Jews throughout Anatolian Turkish history should have earned for the Turks general Jewish good will.

When Jewish holders of Turkish passports began to leave Turkey in thousands—something more than forty thousand have gone to date—the Arab states objected. Turkey responded by stamping passports of departing Jewish citizens "not valid for travel to Israel," confident that this would not deter the Israeli authorities from admitting immigrants, but at the same time giving the Arabs technical satisfaction.

Those who argue that the "Middle East" or the "Moslem World" is today an abstraction meaningful not in itself but only as a passive element in the calculations of strong powers can at least buttress their case by citing Turkey's attitudes towards her Moslem neighbors. The community of interest which fellowship in Islam and geographical propinquity give is not a consideration weighty enough to influence Turkish attitudes or Turkish policy seriously today, nor does it appear that it is likely soon to do so. So long as the Moslem world remains a power vacuum and so long as Turkey tries to save herself from the woes of a state without the power even seriously to deter foreign aggression, Turkey will not strive seriously to link herself directly to other Moslem states. Nor has she overriding economic motives for a closer relationship with Persia or the Arab world.

Thus the Turks' general view of the rest of the Moslem World goes a long way to explain to us why Turkey should not be regarded today *only* as a Moslem land or even primarily as a Moslem land. Turkey's eyes are on the west and on the future, not on the east and on the past.

Apart from Russia, almost every major country of Europe has at least some admirers in Turkey today, and a realization of the difference between one and another European power is felt on even the lowest peasant level of Turkish life. As a rule, strong Turkish admirers of any European country have had some personal connection with that country, either having studied there or else having come into contact with that country's citizens in the cosmopolitan society and the foreign schools of Istanbul. Turks who have had European "advantages" of this sort are naturally only a fraction of the upper class, not to say of the total population. They are, however, an important and an influential element in the country—in government, in commerce and finance, and in intellectual and artistic life. Most Turks of this description are accomplished linguists. Their air of easy cosmopolitanism often leads the foreign observer to feel that they are not "really Turkish." In this, the foreign observer is usually wholly wrong.

For example, it is true that many leading Turks deeply admire Germany. They admire her genius for system. They respect her science and her education. Turkey has many professional men who have had training in Germany as well as in German schools in Turkey, and many business men with experience in Germany. The older officers of the Turkish army are many of them trained in the German tradition. Above all, and this, as we have seen, is a point whose force is fully felt on every level of Turkish society: no Turk forgets that it is Germany, and he would likely add "Germany alone," who twice within the past half century has brought Russia to her knees. This alone would give Germany prestige in Turkish eyes.

Even so, German-trained Turks and Turkish admirers of things German should not be regarded as also being strongly *pro*-German. Germany's ambitions to dominate in Turkey and to exploit the country have always been well understood. Many informed Turks will assert that Germany consistently tried to obstruct the development of Turkey, preferring to keep her as a primitive source of raw materials and as a market rather than to see her exploit her own resources. Few responsible Turks would attempt to claim that Germany's genius has ever extended to the sphere of her own government. More important still, the Turks are fully aware that Germany has lost her wars. Hence her prestige in Turkey is, to say the least, seriously qualified. Turkey produced no potential Quislings who were ready to sell her out to Nazi Germany, any more than she produces communist leaders ready to sell her out to Russia.

The same sort of detached admiration holds true in the case of France, although the background here, of course, is different. French culture has traditionally been regarded in Turkey as *the* European culture. French remains the second language of most Europeanized Turks, although the study and use of English have made increasing strides since the end of World War II. France's military and naval prestige among Turks perished with the fall of France in the recent war. French economic prestige has suffered almost to a corresponding degree. More than a remnant of the influence of French culture, however, does still persist, and the French government is exerting itself to maintain this prestige, but is finding the attempt a losing fight. It is just as true in Turkey as elsewhere that nothing succeeds like success. And in Turkish opinion—especially in the eyes of younger Turks—France has largely failed. Today's young Turk does not try to dress or wear his hair and beard and glasses like a Frenchman or like a German, as he was likely to do in 1910. Events have moved since then, and he moves with them.

England has always been admired by many Europeanized Turks for her *centilmanlik* (the quality of being a gentleman), her sportsmanship and self-control, her Empire, and also for the success of her parliamentary government and for her law, but the British have not until recently enjoyed a degree of widespread esteem comparable to that of France, or even that of Germany. The study of English language and literature in the nineteenth and early twentieth centuries was less common in Turkey than the study of French or German, and most of what was carried on was in the hands of American Protestant missionaries whose energies were directed principally to non-Turkish minorities. These missionaries enjoyed a measure of private British support, and frequently also had more British official support than they did American.

In the twentieth century the picture has changed. Especially since the founding of the Republic, the study of English has spread, and with the Anglo-American victories of World War II, British and American prestige in Turkey reached new highs. Anglo-American support of Turkey against Russia, of course, consolidates this prestige. There could be no more eloquent testimony to the esteem in which the Anglo-American concept of representative government is held in Turkey than that furnished by the 1950 Turkish elections. The amount of information on England and America available in the Turkish press and the volume of literature published in translation from English are truly surprising. There is no doubt that the western nations who have the greatest degree of prestige in Turkey today are first America and England—the one distinctly surpassing the other—and then, at a considerable distance, France. Italy's rank is insignificant.

We should, however, repeat that few Turks are emotionally pro-American or pro-British or pro-anything except Turk. They admire many things about the west, but they are also aware of many of the west's faults. To say that Turkey today regards the United States as the currently functioning western Eldorado, respects and envies what she considers our successes, and attempts not only to discover and emulate our "secrets" but also to keep our good will and help is a somewhat hard-bitten and unsympathetic judgment, but for the mass of the Turkish population it is probably reasonably accurate.

Turkey's attitude towards the United Nations today reflects her attitude towards the League of Nations before World War II. It also summarizes her view of the world in which she exists. To attain her long-range hopes, she must live in a peaceful and secure world. What she can do to achieve international peace and security, she does. Her conduct on international bodies is exemplary—actively constructive, farsighted, and realistic. Its motivation is not at base idealistic or humanitarian but is enlightened self-interest. It is hard to see how any reasonable person could expect her to do more. What she does is based on no illusions, and she does not allow her activity to lead her into an illusory belief that she is secure. Turkey can no more afford illusions than she can afford idealism. She expects her foreign policy, in the United Nations or outside it, to pay dividends, and she exerts herself to make it pay.

The principal point of weakness in Turkey's view of the world (in so far as one can speak of a coherent, nationwide "world outlook") rests in the fact that most of her population is still so unaware of world-wide realities that it consistently overestimates Turkey's own world importance and seriously exaggerates the significance, in world-wide terms, of Turkey's recent role and accomplishments at home and abroad. There is no doubt that this provincialism is a weakness, and that it may become a greater weakness as the Turkish electorate begins to exercise more immediate control upon Turkish foreign policy. One has only to reflect upon the potential implications of the Turkish student demonstrations for the return of Cyprus. This is not, however, now a major weakness, nor need it necessarily ever become one. Even to call this relative lack of information about the rest of the world—a phenomenon due largely to Turkey's situation as a retarded area and a largely peasant state—a weakness is a two-edged knife, for we have already noted that egocentricity has its uses in the domain of national courage and resolution, and that it is Turkey's national resolve to remain sovereign, rather than her absolute strength, which best equips her for her present role of the easternmost bastion of western democracy.

4. RELIGION

To round out any sketch of the modern Turk one must of course consider his personal religion. And in this matter, above all others, the foreigner must confess himself at a disadvantage which obliges him to advance with the greatest care. We have already observed that the religious institutions most characteristic of true Ottoman life were discarded along with much else in the true Ottoman heritage,

that the former prestige of the Ottoman Ulema has almost wholly
vanished, and that the dervish orders have not only been officially
banned but have also in fact dwindled. In all these cases the salt had
in truth lost its savor and today has been cast out and trodden under
foot. But all of these, of course, were matters primarily touching only
the upper classes. On the lower levels, whether in the villages or the
cities and towns, the salt of folk Ottoman religion has remained much
more savory. It is true that the professional practitioners of folk
Islam (to speak in this connection of a "clergy" calls forth too many
error-producing overtones in the mind of the western reader) have
been officially demoted from their ranks of high social esteem and
are, indeed, under careful supervision. These measures have done
something to impoverish such folk religious leaders, not many of
whom were for that matter ever particularly well-to-do by true Ottoman standards, but at the very least it would be distinctly premature
to assert that the hold of folk Islam over the Turkish peasant has
been much impaired. Village life persists largely unchanged, and the
importance of traditional religious sanctions in it has not greatly
altered.

When the foreign observer confines his view to the upper social
levels, he has ample reason to assert that younger educated people
seem generally characterized by an ignorance of the content of Moslem belief and the nature of Moslem religious practice—that they do
not know what Islam as a personal religion is—and that they not
only fail to attend mosque or to pray at home, but even believe that
all organized religion, of whatever faith, is old fashioned and in some
respects socially undesirable. These assertions appear to be reasonably well-grounded in the case of the ordinary, educated, upper-class
young Turk of today, but they are misleading in their failure to allow
for the many non-ordinary people of that description. Numerous
Turks, young as well as old and ruling class as well as peasant, are
personally devout individuals. Mosque attendance, at least on special
holy days, is actually quite heavy in cities as well as in villages, and
one hears frequent assertions—always without statistical underpin-
ning—that mosque-going is increasing. Certainly the erection of new
mosques has increased since the end of World War II. Under President İnönü a somewhat tenuous form of voluntary religious instruction was permitted in the public schools for those who wished it. This
was done in response to a fairly widespread popular demand. When
the Democratic administration came to office, it in its turn lost not a

moment in abolishing the restrictions upon the use of Arabic in religious services, as we have already noted. There has been a marked increase in the number of simple religious manuals appearing from the presses, and presumably in the sale of such literature as well. Pious passages printed in the old letters (the "sacred" Arabic script) and suitable for use as talismans are also again available and are sold widely.

Hence to say that Islam is dead or dying in the Turkish Republic is plainly an untruth. Many thinking Turks obviously have their doubts about the wisdom of efforts to revive Moslem religious institutions, for to them those institutions understandably represent the chains of the past with which the true Ottomans bound themselves as they strove to combat the European new by means of a return to the Moslem old. At the same time many such individuals are also fully aware that a nation without religion courts the peril of substituting the state's good for God's will in questions of right and wrong. Not a few Turks consider such idolization of nationhood as the greatest of all twentieth-century perils.

Certainly Turkish Islam of today cannot be dismissed simply as an inert heritage from earlier times. It is too strong and too vigorous for that. But in granting that Turkish Islam is quite vigorously alive, one is not of course also subscribing to the ideas that the Turks therefore feel a close kinship with other Moslem peoples or that a Turkey-centered "Reformation" in Islam is on the way. No facts support such inferences as these.

One best concludes that for almost all Turks Islam represents the nominally true faith and serves as one of the ultimate bases upon which they draw covert discriminations for or against other individuals. In addition, for many, many Turks, Islam also represents a way of personal life, in this world and in the world to come, which these men and women follow sincerely and reverently whether they chance to live in a most westernized or in a most old-fashioned style.

Religion more than anything else brings home to the western, non-Moslem observer the complexity of Turkish character today. In this aspect, beyond and above all others, Turkish individuals are infinitely varied. The new and old, the Ottoman heritage and the Republic's westernization and nationalism, are inextricably intertwined. Herein resides much of the modern Turk's human charm and appeal for those who know him best. Here, too, Turkey today defies broad generalizations. Among this people one has ever with him the rich and the poor, the wise and the dull, the old and the new, the pious and the impious. Turkish life today gives the individual wide latitude if he seeks to reach a closer personal relationship with God. Here, too, one justly sees an abundant source of Turkish strength.

We have now assembled enough information about the Turks at least to know that their land is not, and cannot be, a *perfect* "eastern-most bastion of western Democracy," physically, economically, or psychologically and that Turkey's record as an exponent of western democracy still leaves much indeed to be desired. At the same time, whenever we have compared present reality with Turkey's own recent past, we have been obliged to register surprise at the strides she has made.

We have seen that in terms of her available physical and human resources, Turkey, despite progress, remains an underdeveloped and retarded area. This is in part thanks to the legacy of the past, for the past is at one and the same time a brake which retards change and a heritage which cannot be jettisoned without losses entailing. We know that the initial success in obtaining Turkey for the Turks did not itself guarantee success in the further struggle to gain enough New Turks to enable New Turkey to survive, and that the development of New Turkey through its extraordinary Operation Bootstraps has been ragged as well as speedy and spectacular. A recapitulation of what Turkey amounts to today has shown us a basically healthy society now actively and consciously engaged in attempting to solve its domestic problems by a new recourse to democracy-in-practice, a more pronounced practice of democracy than the Turkish Republic has previously attempted or has previously had the opportunity to attempt. We know, too, that the Democratic administration of President Bayar has more than domestic problems to solve: its final success in every sphere will depend ultimately upon the international situation, upon factors which Turkey herself can, at best, only partially control. Turkey cannot gain the security which will ensure her continued sovereignty by her unaided efforts. She cannot gain it by submitting to her foe, Russia. Neither can she gain it by attempting to lead any coalition of her neighbors. Her only hope is to join forces with and seek the aid of a power strong enough to withstand Russia. And that power today, if it exists at all, is the Anglo-American world and especially the United States.

7. The United States and Turkey

Relations between the United States and Turkey date from 1830 technically, from the very beginning of America's national existence in fact. Through the nineteenth century those relations were never of prime importance to either party. Improvements in transportation and communications did make the two countries more accessible to each other, but there was no real community of economic, political, or cultural interests to bring them genuinely together.

Even in the twentieth century, Turkey and America remained virtually worlds apart. During the first World War our diplomatic relations with Turkey were, of course, broken, but in part as a result of President Wilson's personal friendship with a family of American philanthropists then residing in the Ottoman Empire, the United States ultimately refrained from a formal declaration of war upon the Turks. During the Allied Occupation of Constantinople at the end of World War I, America's token participation, thanks largely to the tact and vision of our ranking representative, Admiral Mark L. Bristol, was unique in that it left the Turks relatively well disposed towards America after the Allied evacuation of Turkey. The manifold activities of the Near East Relief organization also contributed to maintain American prestige in post-World War I Turkey. Underlying all these was the obvious fact that the United States was not only refusing to participate in the Mandates system but also had no designs in the Middle East of any description. After the first World War, as before, economic and political ties with Turkey were of negligible importance to the United States, while ties with America were of comparatively small, although still of substantial, importance to Turkey. Not until World War II did Turkey become of real importance to the United States.

Such sentiment towards Turkey as existed in America was largely anti-Turkish. We had of course inherited the ordinary western European prejudice against the Turks as champions of Islam. In addition, many groups in America had espoused the cause of one or another of those Ottoman subject peoples who in the nineteenth century were fighting to gain their independence from the Empire. Immigrants from that Empire had helped foster pro-Greek or pro-Macedonian or pro-Bulgarian sentiments in this country. What had principally aroused American interest in Turkey, however, and what had especially directed that interest towards the non-Turks were certainly the long-standing presence and activities of American missionaries in the Ottoman world. It was chiefly the Armenians' aspirations and woes to which those missionaries gave currency.

American missionary activity in Turkey dates from the 1830's. It is one of the most fascinating and astonishing as well as inspiring chapters in the entire history of American Protestantism. The principal endeavor was not to convert Moslems to Christianity, but rather to reinfuse life into the native Christian churches of the Ottoman east. Of the native Anatolian Christians, the Armenians proved most responsive. In time, an Ottoman Protestant church was created. This was not exactly the reinvigoration of native churches for which the more farsighted missionaries had hoped, but it represented a feasible solution in the face of the hostility of those churches toward the missionaries and their new converts. The Ottoman authorities eventually accorded these Protestants full status as a *millet* in the Empire's system. The Protestant *millet* never reached numbers great enough to rival the older forms of Christianity in the Empire, but what it lacked in size it tended to make up in its westernization and in what the missionaries themselves would refer to as old-fashioned Yankee "git up and git." Greek Protestants, Arabic-speaking Protestants, Bulgarian Protestants, and so on—all came into existence in response to the American movement, and all exist today. But the major response came from the Armenian people.

The early missionaries arrived in a wholly foreign world almost wholly unprepared, and they showed extraordinary speed and insight in adapting themselves to the strange realities they had to face. The more able of them realized from the first that exhortation and what might be only lip-service conversion—that simply evangelization— were not what Turkey's Christian populations needed, but rather that education of native leadership was the essential. Education entailed the translation and publication of the scriptures in the vernaculars, and this in turn meant no less than the development of local lan-

guages such as Armenian and Bulgarian into modern literary languages. Here, of course, the missionaries, knowingly or unknowingly,
were pulling in harness with local nationalist agitators, for the cultivation of "national" languages was an essential element in the deliberate evocation of conscious nationalisms among the Ottoman peoples of the nineteenth century. In this matter the American Protestant
missions registered sustained and productive activity, and no one
who knows the facts is likely to try to minimize their role, although
they were not of course the only or the leading forces at work.

Health education and the provision of medical service were also
essential. Addressing themselves to these problems, the American
missionaries eventually produced medical missions, hospitals, and
orphanages staffed with Christian doctors and workers, which have
done and in many cases continue to do untold good throughout much
of the former Ottoman world. To these and to the missionaries' activities in translation, publication, and evangelization we must also add
general education. Mission schools finally included almost every type
of institution from kindergarten to theological seminary, American-
supported and American-controlled. Their effectiveness in the popu-
larization of athletics and sports deserves special mention.

Early in the history of American Protestant activity in the Ottoman
Empire, certain of the more gifted and broad-visioned missionaries
had come to differ somewhat strenuously from most of their breth-
ren on questions of educational policy and purpose. One of these, the
Reverend Cyrus Hamlin of Constantinople, eventually found American financial support for his ideas, and resigned from the mission
in order to take in hand the project of founding in the capital of the
Empire an American college open to all, a college which would be
Christian in purpose and character, but which would not be a missionary institution either in the nature of its financial backing in
America or in the sense of actively proselytizing. Established during
our Civil War, the Hamlin college—called Robert College in honor
of Christopher Robert of New York, its principal American supporter, and incorporated under the Regents' Board of New York
State—has existed to the present day and is now a thriving American-
Turkish institution. Robert College has the distinction of being the
pioneer American college abroad.

At the outset, the College's appeal was principally to non-Moslems
of the Empire, although it welcomed any Moslem student who applied. Under Abdul Hamid II, Moslem Turks were officially forbid-

den to attend. Not until the time of the Republic did American educational institutions in Turkey begin to attract large numbers of Moslem Turks. Before 1914 Robert College had seen periods in which it principally served Armenians, Greeks, and Bulgarians. Eventually it produced offshoots in Athens (a thriving institution today) and Sofia (now defunct as a result of German and Russian measures). In the Arab portions of the Empire the work of the Syrian Protestant College, currently the American University of Beirut, first emulated Robert College and eventually, as Beirut became the greatest American university abroad, surpassed it. In Turkey before World War I numerous other American educational institutions had grown up, some of them colleges, almost all of them under mission control, and all of them attended principally if not wholly by non-Moslem students. Like Robert College, many of them were for men only, but some were women's schools, notably the school which finally became the Istanbul American College for Girls. Like Robert College, this institution was also not essentially a mission school.

The Young Turk Revolution and especially the Turkish War for Sovereignty brought great problems and changes to American educational-philanthropic-missionary activity in Turkey. With the creation of the Turkish Republic, all foreign schools came under the control of the Turkish Ministry of Education. Somewhat chauvinistic legislation (which, however, was certainly needed in the cases of several minority and European-propaganda "private" schools) restricted the teaching of various subjects to the Turkish language and put it exclusively into the hands of Turkish citizens. Restrictions intended primarily to curb the Moslem clergy also impinged upon missionary activity and forbade proselytizing. More important, the minority communities among whom American missions principally worked had now practically disappeared. Hence American mission activity in Turkey under the Republic is only a fraction of what it was under the Empire. The mission stations now operating are, for the most part, either schools or hospitals. Their patrons are largely Moslem Turks, and their work is principally educational and philanthropic. They are probably regarded with favor and with esteem by most Turks, although chauvinist blasts against them are not unknown. The principal factor which today curtails these American activities is not Turkish control but lack of financial resources.

The once thriving American College at Izmir did not continue to function in Turkey for long after the foundation of the Turkish Republic, but the two Istanbul colleges, Robert College and the Girls' College, both of which had remarkable leaders who kept them well ahead of the changing times, have survived, and now thrive. In Turkish law they now form one corporation under an American President and a Turkish Vice-President. They retain their own separate campuses and administrations, and today are esteemed joint American-Turkish ventures. Their finance, an ever thorny problem, comes in some degree from Turkey but in the main from American endowment and gifts, and their student bodies are increasingly Moslem-Turkish in nature.

Taken as a whole, America's still extensive missionary-philanthropic-educational activities in Turkey have shown increased ability to adjust to the kaleidoscopic changes of the last half century. It is worth remarking that this record has been made in the almost total absence of United States governmental support, financial or otherwise. Even today when the importance of America's reservoir of good will in Turkey is fully realized by Washington, the colleges in Turkey still depend upon wholly inadequate private contributions from America and operate under the most stringent financial handicaps.

As before World War I, so during the interval between the two wars, apart from the Foreign Service, American interest in Turkey and Americans informed about Turkey centered in the colleges and missions and in the restricted number of American businessmen whose work, chiefly the purchase of tobacco and the marketing of petroleum products, led them to reside in Turkey. Until World War II, Turkey remained for most Americans a truly distant land.

Our policy in Turkey during World War II thus scarcely stemmed from much previous American interest in or concern for Turkey. Instead it might properly be characterized as one of backing up Britain, enabling her to fulfill her commitments to the Turks, and incidentally exploiting Turkey's neutrality in our own interests as best we thought we might. When, however, the end of the war produced a world severed into two hostile groups by the Soviet-constructed iron curtain, Turkey for the first time began to bulk large in her own right as a potentially important factor in American foreign policy. It is really only with December 1941 when wartime pressures led President Roosevelt to declare the defense of Turkey vital to the security of the United States that Turkish-American relations acquired sufficient importance to be a very tangible subject of discussion, and only with May 1947, when the Congress approved the

first $100,000,000 of American aid to Turkey in implementing the
"Truman Doctrine" of support for Greece and that country, that
American-Turkish relations were officially recognized as of key im-
portance in America's efforts to contain Russian expansion.

And in 1947, as in 1941, it was still true that Turks knew much
more about America than Americans knew about Turkey. This remains true today, and those things which Americans do know about
Turkey, only the logic of events has taught us. It would pay us to
learn more.

After May 1945, when Soviet pressure on Turkey could increasingly be identified as a clear threat not only to the Turks but also to
all of Russia's foes, and especially to her arch-foe, ourselves, informed Americans in the government or outside it (they were few,
but some of them—fortunately—were in it) could lay down a number of guiding principles for America's action in Turkey.

For example, they argued that the general policy which the United
States in its own best interests should follow towards Turkey would
also largely be in the best interests of Great Britain and of the other
members of the British Commonwealth. Therefore, American activity
in Turkey need not involve us in important differences with our great
English-speaking allies in a global struggle with Russia. Events since
1945 have confirmed this assertion, and we may reasonably assume
that it will continue to hold true.

Similarly in the area of which Turkey is the center—the area of
the Straits, the Middle East, and the lower Balkans—Turkey now
began to be fully recognized as not only the strongest local power,
but also as the most firmly anti-Russian power. We know, within the
limits of human fallibility, that she will do her best to resist Russian
aggression. The more we can strengthen her, the more will she be
able to deter Russia from attacking her or, alternatively, in case attack does come, to ensure that that attack will have to be a clear-cut
case of aggression by an admittedly official Soviet army (or just possibly by the Bulgarian satellite army) invading an unquestionably
sovereign country. It is true that as early as 1947 it was recognized
that once we should start arming and aiding Turkey, we would have
a long-term commitment on our hands, for Turkey cannot in the foreseeable future even begin to equip herself with modern weapons or to
replace any significant fraction of the equipment she wears out.
Therefore, before the Truman Doctrine program was ever embarked
upon, it was fully understood that the longer our attempt to contain

Russia should go on, the more of an investment we would have to make in Turkey. But in 1947 it could also be argued that there was another side to this coin, that when and if our opposition to Russia should cease, our support of Turkey could also cease, for our community of interest with Turkey stems from no natural affinities but only from the circumstance that we both are opposing Russian expansion. Hence, America's interest in Turkey was and is a *term* interest. How long that term will last depends in the first instance not upon the Turks, but rather on the Russians and on ourselves. However, this argument that we could assume only a narrowly limited liability in Turkey was never, in fact, very convincing. If nothing else, it was too cold-blooded, far too Machiavellian to suit the prevailing American taste.

Events of course did impose limits. When we came to apportion our total resources for a global struggle, we had at once to recognize that the area in which Turkey is the center was (and at the present writing still is) actually only of *secondary* importance for us—secondary as compared, say, to Germany or China-Japan—but that it nonetheless might at any instant become for a time an area of primary importance. Our other available friends in the area—Greece and Iran—were and are vastly weaker than Turkey. Hence, questions arose: Should we attempt to strengthen the weakest, or instead concentrate our available resources upon the strongest available partner, Turkey? How much of our available total resources should we allot to this entire area? How important was and is it to us to be ready there?

Solomon himself could scarcely have answered those questions, adequately, in 1947 or today. As far as Turkey was concerned, we could at least first try to appraise what our vital interests in the country are. When this was attempted, three basic considerations emerged. First, Turkey was and is of obvious strategic importance to us because her geographic position affords command of land, sea, and air communications in much of the Balkans and the Middle East, because she forms an obstacle to Soviet expansion towards the Mediterranean and the oil lands of the Middle East, and because in the event of war Turkey could be a major military obstacle to Soviet aggression or alternatively a valuable staging area if operations against the Soviets were necessary.

In the second place, Turkey was and is certainly the most resolute, independent, and stable element and also unquestionably the most democratic and the most western element in a semi-oriental area of widespread political and economic unrest. Obviously each of these points was and is highly desirable in an associate for a struggle such as that which the United States had to face. It becomes increasingly evident that *Time* was close to the mark when it dubbed the Turks "Finns with Mountains."

Finally, there was the negative consideration that America's other interests in Turkey were restricted to educational and philanthropic activities plus commercial ties—all of which are important from the Turks' point of view but are relatively unimportant in terms of America's total world interests.

Thus when America's basic interests in Turkey were analyzed, it became clear that she was distinctly America's best bet in an important area, but it could still be argued that American-Turkish association would be a term association, active only for the term during which America would strive to contain Russia. On the face of it, America theoretically could, if she wished, then try to make the maximum short-term use of Turkey and then pull out, *once Russia had been dealt with.* In practice, however, this was never really the case. To begin with, who could—and who can—say just when Russia will have been dealt with, or how hard a task dealing with her satisfactorily will ultimately prove to be? And since this is true, would short-term measures in Turkey be what the United States really wants? In fact, by first attempting what was primarily a program of military assistance, and even of short-term military assistance, the Truman Doctrine, since 1947, has already demonstrated that any attempt to make the best possible short-term use of Turkey and then pull out is not feasible.

The original $100,000,000 appropriation for Turkey was allotted 95 per cent to military requirements, 5 per cent to improve transportation and communications facilities with the hope of thereby increasing Turkish military efficiency. It was also hoped that all these measures would soon enable the Turks partially to demobilize, and that this in turn would somewhat relieve a prolonged strain upon their economy. Since that time, America's interests in Turkey have inevitably broadened. To date a total of some $700,000,000 has been at least earmarked for Turkey, and the American assistance program has grown far beyond its original limits. It is still growing and will continue to grow. Turkey has been included in the Economic Coöperation Administration program, and is the object of ever wider measures on our part to aid her to help others by helping herself.

Attention is being given officially to the improvement of agriculture, of land transportation (both road and rail), of coal mining and distribution, and so on—down the line.

Earlier hopes that American private enterprise and investment would be of immediate and substantial aid to Turkey's economy have largely been disappointed. The Turkish government, under Inönü as well as under Bayar, has increasingly exerted itself to provide the conditions considered most likely to attract American capital—legal conditions, assurance of noninterference on Ankara's part, guarantees that a reasonable share of profits may be exported, and the like. Eventually these measures may at least help to make Turkey a more attractive field for the American investor, but this certainly will not happen until the Russian menace to that country has definitely and incontestably been lessened. Meantime, our activities as well as our interests in Turkey are sure to remain preponderantly official.

American businessmen, for their part, as they have investigated possibilities for investment in Turkey or else when employed by the American government in official capacities in Turkey, have been coming into increasingly direct contact with the massive residue of true Ottoman mentality and practice embodied in Turkish administrative concepts and methods and in the economic impedimenta and mores of the Turkish businessman. When he first stumbles into this new, foreign, and highly uncongenial world, the American tends to feel that inordinate difficulties are deliberately being put in his way. Further experience convinces him, however, that although the difficulties are certainly inordinate, they are not solely or especially in his way, but are the milieu in which business is done in Turkey. Many westernized Turks are as eager as are Americans in Turkey to see fundamental changes made in matters of taxation, cost-accounting, corporate finance, above-the-table competition—in short to see the growth in Turkey of a system of private enterprise and fiscally responsible government such as we take for granted in the United States. But the westernized Turks realize, as few Americans on the spot have yet come to understand, how massive the residue of the Ottoman old in these fields is, and how relatively little of the new façade has as yet truly displaced the old. They do not therefore discount the possibility that Turkey's government and economy will eventually evolve in directions congenial to American enterprise and advisers, but they do realize what a large-scale displacement of traditional practices such evolution will entail. All of these considerations, however, should not be overemphasized. Their impact upon the short-term matters now prominent in American-Turkish relations is of only secondary importance.

As more and more Americans are active in Turkey, the realization grows in unofficial as well as in official quarters that Turkey is, in many important aspects, truly and outstandingly a "natural" for effective United States coöperation, a natural not only for the term interest of containing Russian expansion—however long that may require—but also for longer-range plans towards a better international order and a better world, the sort of plans which are still somewhat nebulously referred to as "Point Four Thinking."

Why Turkey should so impress Americans on the spot is obvious. She is unquestionably a backward and an underdeveloped area. At the same time, and to a degree probably unrivaled by any comparable region anywhere, she has herself actively been facing her problems for the last twenty-odd years, and has already managed to make an appreciable dent upon many of them. In the process she has deliberately and voluntarily striven to remake herself in a new mold, a mold whose general design the ordinary American, once he grasps it, instinctively understands and approves because it so frequently at least approximates his own conception of how things really should be.

In dealing with a country which is in the midst of its own energetic Operation Bootstraps, the American abroad is on incomparably more congenial ground than when he works in a retarded area where everything is to do and nothing has yet started to be done under local auspices and by local initiative. Here one finds the reason why it is that of the many Americans now active on the spot in the Turkish program, those who are most enthusiastic about possibilities and accomplishments are likely to be precisely those who have had enough experience of countries other than Turkey so that they bring with themselves to Turkey some standard upon which to base comparisons.

In the matter of containing Russian expansion, the Turks—like ourselves and like the British—are unfeignedly, wholeheartedly, in sober, serious earnest. Of what other peoples can the same be said?

Many American officials in Turkey will tell one—and the more the individual official's work gives him an overall grasp of the picture, the more likely he is to hold this view—that there is no other place in the entire world where the American tax dollar spent abroad for military purposes buys as much as it does in Turkey today, and also that there is no place in the world where the American tax dollar spent to strengthen a foreign country in a nonmilitary sense finds a better potential use than it does in Turkey.

Naturally, such assertions are subject to some allowance for the enthusiasm of a hard-working man for the job he has in hand. They are also subject to another, and a much more important, reservation. That is the tendency of the American expert abroad to be fooled by his own expertism. When, for example, the American agricultural expert working in Turkey (not to mention the expert who has never worked in Turkey, or who has been there for only two weeks) asserts that "if we do X, Y will happen," his listener must at once find out whether the meaning is (a) if X is done in Iowa (or Uganda, or wherever this man has worked), Y will happen, or whether he means (b) "we know upon the basis of adequate experience in Turkey that if we do X here, Y will happen here." It is only if he means (b) that that man is a true expert for Turkey—whether his field be agriculture or harbor works or banking. And as a matter of fact, as yet there are very, very few qualified American experts on Turkey of any description. To create them will take time. Pending their creation, an absence of dogmatism in official assertions that such and such "will happen" will be reassuring to all concerned, for it will mean that Americans charged with our mission to Turkey are fully aware that, despite various partly superficial appearances, Turkey is still a most foreign and complicated land to the citizen of the United States.

The essential weakness in all long-range plans for American-Turkish coöperation is of course that they assume there will be a long range of time in which we can coöperate. Such is plainly not necessarily the case. If Russia tomorrow firmly resolved to conquer Turkey at any cost, she eventually could. It is true that the Turks would resist to the uttermost of their ability. It is true that thanks to American military and nonmilitary aid already received, and to American techniques already learned, their resistance would be more formidable than could have been the case in 1945. It is true that even if Turkey were completely occupied by Russia, resistance would undoubtedly continue. It is also true that such an attack on Turkey would at once involve the United States. But all these things, true though they are, do not mean that Russia could be denied Turkey if she were sufficiently determined to occupy the country.

What this prospect means to thinking Turks can be realized only by those with firsthand knowledge of modern warfare and of Soviet

methods. Not many Turks blame us that their situation should be
as it is. Rather, they thank us that they are as well off as they are.
They politely keep to themselves their opinions on how slow the
people and government of the United States were in effectively realizing the nature and dimensions of Russia's threat to us. They probably
believe that we are not yet entirely awake. Privately they are not
above saying "We told you so" to those Americans who throughout
the war were assuring them of the coming glories of American-British-
Russian coöperation. Above all, the Turks plainly now sense that the
United States is swiftly becoming not only an aroused associate in the
struggle against the U.S.S.R. but also a disillusioned and hence a
more sophisticated and wily associate in what Turkey has long known
is a struggle for her own life. These changes in America's temper delight the Turks, and they react to our reverses not with dismay but
by the implemented voluntary offer of what immediate aid they can
send even as far afield as to the Korean theater of war. In short, Turkey is proving that she is not a fair-weather friend. But the Turks do
wish ardently that they had some *formal* guarantee from us that we
would (a) go at once to their aid to the best of our ability in case of
attack, and (b) commit ourselves formally to their ultimate liberation and restoration in the tragic event that they are nevertheless
overrun. They feel that just to the extent that it is they, and they
alone, who today are able to serve, and do willingly serve, as the
easternmost bastion of western democracy, so to that degree do they
merit formal assurance that their bastion will not be regarded as ultimately expendable. Their irreducible minimum demand is admission
to the North Atlantic Pact. For this they are pressing with all means
at their disposal, and it is wholly probable that they soon will receive
the recognition and the degree of formal assurance that admission
to that mutual defense pact will entail. To date, they have only
qualified status therein.

Some legally minded Americans argue that such recognition of
Turkey will also entail recognition of Greece, inasmuch as the original
Truman Doctrine was intended for Greece *and* Turkey, and even that
it will also entail recognition of Iran, since Greece, Turkey, and Iran
now form an "area" in our official terminology. To this the Turks
can reply, "All right—Greece and Iran and the Yemen too, if you
will. But isn't the real point that we, and we alone in this part of the
world, are strong enough and dependable enough in ourselves effectively at least to deter Russian aggression, that we and we alone actu-

ally are the functioning easternmost bastion of western democracy? Obviously you want to strengthen the areas adjacent to us. Obviously you want, as you can, to strengthen *all* areas. We hope you will. We are extremely anxious to see you strengthen Greece and Iran, and to see the situation of Syria and Iraq clarified, but—how much time do you have? Would you not do better to put more of your eggs into our relatively strong basket, and to admit that ours *is* strong and therefore immediately useful to *you* as well as to us, rather than to distribute your precious and limited eggs into basket after basket, regardless of whether they are strong or weak, relatively useful or relatively useless receptacles for these perilous times? Is it not true that we, today, are of more genuine value to the United States than is France?"

The reader will probably join the writer in a feeling of relief that *he* does not have to answer that question, and in a sense of respect for those of our fellow citizens whose positions of authority compel them to answer and to answer soon.

It is probably true that if Turkey had had a better press in this country for the last twenty years, if her present nature and outlook were better known to Americans generally, she would today bulk far larger in our plans and in our actions than is now the case. The Turks, for their part, are now somewhat belatedly doing all in their power to arouse American public interest and opinion in their favor. The Turkish Information Office in New York City is definitely one of the most ably conceived and operated friendly foreign propaganda services in America today. Its entire purpose and method are not only legitimate and aboveboard, they are congenial to Americans because the men who operate the office are themselves in sympathy with American values as well as those of their own land. But this Information Service is new. It is tiny. And its budget is limited. Over the years, brick by brick, it can aid in the slow construction of a solid edifice of American-Turkish coöperation and understanding. But it is not a short-order restaurant.

There is very little anti-Turkish feeling left in America. The occasional Greek-American may still remark that Constantinople was better before 1453, to which the obvious rejoinder is that it is now almost 1953; and the occasional Armenian-American society may direct a resolution to the Secretary of State, censuring him for dealing with the Turkish barbarian. But these things mean little.

The Secretary of State is dealing with New Turkey, the Turkish

Republic which continues to strive to produce enough New Turks to ensure its own future, the Turkey of Atatürk, Inönü, and Bayar—the Turkey of the Turkish people and the Turkish electorate. Above all, in extremely critical times, he is dealing with a country which is functioning to the best of its ability, and with as much help from us as it can get and as we are currently willing to give, as the easternmost European bastion of our cause against our own implacable foe. Turkey is not perfect. After all, she is only a collection of human beings, even as are we. But imperfect as she is, she is a land of unusual promise for important values close to many cherished American values, an associate more helpful than demanding, self-respecting and resolute and reliable.

Her house today is in relatively good order and in surprisingly good order by any reasonable standards. Compared to the houses of her neighbors, it is in outstandingly good order. For this, for the fact that such a country exists in the world today to be our associate in a common struggle, the United States can take a very small and recent share of credit indeed. On some counts the Turks merit reproach, but on far more counts they merit praise. Dare we say better of ourselves?

The American who attempts to form a final judgment on what the relationship of the United States with Turkey should be in the near future and, God grant, in the distant future, will do well to listen to a wise voice from that country's own distant, pre-Turkish past, to Herodotus of Halicarnassus who said:

I shall devote as much attention to small countries as to great, for those which were great in the past have mostly become small, while those which were great in my time had been small before. Conscious as I am of the perpetual instability of human fortunes, I shall make no distinction in my treatment of the two.*

* Herodotus, I, 5: translated by A. J. Toynbee, *Greek Historical Thought,* 5–6.

Appendix I.　General Information
about Turkey

AREA: 296,503 square miles.

POPULATION: According to the 1945 census, 18,860,222. Preliminary announcement of the 1950 census gives a total of 20,902,628. This gain is probably partly due to the fact that the 1950 count reached regions which earlier censuses had only partly covered.

The most recent breakdown available for the principal religions of Turkey dates from 1935 and hence fails to indicate the growth of the Moslem group and the diminution of other religious groups which have taken place since that date. In 1935 the religious percentages of the total population were

Islam	97.43
Christianity	1.39
Judaism	.46
"Others"	.72

The latest percentages for the mother tongues of Turkey's inhabitants are also for 1935 and thus extremely out of date. They were

Turkish	85.98
Kurdish	9.09
Greek	.63
Armenian	.37
Georgian	.36
All others	3.57

COMPOSITION OF THE GRAND NATIONAL ASSEMBLY BY PARTIES

	Prior to 1950 Election	*After 1950 Election*
Democrat	54	408
People's Republican	403	69
Nation		1
Independent	8	9

ELECTIONS OF 1950

Voters registered	8,905,576
Ballots cast	7,916,091
Democratic	4,242,831
Republican	3,165,096

The percentage of registered electorate who voted was 88.88.

GOVERNMENT (as of February 1951)

President	Celal Bayar
Prime Minister	Adnan Menderes
Minister of State and Assistant Prime Minister	Samed Ağaoğlu
Minister of	
State	Fevzi Lûtfi Karaosmanoğlu
Justice	Halil Özyörük
Defense	Refik Ş. Ince
Interior	Rüknettin Nasuhioğlu
Foreign Affairs	Fuat Köprülü
Finance	Hasan Polatkan
Education	Tevfik Ileri
Public Works	Kemal Zeytinoğlu
Economics	Zühtü H. Velibeşe
Health and Social Welfare	Dr. Hayri Üstündağ
Customs and Monopolies	Nuri Özsan
Agriculture	Nihat Iyriboz
Communications	Hulûsi Köymen
Industrial Development	Muhlis Ete

TURKISH REPRESENTATIVES IN THE UNITED STATES

Ambassador	Feridun Cemal Erkin
Military Attaché	Col. Arif Güvenç
Naval Attaché	Capt. Bahri Geyer
Air Attaché	Maj. Saim Arman
Financial Councilor	Nahit Alpar
Press Attaché	Nüzhet Baba
Commercial Attaché	Nail Artuner
Cultural Attaché	Cezmi Berktin
Permanent Delegate to the United Nations	Selim Sarper
Director, Turkish Information Office	Nuri Eren
Consul General, New York	Necdet Kent
Consul General, Chicago	Hikmet Anlï

EDUCATION

	1948–49	1949–50
Number of Schools	13,311	17,029
Total Enrollment	1,474,781	1,625,452

LITERACY: Of the total male population above 7 years of age, in 1935, 31 per cent were literate; in 1945 the percentage was 39.50. Of the total female population above 7 years of age, 10.50 per cent were literate in 1935; 14.60 per cent in 1945.

TURKISH STUDENTS in the United States in 1948 totaled 676 and were registered in 120 different educational institutions. Of the 676 students, 393 were financed by the government.

FINANCES OF THE CENTRAL GOVERNMENT OF TURKEY

	1948	1949
Total revenue (Turkish Liras)	1,261,000,000	1,252,000,000
Total expenditure	1,368,000,000	1,372,000,000
Deficit	107,000,000	120,000,000

TURKEY'S FOREIGN COMMERCE, 1940–1948
(Turkish Liras)

	Exports	Imports
1940	111,446,486	68,922,708
1941	123,080,868	74,815,069
1942	165,034,442	147,713,229
1943	257,151,661	203,045,170
1944	232,530,350	164,944,863
1945	218,928,951	126,168,357
1946	432,094,468	223,931,229
1947	625,243,952	685,003,317
1948	551,038,451	770,148,535

INDEX OF COST OF LIVING (1938 equals 100)

1947	344
1948	346
1949	397

Note: the above information is abstracted from Turkish official publications, particularly the 1949 edition of the *Istatistik Yilligi* (*Annuaire Statistique*), vol. 17 (Ankara, 1949), and from information made available by the Turkish Information Office. The compilation of exact and meaningful statistical information concerning Turkey is, in reality, only now beginning, and it is to be expected that the next ten years will see great strides made in these matters. In the meantime, material such as that given above should be regarded as an honest beginning, but not necessarily as definitive.

Appendix II. The Turkish Constitution

Chapter I. Fundamental Provisions

Art. 1. The Turkish State is a Republic.

Art. 2. The Turkish State is republican, nationalist, populist, etatist, secular and reformist. Its official language is Turkish and its capital is the city of Ankara.

Art. 3. Sovereignty belongs unconditionally to the nation.

Art. 4. The Grand National Assembly of Turkey is the sole representative of the nation, on whose behalf it exercises the rights of sovereignty.

Art. 5. Legislative authority and executive powers are concentrated and manifested in the Grand National Assembly.

Art. 6. The Grand National Assembly exercises direct legislative authority.

Art. 7. The Grand National Assembly exercises its executive authority through the person of the President of the Republic elected by it, and a Council of Ministers chosen by the President.

The Assembly may at any time control the activities of the Government (Council of Ministers) and dismiss it.

Art. 8. Judicial authority is exercised by independent tribunals in the name of the nation in accordance with the laws and regulations in force.

Chapter II. Legislative Powers

Art. 9. The Grand National Assembly is composed of deputies elected by the nation in accordance with a special law.

Art. 10. Every Turk, man or woman, who has completed his twenty-second year, has the right to vote in the election of Turkish deputies.

Art. 11. Every Turk, man or woman, who has completed his thirtieth year, may be elected deputy.

Art. 12. The following persons are not eligible for election to the post of deputy: Persons in the service of a foreign state; persons who have received a sentence of a defamatory nature or a sentence for theft, fraud, swindling, abuse of confidence, or fraudulent bankruptcy; persons over whom a guardianship has been established; those claiming foreign citizenship; persons deprived of their civil rights and, lastly, those who are unable to read and write Turkish.

Art. 13. Elections of representatives to the Grand National Assembly are to be held once every four years. Deputies whose terms have expired are eligible for re-election. The outgoing Assembly exercises its functions until the meeting of the newly constituted Assembly. Should the holding of new elections prove impossible, the legislative term may be extended for another year. A deputy is the representative not only of his constituency but of the entire nation.

Art. 14. The Grand National Assembly shall convene on the first day of November each year, without being summoned.

The period for which the Assembly may adjourn to enable the deputies to visit the country and to collect material for their supervisory functions, as well as to provide for their personal rest, shall not exceed six months.

Art. 15. The right to introduce laws belongs to the members of the Assembly and to the Council of Ministers.

Art. 16. Deputies shall take the following oath of office when joining the Assembly:

"I swear on my honor that I shall not pursue any course contrary to the prosperity and safety of the country and nation, or contrary to complete national sovereignty, and that I will be loyal and faithful to the principles of the Republic."

Art. 17. Deputies are not responsible for their votes, opinions and statements in the Assembly, nor are they responsible for making known these statements, opinions or votes outside the Assembly. The examination, arrest, or trial of a deputy who is charged with an offense previous or subsequent to his election, can only take place following a decision by the Grand National Assembly. Cases of a criminal nature *in flagrante delicto* are excepted from this provision; however, in such instances, the competent authorities are expected immediately to inform the Assembly of the charges. The application of a penal sentence pronounced against a deputy prior to or after his election shall be postponed until the expiration of his membership. The statute of limitations is not operative during the term of deputyship.

Art. 18. The annual compensation of deputies is determined by special law.

Art. 19. If the Grand National Assembly is in recess, it may be convoked in special session by the President of the Republic or the President of the Assembly whenever deemed necessary; it may likewise be convened by the President of the Assembly upon the request of one-fifth of the members of the Assembly.

Art. 20. The debates in the Assembly shall be open to the public and shall be published word for word.

However, the Assembly may also hold closed sessions in accordance with the rules of procedure. The publication of the minutes of closed sessions is subject to a decision of the Assembly.

Art. 21. The Assembly conducts its debates in accordance with the provisions of its rules of procedure.

Art. 22. Questions, interpellations, and parliamentary inquiries lie within the province of the Assembly and are governed by the provisions of the rules of procedure.

Art. 23. A person is not permitted to be a Deputy and hold another Government post at the same time.

Art. 24. The Grand National Assembly of Turkey elects in a plenary session at the beginning of each November a president and three vice-presidents of the Assembly for one year.

Art. 25. In case of new elections before the expiration of the term by a decision of a majority of the Assembly, the term of the incoming Assembly begins the following November.

The session preceding November shall be considered as an extraordinary session.

Art. 26. The Grand National Assembly directly exercises such functions as enacting, modifying, interpreting and abrogating laws; concluding conventions and treaties of peace with foreign states; declaring war; examining and approving laws relative to the General Budget and the Final Accounts of the State, coining money, approving or annulling contracts and concessions involving financial obligations; proclaiming partial or general amnesty; reducing or modifying sentences, postponing legal investigations and penalties and executing definitive death sentences pronounced by the courts.

Art. 27. A deputy who is found guilty of treason or other crimes committed during his term of deputyship by a decision of two-thirds of the members of the Grand National Assembly, or who is convicted for any crime mentioned in Art. 12 of the present law, and whose sentence becomes final, loses his deputyship.

Art. 28. A member of the Grand National Assembly shall forfeit his deputyship by resignation, by being placed under guardianship, by absence from the Assembly without permission or admissible excuse for a period of two months, or by acceptance of government office.

Art. 29. Whenever a deputy loses his deputyship for any of the reasons stated in the preceding Articles, or in case of his death, another deputy will be elected in his place.

Art. 30. The Grand National Assembly organizes and directs its policy through its President.

CHAPTER III. EXECUTIVE POWERS

Art. 31. The President of the Turkish Republic shall be elected for one Assembly term by the Grand National Assembly in a plenary session from among its members. The outgoing President shall remain in office until the election of the new President of the Republic. A President is eligible for reëlection.

Art. 32. The President of the Republic is the chief of the State. In this capacity he may, during special ceremonies, preside over the Assembly and whenever he should deem it necessary may also preside over the Council of Ministers. The President of the Republic may not participate in the debates and discussions of the Assembly nor cast his vote as long as he occupies the position of President.

Art. 33. If the President of the Republic is prevented from exercising his functions due to a reason such as illness or a journey abroad, or if the Presidency becomes vacant through death or resignation or for some other reason, the President of the Grand National Assembly shall provisionally exercise the duties of the President of the Republic.

Art. 34. Should the Assembly be in session when a vacancy occurs in the Presidency of the Republic, it shall immediately proceed to the election of a new President. If the Assembly is not in session a special session thereof shall be immediately convoked by its President for the purpose of electing a President of the Republic. If the term of the Assembly has expired, or if new elections have been decided on, the succeeding Assembly shall elect a President of the Republic.

Art. 35. The President of the Republic shall promulgate the laws voted by the Grand National Assembly within a period of ten days.

With the exception of the Organic and Budget Laws the President may return to the Assembly for reconsideration—likewise within ten days and accompanied by an explanation of reasons—such laws whose promulgation he does not approve.

Should such a law be voted by the Assembly for a second time, the President of the Republic is obliged to proceed to its promulgation.

Art. 36. The President of the Republic shall, in November of each year, deliver personally or have read by the Prime Minister an address to the Assembly regarding the activities of the Government during the past year, and the measures recommended for the coming year.

Art. 37. The President of the Republic shall appoint the diplomatic representatives of the Turkish Republic to foreign states, and shall receive like representatives of other powers.

Art. 38. The President of the Republic shall, immediately after his election, take the following oath before the Grand National Assembly:

"As President of the Republic I swear upon my honor that I shall always respect and defend the laws of the Republic and the principles of national sovereignty, faithfully strive with all my strength for the welfare of the Turkish nation, ward off with vigor any threat or danger to the Turkish State, protect and magnify the honor and glory of Turkey and devote myself to the duty which I am assuming."

Art. 39. All decrees promulgated by the President of the Republic shall be signed by the Prime Minister and the competent Minister.

Art. 40. The Supreme Command of the Army is vested in the Grand National Assembly and is represented by the President of the Republic. In time of peace the command of all armed forces is entrusted by special law to the Chief of the General Staff, and in time of war is given to the person appointed by the President of the Republic upon the proposal of the Council of Ministers.

Art. 41. The President of the Republic is responsible to the Grand National Assembly in case of high treason. All responsibility for decrees promulgated by the President of the Republic is incumbent on the Prime Minister and on the Ministers who, according to the stipulations of Art. 39, placed their signature on the decree in question. Should the president be held responsible for matters of a personal nature the provisions of Art. 17 of the present law pertaining to parliamentary immunity will be applied.

Art. 42. The President of the Republic may, on the proposal of the Council of Ministers, suspend or reduce sentences of convicts for personal reasons such as incurable illness or infirmity. However, the President of the Republic cannot exercise this right on behalf of Ministers who have been convicted by the Grand National Assembly.

Art. 43. The compensation of the President of the Republic is determined by a special law.

Art. 44. The Prime Minister is designated by the President of the Republic from among the members of the Assembly. The other Ministers are chosen by the Prime Minister from the members of the Assembly and presented collectively to the Assembly following the approval of the President of the Republic.

In the event that the Grand National Assembly is not in session, the presentation (of the Council of Ministers) is postponed until the meeting of the Assembly.

The Government must submit its program and policy to the Assembly within one week at the latest and request a vote of confidence.

Art. 45. The Ministers form, under the presidency of the Prime Minister, the Council of Ministers (Executive Council).

Art. 46. The Council of Ministers is collectively responsible for the general policy of the Government.

Each Minister shall be individually responsible for the affairs falling within his jurisdiction and for the acts and functions of his subordinates as well as for his general policy.

Art. 47. The duties and responsibilities of the Ministers shall be defined by special law.

Art. 48. The number of Ministries is likewise defined by law.

Art. 49. If because of leave of absence or for another reason a Minister is not in attendance, another member of the Council of Ministers shall temporarily act on behalf of the said minister. However, a Minister may not act temporarily on behalf of more than one Minister simultaneously.

Art. 50. If the Grand National Assembly of Turkey decides to summon for trial before the High Tribunal a member of the Council of Ministers, this decision shall likewise involve his relinquishment of office as Minister.

Art. 51. A Council of State shall be formed, the duties of which will be to examine and decide administrative suits and conflicts; to express its opinion in regard to draft laws and terms of contracts and concessions to be granted by the government, and to discharge any duties which may be incumbent on it in accordance with the law providing for the constitution of the Council, or by virtue of subsequent laws. The President and members of the Council of State are chosen by the Grand National Assembly from such persons of distinction as have filled high administrative posts and who possess special knowledge and experience.

Art. 52. The Council of Ministers shall draw up regulations determining the mode of application of existing laws or particular sections in the law, provided the said regulations do not contain new legal provisions and are approved by the Council of State.

These regulations become effective after signature and promulgation by the President of the Republic. In case of an alleged conflict between the regulations and the laws, the Grand National Assembly shall have jurisdiction in the matter.

CHAPTER IV. JUDICIAL POWERS

Art. 53. The organization of courts, their functions, and their jurisdiction is determined by law.

Art. 54. The magistrates of courts are independent in the trial of all cases and in the rendering of their verdicts; they are free from all kinds of interference and are dependent only upon the law.

The decisions of courts may not be modified in any manner whatsoever by the Grand National Assembly or by the Council of Ministers nor be postponed or their application be obstructed.

Art. 55. Magistrates of courts may not be dismissed under any circumstances or manner other than specified by law.

Art. 56. The qualifications of magistrates, their rights, duties, compensations, and the manner of their appointment and dismissal are determined by special law.

Art. 57. Magistrates may assume no private or public functions other than those provided for by law.

Art. 58. Court hearings are public; however, the court may decide to hold closed sessions in accordance with the law on Court procedure.

Art. 59. Every individual has free recourse to all legal means which may be deemed necessary for the defense of his rights before a court.

Art. 60. No tribunal may refuse to examine cases which lie within its competence and jurisdiction. Cases not coming within the court's jurisdiction can be rejected only following the rendering of a decision (by the Court itself).

HIGH TRIBUNAL

Art. 61. A High Tribunal is constituted and the jurisdiction thereof shall extend to the trial of members of the Council of Ministers, the President and members of the Council of State and of the Court of Cassation as well as the Chief Public Prosecutor in all matters arising from the performance of their duties.

Art. 62. The High Tribunal shall be composed of twenty-one members, eleven from the Court of Cassation and the remaining ten from the President and members of the Council of State. The said members shall be elected by the above bodies from among their members and presidents, in case of necessity by secret ballot.

The said members of the High Tribunal shall in their turn elect from among themselves by secret ballot and majority vote a president and a vice-president.

Art. 63. High Tribunal trials shall be held before the President and fourteen members, and the Court's decisions shall be determined by majority vote.

The six remaining members shall constitute alternates intended to complete the court in case of vacancies. The said members will be chosen by lot, three from among those elected from the Council of State and three from those elected from the Court of Cassation. The members elected to the Presidency and Vice-Presidency shall not be included in the said drawing of lots.

Art. 64. The functions of Prosecutor General of the High Tribunal will be fulfilled by the Prosecutor General of the Republic.

Art. 65. Decisions of the High Tribunal are final.

Art. 66. The High Tribunal shall conduct trials and render verdicts in accordance with the laws currently in force.

Art. 67. The High Tribunal shall be constituted by decision of the Grand National Assembly of Turkey whenever it is deemed necessary.

CHAPTER V. GENERAL RIGHTS OF TURKISH CITIZENS

Art. 68. Every Turk is born free, and free he lives.

Liberty consists of any action which is not detrimental to others.

The limits of an individual's liberty, which is his natural right, extend only to the point where they infringe on the liberties enjoyed by his fellow-citizens. The said limits are defined solely by law.

Art. 69. All Turks are equal before the law and are expected conscientiously to abide by it.

Every type of group, class, family, and individual special privilege is abolished and prohibited.

Art. 70. Personal immunity, freedom of conscience, of thought, of speech and press, the right to travel, to make contracts, to work, to own and dispose of property, to meet and associate and to incorporate, form part of the rights and liberties of Turkish citizens.

Art. 71. The life, property, honor, and residence of each individual are inviolable.

Art. 72. No individual shall be seized or arrested under any circumstance or in any manner other than provided by law.

Art. 73. Torture, bodily mistreatment, confiscation and forced labor are prohibited.

Art. 74. No person may be deprived of his possessions and property or have them expropriated unless it be formally established that it is required for public benefit and unless he has first been indemnified in cash for the value of the property in accordance with the pertinent laws.

The expropriation indemnity and the manner of payment of such indemnity for land and forests to be expropriated in order to make the farmer proprietor of land and to place administration of forests under the State, shall be determined by special laws. No person shall be constrained to make any sort of sacrifice except such as may be imposed in kind, or money, or in the form of labor in extraordinary circumstances and in conformity with the law.

Art. 75. No one may be censured for the philosophical creed, religion or doctrine to which he may adhere. All religious services not in contravention to public order and morals and the laws are authorized.

Art. 76. No one's domicile may be entered or his person searched except in the manner and under the conditions stipulated by law.

Art. 77. The press shall enjoy freedom within the framework of the law and shall not be subject to any censorship or control prior to publication.

Art. 78. Travel is subject to no restriction whatsoever except in cases of general mobilization, martial law, or legislative restrictions of a hygienic nature necessitated by epidemics.

Art. 79. The limits imposed on the freedom of making contracts, of labor, of ownership, of meeting and associating, and of incorporating shall be determined by law.

Art. 80. Instruction of any kind is free within the limits laid down by law under the supervision and control of the State.

Art. 81. Documents, letters and all kinds of parcels delivered to the postal authorities may not be opened without a decision by a competent examining magistrate and tribunal. Likewise the secrecy of telegraphic and telephonic communication may not be violated.

Art. 82. Turkish citizens shall have the right, should they notice any instances which are in contravention to the laws and regulations in force, to report such cases or complain, individually or collectively, either in their own interest or in the interest of the community, to the competent authorities or to the Grand National Assembly. The reply to a personal application must be communicated to the petitioner in written form.

Art. 83. No one may be summoned before or taken to a court other than to that court having jurisdiction in the question in accordance with the law.

Art. 84. Taxes shall be understood to be the participation of the people in the general expenditures of the State. The collection of tolls, tithes, or any other kind of taxes in a manner incompatible with the aforestated principle by individuals or corporations or in their behalf is prohibited.

Art. 85. Taxes may be levied and collected only by virtue of a law.

However, the collecting of such taxes as have been customarily levied by the State or by provincial and municipal administrations may be continued pending the enactment of new laws.

Art. 86. In the event of war or rebellion, or in the case of convincing evidence of a positive and serious conspiracy against the country and the Republic, the Council of Ministers may proclaim partial or general martial law on condition that this does not exceed one month and that this measure is submitted without delay to the Grand National Assembly for approval. The Assembly may, if deemed necessary, extend or reduce the duration of martial law. Should the Assembly not be in session, it shall be convened immediately.

The prolongation of Martial Law is subject to the decision of the Grand National Assembly. Martial Law implies the temporary restriction or suspension of personal and residential immunity, of inviolability of correspondence, of the freedom of the press and of the right of assembling and associating.

The area over which Martial Law may be proclaimed, the application of the provisions of this regulation over the said area, as well as the mode of the restriction or suspension of immunity and freedom in time of war is determined by law.

Art. 87. Primary education is compulsory for all Turks, male or female, and is free in public schools.

Art. 88. The people of Turkey, regardless of religion and race, are Turks as regards citizenship.

Any person born of a Turkish father, in Turkey or elsewhere, as well as any person born of an alien father domiciled in Turkey and who, residing in Turkey, formally assumes Turkish citizenship upon attaining his majority, as well as any person granted Turkish citizenship by law, is a Turk. Turkish citizenship may be lost under circumstances defined by law.

CHAPTER VI. MISCELLANEOUS

PROVINCES

Art. 89. Turkey is divided on the basis of geographic conditions and economic relations into Vilayets, the Vilayets into Kazas, the Kazas into Nahiyes which are made up of Kasabas and villages.

Art. 90. Vilayets, towns, Kasabas and villages are considered to be corporate persons.

Art. 91. The Vilayets are administered according to the principle of decentralization and division of functions.

GOVERNMENT OFFICIALS

Art. 92. Any Turk in full possession of his political rights may be employed in the service of the Government with due consideration as to his qualifications and capacities.

Art. 93. The qualifications of Government officials, their rights and duties, their salaries, the mode of their appointment, dismissal, and promotion are determined by law.

Art. 94. In case of an infraction of the law, an official or employee of the Government may not escape responsibility on the ground of compliance with instructions from superiors.

FINANCIAL AFFAIRS

Art. 95. The bill relating to the Annual Budget, as well as all draft budgets, tables, and annexed budgets connected therewith, shall be submitted to the Grand National Assembly at least three months before the beginning of the fiscal year.

Art. 96. Public funds may not be spent in excess of the provisions of the Budget Law.

Art. 97. The provisions of the Budget Law are valid for the duration of one year.

Art. 98. The Final Accounts shall show the actual figures of revenues collected in the course of the fiscal year of the pertinent budget, as well as disbursements effected during the said fiscal year. The form and rules relative to the drawing up of the Final Accounts must be analogous to those provided for in the Budget Law.

Art. 99. The draft of the Final Accounts shall be submitted to the Grand National Assembly not later than the beginning of November of the second year following the end of the fiscal year which it covers.

Art. 100. A Bureau of Accounts attached to the Grand National Assembly is charged with the control, in accordance with the law *ad hoc,* of all revenues and disbursements of the State.

Art. 101. The Bureau of Accounts shall submit to the Grand National

Assembly, at the latest within six months following the submittal of the Final Accounts, a general statement of verification.

PROVISIONS RELATING TO THE CONSTITUTION

Art. 102. Amendments of any of the provisions of the present Constitution can be made only under the following conditions:

The motion for amendment must be signed by at least one-third of all the members of the Assembly. The amendment must be supported by the vote of a majority numbering two-thirds of the total members of the Assembly.

An amendment or a modification of Art. 1 of the present law, stating that the form of Government of the country is a Republic, cannot be proposed under any circumstances or in any form whatsoever.

Art. 103. No provision of the Organic Law shall be disregarded nor its application suspended for any reason or under any pretext whatsoever.

No Law may contain provisions contrary to the Organic Law.

Art. 104. This law takes the place of, in simplified Turkish and without instituting any change in meaning and understanding, Organic Law No. 491, dated April 20, 1924.

Art. 105. The present law enters into force on the date of its publication.

Date of Publication:
  January 10, 1945

[Translation issued by the Turkish Information Office, 444 E. 52nd St., New York City.]

Appendix III.   Suggested Reading

1. General: The reader who wishes to continue the study of the Middle East in general and of Turkey and Iran in particular will find the following to be of the greatest value.

The *New York Times,* available in most libraries and probably unrivaled in its coverage of foreign news. Reference use of the *Times* is simplified by the Index which it publishes monthly (and in quarterly and annual cumulations).

Foreign Affairs, the quarterly published by the Council on Foreign Relations, 58 E. 68th Street, New York 21, N. Y. This magazine is available in most good libraries and is an invaluable aid for all who are seriously interested in America's course abroad. Its quarterly bibliographies of books and source materials are especially useful and important.

The Middle East Journal. For the specific field of the Middle East, including Turkey and Iran, Americans have been uniquely fortunate to have at hand, since 1947, this authoritative quarterly published by the Middle East Institute, 1830 Nineteenth Street, N. W., Washington 9, D. C. The *Journal,* which deserves to be far more widely known than is yet the case, carries frequent first-rate articles on Turkey and Iran. Its fundamental value, however, lies in its careful lists of current developments and in its systematic and comprehensive tabulations and descriptions of current publications on the Middle East—books, magazine articles, and government documents. The importance and the utility of *The Middle East Journal* cannot be overstressed.

Mention also should be made of at least two publications of the London Royal Institute of International Affairs (sometimes also called Chatham House), the British counterpart of the American Council on Foreign Relations. First, a handbook useful for Turkey and Persia is the up-to-date *The Middle East, A Political and Economic Survey* (London, 1950); second, the monumental *Survey of International Affairs,* 23 volumes, 1925— (in progress), edited by Arnold J. Toynbee.

2. Turkey: American readers who wish to undertake a study of Turkey are especially fortunate to have at their disposal an up-to-date bibliographical handbook designed expressly for their needs: John Kingsley

Birge, *A Guide to Turkish Area Study* (American Council of Learned Societies, Washington, 1949). In this handbook Dr. Birge enumerates and describes the basic works available in English, and adds considerable information concerning materials in other western European languages, surveying the field under thirteen headings: 1. Sources of General Information; 2. Geography; 3. Population and Races; 4. Language and Literature; 5. History; 6. Political Structure of Turkey; 7. Social Organization; 8. Transportation and Communications; 9. Finance, Industry, and Commerce; 10. Education and Intellectual Life; 11. Religion; 12. Art; and 13. Music. The *Guide to Turkish Area Study* includes works published up to the end of 1945. For what has appeared since, the authoritative source is *The Middle East Journal,* whose importance was stressed in the first section of these bibliographical notes.

In the Birge *Guide* and *The Middle East Journal* the American student has a remarkably useful pair of tools. When he turns to hunt for a recent, reliable, balanced, and reasonably short history of the Turks, however, nothing really adequate will be found at all. Probably the best which can be recommended are the sections dealing with the Turks in the two following works, each of which is likewise useful for a study of Iran: first, George E. Kirk, *A Short History of the Middle East from the Rise of Islam to Modern Times* (Public Affairs Press, Washington, D. C., 1949), and second, Carl Brockelmann, *History of the Islamic Peoples with a Review of Events, 1939–1947, by Moshe Perlmann,* translated by Joel Carmichael and Moshe Perlmann, Putnam's Sons, New York, 1947.

The three standard histories of the Turks are all in German, are usually very hard to obtain, and are always dismaying because of their great detail. All but the first one also lack an index, and all are seriously out of date and of course fail to cover modern times. They are: first, Joseph von Hammer-Purgstall, *Geschichte des Osmanischen Reiches* (10 vols.; Pest, 1827–1835), the classic European presentation, marked by a copious use of oriental sources which remains unexcelled and which has made this and others of von Hammer's works inexhaustible treasure-troves for generations of later writers; second, Johann Wilhelm Zinkeisen, *Geschichte des osmanischen Reiches in Europa* (8 vols.; Hamburg, 1840–1863), a treatment concerned primarily with the Turks in Europe and which adds to von Hammer's foundation abundant materials gleaned from a large range of European official documents; and third, Nicholas Iorga (or Jorga), *Geschichte des osmanischen Reiches* (5 vols.; Gotha, 1908–1913), a work which pays considerably more attention to social and economic problems than do the two preceding titles.

Of the several shorter English histories which represent, in large part, abbreviations of von Hammer, the most useful is Lord Eversley (George J. S.) and Sir Valentine Chirol, *The Turkish Empire from 1288 to 1922* (years 1288–1914 by Eversley, 1914–1922 by Chirol; New York, Dodd Mead & Co., 1923). Also to be noted are: Edward S. Creasy, *History of the Ottoman Turks* (Holt, New York, 1878); Stanley Lane-Poole, *The Story of Turkey* (The Story of the Nations series), assisted by E. J. W. Gibb and Arthur Gilman (New York, Putnam, 1888); William Miller, *The Ottoman Empire and Its Successors* (Cambridge, University Press, 1936); William Stearns Davis, *A Short History of the Near East from the Founding of Constantinople (330 A.D. to 1922)* (New York, Macmillan, 1933); and Sir John Arthur Ransome Marriott, *The Eastern Question* (4th ed., Oxford, Clarendon Press, 1940). Much also is to be gained from Leopold Ranke, *The Ottoman and the Spanish Empires in the Sixteenth and Seventeenth Centuries* (translated by Walter K. Kelly) (Philadelphia, Lea & Blanchard, 1845).

Elias John Wilkinson Gibb, *A History of Ottoman Poetry* (6 vols.; London, Luzac & Co., 1900–1909; vols. 2–6 edited by Edward G. Browne) is the standard European guide to formal Ottoman literature. For Ottoman religion, especially for the popular religion of the Anatolian Turks, there exist: John Kingsley Birge, *The Bektashi Order of Dervishes* (London and Hartford, Luzac and Hartford Seminary Press, 1937), and F. W. Hasluck, *Christianity and Islam under the Sultans* (2 vols.; Oxford, Clarendon Press, 1929). Two important works dealing with the Ottoman state at the time of its greatest magnificence are Ogier Ghiselin de Busbecq (Imperial Ambassador at Constantinople, 1554–1562), *The Turkish Letters of . . . Busbecq*, translated by Edward S. Forster (Oxford, Clarendon Press, 1927), and Roger Bigelow Merriman, *Suleiman the Magnificent* (Cambridge, Harvard University Press, 1944). Walter Livingston Wright, Jr., *Ottoman Statecraft: the Book of Counsel for Vezirs and Governors of Sari Mehmed Pasha, the Defterdar* (Princeton Oriental Texts, vol. II, Princeton University Press, 1935), and Albert Howe Lybyer, *The Government of the Ottoman Empire in the Time of Suleiman the Magnificent* (Cambridge, Harvard University Press, 1913), are excellent introductions to the study of the decline of the Ottoman Turks.

Among the distinguished historians of the Turks who are now publishing, mention must be made of Professor Paul Wittek of the University of London and of Professor Fuat Köprülü (Köprülüzâde Mehmed Fuad Bey), formerly of Istanbul University and now Foreign Minister of Turkey. Of Wittek's publications in English, the most interesting for the general reader is *The Rise of the Ottoman Empire* (Royal Asiatic Society, London, 1938). A complete bibliography of Professor Wittek's publications, largely in German and French, up to 1936 may be found in the *Annuaire de l'Institut de Philologie et d'Histoire Orientales et Slaves* (vol. IV (1936), Université Libre de Bruxelles, Brussels). Of Professor Köprülü's publications in languages other than Turkish the outstanding volume is *Les Origines de l'Empire Ottoman* (Paris, 1935). A complete bibliography of this scholar's publications up to 1935 was published in Istanbul (1935) by Şerif Hulûsi Sayman.

For the study of Ottoman history, and indeed for most aspects of the Moslem world, the indispensable encyclopaedia is *The Encyclopaedia of Islam. A Dictionary of the Geography, Ethnography, and Biography of the Muhammadan Peoples* (4 vols.; Leyden, 1915–1934 plus one supplement volume, Leyden, 1938). This standard reference work is now being replaced by the greatly expanded and improved Turkish edition which has been appearing at Istanbul (*Islâm Ansiklopedisi,* 1941–   ) under the direction of the distinguished scholar Dr. Abdülhak Adnan-Adĭvar.

For the study of more recent times in Turkey, the most important works are: Sir Charles Eliot, *Turkey in Europe* (London, Edward Arnold, 1908); Arnold J. Toynbee, *The Western Question in Greece and Turkey: a study in the contact of civilizations* (Boston, Houghton, 1922); Count Leon Ostrorog, *The Angora Reform* (London, University of London Press, 1927); Stephen P. Ladas, *The Exchange of Minorities: Bulgaria, Greece, and Turkey* (New York, Macmillan, 1932); Ahmed Emin (Yalman), *The Development of Modern Turkey as Measured by Its Press* (New York, Columbia University Press, 1914); the same, *Turkey in the World War* (New Haven, Carnegie Endowment for International Peace, 1930); Harry N. Howard, *The Partition of Turkey: A Diplomatic History, 1913–1923* (Norman, University of Oklahoma Press, 1931); Sir Harry Luke, *The Making of Modern Turkey* (London, Macmillan, 1936); Donald E. Webster, *The Turkey of Atatürk, Social Progress in the Turkish Reformation* (Philadelphia, American Academy of Political and Social Science, 1939); Barbara Ward, *Turkey* (London, Oxford University Press, 1942); and Max Thornburg and others, *Turkey: An Economic Appraisal* (New York, The Twentieth Century Fund, 1949).

Any reader who wishes to address the Turkish Information Office, 444 East 52nd Street, New York 22, N. Y., will receive the useful publications issued by that organization free of charge.

THE UNITED STATES AND IRAN

by

RICHARD N. FRYE

PREFACE

This section was written at the request of the late Walter L. Wright, Jr., my teacher of Turkish, who was to have written the part on Turkey. I turned from my study of Middle Persian inscriptions to undertake its writing with some trepidation, for it is not easy to write about such a complex subject in so few pages.

From this brief account much useful and interesting factual and interpretative material has of necessity been omitted. Some of the omitted facts are perhaps necessary for an adequate understanding of the Iranian scene and of the events recounted; the history and culture of Iran have been especially slighted. Additional information on Iranian oil and Point Four can be found in many publications. I must apologize for the obvious shortcomings of this truncated version of the story of Iran and the United States, a story which deserves fuller treatment. Look, therefore, upon these pages as sketching out, roughly and imperfectly, only a part of the picture. The reader who recognizes the value and significance of Iran, both in and of itself and as related to the larger destinies of the world, must seek out the details for himself.

Many authorities on Iran will disagree with my conclusions, and perhaps even with some of my data, which, particularly for the recent period, are conflicting and unreliable. The rapid course of events in Iran makes prediction of the future hazardous. All will wish that more space could have been devoted to what is to them, as to me, a fascinating and inexhaustible area of study.

The manuscript was completed in February 1951 before the assassination of Prime Minister Razmara, the nationalization of oil, and the violent strikes and anti-Western demonstrations. I have made only slight additions and changes in the proofs to bring the text up to the events of April 1951.

I wish to thank the Rockefeller Foundation and the Social Science

Research Council for grants which enabled me to visit Iran in the summer of 1948. My debt to past writings and to scholars on Iran is obvious. To my critics who have been helpful in the preparation of this manuscript, and especially to Professors W. Cantwell Smith and T. Cuyler Young, who read parts of the manuscript and offered helpful suggestions, I proffer my sincere thanks. To my wife I owe a special debt of gratitude. I alone, however, am responsible for any errors and shortcomings.

Richard N. Frye

1. Introductory

The customs office on the frontier between Turkey and Iran stands in solitude within the shadow of Mount Ararat, fabled resting place of Noah's Ark, near the point where these two countries are joined by their neighbor to the north, the Soviet Union. In this unmarked spot on the map the contrast between the strict state organization of Turkey and the lack of such organization in Iran is indeed striking. The Turkish section of the customs area has been built according to plan; the buildings are occupied and in use. A Turkish sentinel with fixed bayonet marches along the border line night and day; a feeling of order and security permeates the air. The Persian half of the enclosure, on the other hand, is a mere shell, bleak and desolate, left unfinished when Iran unwillingly became enmeshed in war in 1941.* Windows and furniture are missing and no Persian soldier is there to match the Turk. At the frontier the scheduled Turkish state bus, with uniformed driver, is met by an undependable private bus with a chauffeur who sets his own fare to carry a passenger to the nearest town in Iran.

The customs office mirrors on a small scale the differences between the Turkish Republic and the Kingdom of Iran—differences, however, which are not always in favor of the former. Turkey has definitely rejected its past and has turned its face toward Europe, where Turkish power was once felt and respected. Iran, on the other hand, is in the heart of the Orient with her eyes on Central Asia and the Persian Gulf. Whereas Turkey has been the bridge between Europe and Asia, Iran has linked the Middle East with India and the Far East. The Persians have been more reluctant perhaps to adopt the ways of the West than the Turks. The past is still very much alive and venerated in Iran, in spite of the efforts of the late Reza Shah to

* The words Iran and Persia, Iranian and Persian, are used interchangeably in this book.

minimize its influence, and it is not easily to be pushed aside. On the other hand, the sometimes stifling atmosphere of Turkish *étatism* is not so evident in the land of the lion and the sun.

One should remember that Iran was occupied by Allied troops during the late war, while Turkey's borders remained inviolate in her neutrality. But this is only the immediate background of the present situation. The new Turkey has been welded into a homogeneous state by the efforts of strong, able leaders, while Iran—with large minorities of Kurds, Turkish-speaking peoples, and unruly nomads—has always lacked the advantages of a unified nation with a unified population. Furthermore, the unfortunate history of Iran in recent years must not be forgotten. For decades she served as the buffer between the conflicting interests of Tsarist Russia and the British Empire. Many Persians claim that as long as there was disagreement between the two great powers, Iran had a modicum of independence, but that once they resolved their differences her independence became a farce. Howbeit, Iran today enjoys a greater degree of independence than she has at any time since the beginning of the nineteenth century—except, perhaps, for the days of Reza Shah. But, although her sovereignty and territorial integrity were reaffirmed in 1943 by Britain, Russia, and the United States, her present position is precarious.

In the nineteenth century the importance of Iran in great power politics was measured solely by her strategic location astride the British lifeline to India and the Far East. For Britain it was imperative that no hostile power should gain a strong position in Iran, either political or economic, which might threaten that lifeline. Yet the goal of Russian ambitions was to obtain a warm water port on the southern seas. The Tsars were blocked at the Dardanelles by the Ottoman Empire, a tottering state supported by the Western European powers. Iran seemed to be the back door through which the Russians could attain their end. Needless to say, this drive to the south did not coincide with British interests. After many months of maneuvering and rivalry in Iran, however, the Russians and British came to an agreement and divided the country into two zones, with a small band of no-man's land between. Russian interests were recognized as paramount in the north, British in the south. This happened in 1907, and the agreement lasted till the fall of the Tsarist government. The years immediately preceding 1914 represent the high-water mark of Russian strength in Iran, the influence of the Tsar's ministers in Teheran then surpassing that of the British.

A repetition of the events of 1907 took place in the last war, but circumstances had changed considerably; oil had been discovered and produced in considerable quantities in southern Iran, and oil was a great prize, a prime necessity for modern war. The oil fields of the Anglo-Iranian Oil Company, which had a monopoly concession in southwestern Iran, are part of the great oil area of southwestern Asia. This area has enormous reserves only partially tapped at present. With the use of oil growing, and the prospects of the future development of atomic energy uncertain, this part of the world assumes a new significance for us.

Before the late war Iran was a *terra incognita* to most Americans. After 1941, however, thousands of our troops who served in the Persian Gulf Command became acquainted with the country. Several times during the war Iran rose to prominence in the news, when for a period it was the most important supply route from the Western Allies to the U.S.S.R., and again when it became the first meeting ground of the "Big Three," at the Teheran Conference in 1943. Several months after the end of the war Iran occupied headlines in the world press as a result of the drama which was being played in her northwestern province. For the events which took place in Azerbaijan were unquestionably dramatic. Even today the story of the Soviet occupation of northern Iran and its aftermath is confused, while the citizens of Tabriz, capital of Azerbaijan, believe that the drama is not yet finished.

Iran, then, is a weak country but strategically important because of its geographical position and large oil reserves. It is today not only a buffer between Russian and British interests, but also between Russian and American. But it is much more than that. What is at stake in Iran is not merely Russian and American power. It is not just that the old British-Russian rivalry has been superseded by American-Soviet rivalry. The contest there is part of a world-wide struggle for supremacy between two opposing and ultimately incompatible ways of life and systems of thought.

No nation, no matter what its desires, can remain untouched by the struggle. Though Iran herself is non-Communist, she is not entirely uninfected by the Communist virus. She has within her borders native Communists and Soviet agents actively seeking to undermine her government, to foment disunity and dissension. Moreover, she has reached a critical stage in her own development and has turned, in her need, to the West. She has sought aid directly from the United

States. Because she is menaced both by communism within and Soviet power outside, and because she is a valuable member of the free world, her welfare and her future cannot be a matter of indifference to us. To serve her and to serve ourselves, to understand her future and our concern with it, some knowledge of her people and her past is indispensable.

2. The Country and the People

1. LAND OF EXTREMES

In Iran, as elsewhere in the Orient, man is close to nature. The Persian has little of the complex material structure of civilization enjoyed by the Westerner to shield him against the onslaughts of nature. The snow and ice of severe winters followed by swollen torrents, parched earth, locusts, and dust storms, all tax the ingenuity of man in his struggle for existence. That man has been able to exist on the bleak Iranian plateau and develop flourishing civilizations is a tribute to his kind.

One senses the submission of man to nature in the East, which perhaps helps to form that attitude in him interpreted by the Westerner as fatalism. It has been said that in the West man revolts against and conquers nature, but in Iran it is otherwise; man accepts the hardships which nature imposes on him. And nature is never loath to test and try him.

Iran is a land of extremes, both natural and human. The great differences between the subtropic lands of the Caspian Sea coast and the wind-swept barren mountains of the plateau are matched by the inequalities of wealth and social position among the people. Yet these contrasts are an integral part of the scene in Iran.

In the crystal-clear sky of the plateau, as blue as one can imagine, there is an indescribable brilliance of light and color. Here the dull red sash of the nomad seems scarlet in the sun, and the glint of a rifle barrel dazzles the eyes. Yet in a nearby oasis the dank, dark atmosphere subdues all color, and one is in a different world. The contrast between the arid wilderness and the shadowy, flowered paradise is so abrupt that one is startled. Indeed the dividing line is so sharp that one may stand with one foot in the desert and another in the garden. And the contrast is often accentuated by the hand of man. The Persian builds tall mud walls to keep the desert or the intruder from his garden, his paradise; for he is a strong individualist, jealous of his privacy. (Incidentally, the word "paradise" comes from Iran and truly the Persian garden is a paradise in contrast to the barren desert outside.)

There is also contrast in sound: between the clamorous activity of the bazaar and the quiet of the garden behind high walls, the contrast suggested by Ketelbey's musical composition, "In a Persian Market." The deafening noise of the metalworkers is matched by the solemn loneliness of the desert always near at hand. The desert leaves its mark on those who venture upon it, and those who roam over the barren tracts of land are more conscious of the infinite expanse of the universe than are the city dwellers. To lie under the stars in the clear, lonely night which was not intended for sleep, is an experience cherished by the traveler in Iran.

In one instance the contrast is not so forceful in Iran as it is in the Occident. This is the division between the living and the dead. Iran is full of memories, and one cannot travel in the country without encountering the vestiges of mighty empires and heroes long since departed. In Iran you have ever present the evidence of the centuries-old hand of man, and it impinges on one's daily life as it does not in the West. The countryside is dotted with ruins, abandoned by people who preferred to move rather than demolish their buildings. Yet the shepherds and nomads camp in them, and one has the feeling that the gulf between living and dead is not so great there. A by no means rare sight in Iran is a road passing a bluff where human bones project out of the ground in all directions.

Mountains dominate the landscape and rarely, if ever, does the traveler lose sight of them. They are barren and their cold loneliness is not conducive to settled life; a nomadic existence is better. In Iran the mountaineer and the dweller on the plain have much in common, for both are face to face with a stern nature, and once the hand of man is removed the gardens decay and the desert conquers, or the flocks are dispersed and die.

The greater part of the country is a plateau in the form of a huge, rough bowl, the edges of which are the high, rugged mountains. Again, the contrast between the snow covered ranges and the deserts close at hand is striking. In the interior the land slopes down to only a few hundred feet above sea level. Here are the Salt Desert and the Lut Desert, or desert of Lot, where no animal, plant, or insect is found, perhaps the most desolate area on the face of the globe. Not far to the north is Mount Demavend (18,600 feet) the highest in Iran, and the legendary home of demons in Persian folklore.

The lack of verdure on the plateau strikes everyone who comes to Iran from Europe or America. Patches of green are found only on the banks of streams or around wells, and stony wastes surround the oases, reminiscent of some areas in the southwestern part of the United States. It is rumored in songs and ancient traditions that the mountains of Iran were once heavily forested, but the trees were ruthlessly cut down by men in search of fuel and building material. Today the makers of charcoal cut down striplings to provide wares to sell, while over-grazing of sheep and goats prevents the growth even of shrubs. This destruction of plant and tree has been followed by erosion and terrible dust storms. It is most unlikely, however, that the inhabitants of the plateau ever experienced the pleasures of a real forest primeval. Rather they have grown up from generation to generation in the midst of the waste land and have been conditioned to it.

The seasons in Iran provide another series of contrasts, for they are sharply divided, like the brilliant day which passes into night with astonishing rapidity. The change from winter to spring in the month of March is especially abrupt, and one can readily understand why the ancient Persians began their new year in the spring when the old changed to the new. The heating of government offices ceases with the beginning of spring, and it is not unusual to have snow on the ground the day before the warm sun renders heating unnecessary. The climate on the plateau is on the whole continental, with hot, dry summers and cold, severe winters. In the winter the mountains are covered with snow, while some peaks are white most of the year. Indeed, many villages are isolated for weeks during the winter owing to the heavy snowfalls in the mountains.

Although the narrow strip of land between the Elburz Mountains and the Caspian Sea is included within the political boundaries of Iran, it is different in many respects from the rest of the country. The provinces of Gilan and Mazanderan, which comprise this territory, have a subtropical climate and excessive rainfall. As a result the land is covered with dense underbrush and trees; the Persians say there are jungles here. The damp forests of Gilan seem a welcome relief from the barrenness of the plateau till one sees the sunken faces of the inhabitants, plagued by dreaded malaria. The people in this part of Iran speak dialects quite distinct from those spoken elsewhere in the country, and they are smaller in stature. Throughout history the Caspian Sea coast has led an existence separate from the rest of Iran, and has frequently been the prey of Russian designs. Most of the world's supply of caviar comes from the rivers of Gilan and Mazanderan.

Azerbaijan is the richest agricultural province of Iran, and, with Khurasan, supplies the country with most of its grain. Dry farming is practiced here, whereas irrigation is the rule elsewhere on the plateau. The border with Soviet Azerbaijan is only a river flowing through a barren plain to the Caspian Sea, an insignificant barrier to any invading force. The great majority of the population of Azerbaijan is Turkish-speaking, which does not mean, however, that the people feel any affinity with Turkey. Their cultural, religious, and historic ties have been with the rest of Iran, while their attitude toward their brothers in Soviet Azerbaijan is best illustrated by the absence of any attempt to form a unified state with them in 1946.

Summers on the Persian Gulf coast are famous for their intense heat; the air is moist but the temperature is so high that there is virtually no condensation, hence no rain during the summer months. This is proverbially one of the hottest spots on the earth, notorious to the troops of the Persian Gulf Command during World War II. The cooler summers on the plateau, however, also have their drawbacks. In eastern Iran, especially in the province of Seistan, from June to September there is a recurrent wind which blows with great violence and completely dries up the land; this is the so-called "wind of one hundred and twenty days." At times the velocity of the wind exceeds sixty miles an hour. Elsewhere dust is an unhappy concomitant of breezes which otherwise make the heat bearable. Dust covers everything, and the dishes on kitchen shelves receive a coating between each meal. Yet in the mountain vales and in the gardens life is all the more pleasant in contrast.

The soil, which the traveler on the plateau frequently swallows, is chiefly a mixture of clay and sand permeated with dust, similar to the soil of north China and much of Central Asia. Iran is not an extension of the Levant eastward from the Mediterranean coast, but rather the continuation of Central Asia toward the west. In the eastern part of Iran the ground becomes sandy, while in the Salt and Lut Deserts the salt deposits are as much as three feet thick. The country along the Indian Ocean coast is particularly forbidding, for the extremely low rainfall prevents any growth of plants or shrubs and the land is as desolate as any landscape on the moon.

Iran, then, appears to be a barren land hardly fit for habitation. Nevertheless, the Persians have not only maintained life for many generations on the plateau, but in the past they have flourished and multiplied beyond their present condition. How have the peasants, nomads, and the townspeople survived, and how have they organized their lives?

2. PEOPLE OF EXTREMES

The division between peasants and non-peasants which characterizes Turkish society also pertains to Iran, although there is a more complicated pattern in the Shah's realm. The most easily discernible difference between the societies of the two countries is the existence of great tribes in Iran. The tribes are a minority of the population but, by virtue of their solidarity and unity of action, their importance is greater than their numbers would indicate.

It would be more accurate to say that the basic cleavage in Iranian society is between townsman and non-townsman rather than peasant and non-peasant. While historically the peasants and nomads may have been bitter enemies, today they are brothers in poverty. It is the city folk who have received the benefits of westernization, and who constitute a group apart. Indeed, the disparity between the townsmen and the people of the countryside is one of the problems of the present government of Iran, which is seeking to decentralize the administration in an effort to distribute authority and benefits more equitably.

The Peasant

Over 80 per cent of the population of Iran is engaged in agriculture and related activities; most of these people live in small villages. Iran has always been an agricultural country, and it has been traditionally the concern of the ruler or governor to foster agriculture. The ancient religious book of the followers of Zoroaster, the *Avesta,* praises agriculture as the noblest of livelihoods, and promises divine rewards to the tiller of the soil. Since agriculture is so important, the progress and development of Iran depend very much on the welfare of the peasantry.

The lot of the average Persian peasant is not an easy one. He finds a traditional pattern of behavior laid out for him by his religion from the time of his birth to the grave, and, as we have seen, he is a child of his environment. He still lives much the same life as his forefathers two thousand years ago. His house from time immemorial has been made of *pisé* mud with one or two rooms. There are no windows and only one door; there may be a hole in the roof in one corner where the food is cooked. The floor is mud, covered with a grass mat or a carpet, usually the only furnishing in the house. Some houses have domed roofs while others have flat ones, and the family sleeps on the roof during the summer. At a distance it is difficult to distinguish the houses of a village from surrounding rocks or hills as the houses blend with the landscape.

If the peasant is well-to-do he may have a samovar which he keeps boiling for friends who pass by. The peasant's food consists of bread, vegetables, such as cucumbers and carrots, curds (the yoghurt of dietitians, *mast* in Persian), and very occasionally eggs, meat, and fruit. If he works in the melon patches of a great landlord during the melon season, he will enjoy various kinds of melons known for their flavor all over the Middle East. The peasant will probably own a wooden plow, a spade and hoe, and a few other homemade tools. If he is wealthier than average he will own some chickens, some livestock, and even a yoke of oxen. Frequently oxen are jointly owned by a number of families.

None of the amenities of city life are to be found in the village; there is no electric power, no communication system, no sanitation, no medical facilities, and usually no money. The barter system prevails in most villages, and naturally enough the peasants are an easy prey to traveling salesmen and hucksters. If it becomes known in a village that a traveler has a supply of quinine with him, he will be besieged by the entire village population seeking the precious pills. Disease is a constant threat which may strike a family when it can least afford the loss. Malaria and typhoid are prevalent, while eye diseases are endemic. Although swamps have been drained and DDT has been used liberally, under the supervision of American health officers, the lack of sanitation as well as the deficient nutrition of the people make the eradication of disease a very difficult matter.

The opium problem should be noted in passing, for it is of great concern to the peasants of Iran. It may be an exaggeration to say, as some have claimed, that over 20 per cent of the population of Iran is addicted to opium. But nonetheless the percentage is high enough to impair seriously the labor potential of the country. The peasant smokes opium to escape from his daily drudgery, but also he reaps a greater profit from the cultivation of the poppy than from other crops.

The poppy can be sown in the autumn and reaped in the spring, thus allowing another crop to grow during the year. Of course, the cultivation of the poppy is an international affair and the Iranian government is greatly concerned about the opium problem, but it is very difficult to control the growing and smuggling of opium. It has been and is sapping the strength of the Persians and is a problem which can hardly be solved by merely limiting the cultivation of the poppy. But this is by the way.

Each village has a head man, who is usually the manager of the estates of the richest landlord in the vicinty. Needless to say, the "governmental" organization of a village with its surrounding lands is very loose. Much of the land suitable for cultivation is owned by absentee landlords. The land in itself is of little value without water, hence ownership of land really means ownership of the water supply. In theory crops are divided into five shares, with one share going to the person who furnishes each of the following: seeds, labor, power, land, and water. By power is meant oxen or other beasts of burden. Often a peasant can furnish only his labor, and then he receives much less than one who can also furnish seeds and his own oxen. The peasant must frequently borrow money at an exorbitant rate of interest to pay the landlord rent for the land he tills, and it is not at all unusual to find families eternally and hopelessly in debt to the landlord. The percentage system of responsibility and profit seems advantageous to the peasant, but in practice it keeps him only slightly above the starvation level. It is a long and difficult process for the peasant to better his state and few are successful.

Land tenure is established firmly in custom and tradition, and to say that it is backward and unfair is an understatement. The age-old social system in Iran has hindered the growth of any sense of responsibility on the part of the landlord for his land and for the people who work the land. Frequently the landowner sells the right of collecting rent from the peasants to the highest bidder. The consequences are not difficult to imagine. The general lack of security in Iran and the consequent disinclination for anyone to make a long-term investment have been important reasons for the low level of economic and social development among the peasants. The Persian's lack of confidence in his fellow man and his unwillingness to assume any responsibility for his own destiny are basic ills which must be remedied if Iran is to progress.

Water is the lifeblood of Iran, as elsewhere in the Orient, or as an economic survey of the country puts it, "for the most part, water in Iran is not a gift of nature but a capital item." * Irrigation has always been important for agriculture, and from earliest times the Persians have been experts in methods of conserving and leading the precious fluid to their fields. Centuries ago they devised a unique system of underground canals which carried water from the comparatively shallow water table in the foothills sometimes as far as thirty miles out into the plains. This is the most prevalent and highly touted as the most efficient method of irrigation. Every fifty or sixty yards a well is dug in the ground and the bottoms of each are connected by a tunnel. The depth of the wells varies but some tunnels are over a hundred feet under the ground. The tunnels are large enough for a man to walk through with bent back, and they must be cleaned constantly of mud and cave-ins. This primitive method of conducting water to the fields involves much cost and labor, but it is relatively efficient since little of the water evaporates before it reaches the fields. Visitors to Iran have been intrigued by these underground canals or *qanats,* as they are called, but a recent survey of the water problems of the country concluded that surface canals could cope with the situation better than *qanats*. More wells need to be drilled, for water does exist in considerable quantities underground; but drilling machines and pipes are needed. A number of large dams would also be useful for irrigation purposes.

About 12 per cent of the land of Iran is under cultivation or is used for pasture, while the rest is mostly waste land. Although much of the land is unfit for crops, large areas would bloom if the water supply were increased and fertilizers and machines used. Many cabinets have proclaimed the necessity of increasing the area farmed per family, as a prerequisite to raising the standard of living, though to date little has been accomplished in this direction. Unfortunately in many places unscientific irrigation has caused erosion, leaving stony ground unfit even for grazing. The government has several large irrigation projects, which it hopes ultimately will reclaim many acres for cultivation and possible reforestation. One is a plan to join two rivers near Isfahan, while another is to utilize the Karun River in the south. In all cases the agency of man is needed to extend cultivation into the waste lands. An old Persian saying claims that when man dies

* *Report on Seven Year Development Plan for the Plan Organization of the Imperial Government of Iran* (Overseas Consultants, New York, 1949), III.

the tree also perishes. Man has to labor unceasingly to overcome the desert.

For the most part the rivers of Iran are unimportant. Only the Caspian Sea coast is well watered by numerous small rivers and streams; on the plateau the seasonal streams lose themselves in the sands or in salt marshes. The only navigable river in the country is the Karun which flows through the plain of Khuzistan to empty finally into the Persian Gulf.

The picture which has been presented of the Persian peasant and his land is not encouraging and may appear hopeless. No people who are undernourished and who have to fight against the scourges of climate and disease can be united and confident of the future. The Persians have been reproached for their lack of martial spirit, yet the peasants of the plateau would be the best of soldiers if they had something to defend, and enough in their stomachs.

The Tribesman and Minorities

The nomads have received more attention from the outside world than the Persian villagers or townspeople because of their more colorful life and their greater freedom and mobility. Yet the problem of the tribes is one of the greatest facing Iran, for the tribes are an element of instability in the organization of the country. Indeed, they seem to be a country within a country, for the tribesmen owe allegiance first to their *khans,* or chieftains, and second to the government in Teheran. Much of the insecurity along the roads in Iran is due to the independence of the tribes, for frequently even the chiefs cannot control the behavior of their men. The ancient antagonism of the nomad and the townsman is not yet dead in Iran. The gullible tribesman will frequently lose all his possessions in the bazaars of a town and will not be loath to recoup his losses from a caravan passing through tribal territory. The nomad leads a primitive life and his code of behavior is different from that of the townsman. In order to survive, the tribe must keep together, maintaining a united front to the world. At the same time any member of the tribe who breaks the strict code of the nomads must be punished or expelled.

Reza Shah subdued the tribes and started a program of settling them on the land, but with his abdication the nomads regained some of their lost freedom. No government in Teheran can afford to ignore the problem of the tribes. At the same time one should not exaggerate their importance; for the nomads are a vanishing race and in the future are destined to be merged with the settled population. Automobiles and other machines of modern life will eventually make the nomadic way of life a thing of the past. Meanwhile the nomads present many problems of administration which sorely tax the ingenuity of government officials seeking to unite the country.

The major difficulty in unification, however, is the language problem, for the multitude of languages and dialects spoken in Iran is a source of confusion to the foreigner. The largest body of non-Persian speakers are the Turkish-speaking people, the majority of whom are found in Azerbaijan, with many also living in the provinces of Fars and Khurasan. A census of them has never been taken (a general census of Persians has never been made), but there may be over two and one half million all together. The Turkish-speaking people of Khurasan are the once-feared Turkoman nomads, although many have now settled in villages and towns. In the south are the powerful Qashqai tribes with many subdivisions.

Another group is the Kurds, sturdy mountaineers who speak a tongue akin to Persian and who live under a strict tribal system. They number perhaps 800,000 and dwell in the Zagros Mountains of western Iran. The Kurds are potentially dangerous to the unity of Iran because of large Kurdish minorities in Turkey and especially Iraq, but they have no unity among themselves. Kurdish nationalism, however, is not dead, for Kurdish intellectuals in Syria, Iraq, and France, as well as in Iran, keep it alive. There has been only one attempt to create a Kurdish state in recent years—the ill-fated Kurdish republic of Mahabad, in Iran. It was created at the same time the rebel government of Azerbaijan came into existence in 1945. The most recent Kurdish revolt was in September 1950 but it was quickly suppressed by government troops. Radio Moscow and Kurds in the Soviet Union gave encouragement to the unsuccessful rebels.

To the south of the Kurds, and speaking dialects closely related to Kurdish, live the Lurs and Bakhtiyari tribesmen. While the Kurds of Turkey may have become "mountain Turks," the Kurds of Iran have not become "mountain Persians." In their relationships with the Kurds, as in so many other respects, the Persians have differed greatly from the Turks. The Persians have disdained to make Persians out of the Kurds, believing, like the French, that their superior culture will always attract and eventually win over minorities and dissident groups.

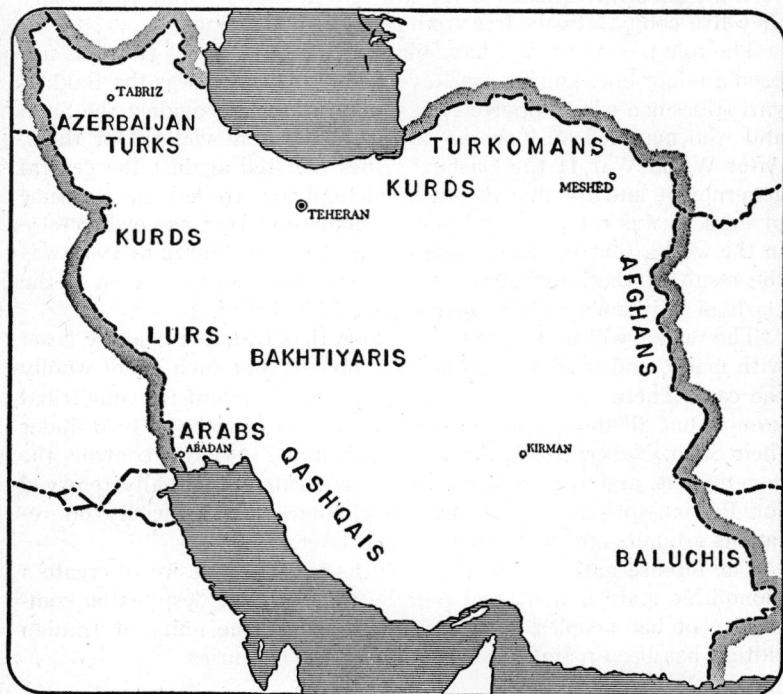

Iran: Minorities and Tribes

On the plains of Khuzistan and the Persian Gulf coast live about 300,000 Arabs. Many of them have been recruited for work in the oil refinery at Abadan, but there are also Arab tribes in the hinterland. This part of Iran is but an extension of the flat plains of Mesopotamia to the foot of the plateau.

Along the Afghanistan and Pakistan frontiers live wandering tribes of Baluchis and Afghans. They are few in number and very poor; they live comparatively free from outside interference.

The role that the tribes have played in the history of Iran has not been a minor one. During the Revolution, in 1909, it was the Bakhtiyari tribesmen who supported the Constitutionalists against the Shah and who marched on Teheran to secure the final victory for them. After World War II the Qashqai tribes revolted against the central government and for many months virtually controlled the province of Fars. It was rumored, and rumors flourish in Iran as nowhere else in the world, that the asphalting of the streets in Shiraz in 1948 was the result of the remonstrances made by Nasr Khan, leader of the Qashqai tribesmen, to the government in Teheran.

The reader will undoubtedly conclude that Iran is a country beset with many, and insoluble, minority problems, but such is not wholly the case. There are, of course, many religious, linguistic, and tribal groups, but all the people consider themselves citizens of Iran under their Shah. Nevertheless, the Persian-speaking majority controls the government, and success in a government career is usually reserved for Persian-speaking Moslems. Discrimination is primarily on religious grounds and will be mentioned later.

The intense nationalism of the Turks and their desire to create a monolithic state find no real parallel in Iran. Yet despite the complexity of her peoples, religions, and tongues, the unity of Iranian culture has been maintained throughout the centuries.

The Townsman and the Bazaar

It is only in the towns that foreign influences touch the lives of the Persians. The townsfolk lead much the same lives as the villagers, however, though generally their lot is somewhat better. Social intercourse, as nearly everywhere in Iran, is largely between members of the extended family. Indeed, the social organization here, and in the villages, seems little removed from the patriarchal society of the tribes.

The town, then, is closer to the village than to the large city, for most of the towns are simply villages which have grown because of their location on important roads or because they are administrative centers. The real distinction between the village and the town is the existence of bazaars with shops of artisans in the latter. But this is an important distinction.

The bazaar in Iran is far more than a market place or shopping center where articles of food, clothing, and luxury are bought, sold, or exchanged. It is also a market place of opinion and discussion, the Hyde Park or Boston Common of the town. Here rumor and gossip are also bought, sold, and exchanged, while they are transmitted from shop to shop with unbelievable rapidity. Before the radio and telephone, the bazaar provided the quickest means of sending news, and it is still the best way of disseminating information among the people. In the center of every bazaar is found the all-important tea house. The tea house is to the Persian what the café is to the Parisian. In a tea house beautiful poetry may be composed in one corner while a plot of assassination is discussed in another.

The reaction of the populace to new laws or decrees can be observed first in the bazaar. Even the late Reza Shah hesitated to go ahead on some of his plans of modernization of the country when the people of the bazaar showed opposition. It was far safer to win over the bazaar by use of rumor and bribery than to risk an open revolt. At the time of the establishment of the Constitution, in 1906, the religious leaders roused the populace of the bazaar in Teheran to oppose the government, and thereby secured their ends.

The bazaars of all towns in Iran have common ties and they always seem in close contact with one another. They are also the meeting grounds between the nomads and the settled folk. In the bazaar of Shiraz, one may meet a Qashqai tribesman at any turn, clothed in his distinctive costume of felt skull cap with projecting wings on either side, and a long robe bound around the waist with a wide cummerbund. The Bakhtiyari tribesman is a frequent visitor to the bazaar of Isfahan.

Bazaar transactions are accompanied by much arguing and the gesticulation so dear to the Persians. The purchase of any article is no simple procedure but involves a matching of wits and tempers in a contest of personalities. He who has the readiest tongue and the nimblest mind, whether it be in a trade transaction or a question of politics, is the winner. Prices, of course, are subject to much dispute. The

Persians enjoy the bargaining involved in the sale of anything, though this is frequently a source of irritation to the American purchaser.

The external appearance of a typical Persian bazaar reveals a convenient grouping of all the shops of one trade or profession in a certain section of the bazaar. All of the booths of the tinsmiths or shoemakers are next to one another, and one can hear their hammers long before that part of the bazaar is reached. Frequently the passages or streets of the bazaars are covered to protect the throngs from the sun, and, rarely, from rain. The shopkeeper usually lives behind or above his shop, while apprentices may sleep in the shop itself. The color, noise, and throbbing life of the bazaar are a never-ending source of wonder to the visitor, while the blending aroma of spices and camel dung is unforgettable.

The bazaars, however, belong to the past. As streets are widened and paved, albeit slowly, shops on the western model are replacing the open booths. Likewise the unity of the bazaar is disappearing, and in the future it will no longer be possible to speak of it as almost a living entity with a character of its own. Still, for many years to come the bazaar will remain an important factor in the life of the people, especially those living in small towns.

Economically, the bazaar operates for the integration of production and distribution, the oldest such institution in the world. Wholesaling and retailing are carried on side by side, and barter exists along with a money economy. The marketing practices of the bazaar are primitive and prices vary considerably; one might say they fluctuate violently. As with the peasants, so in the towns credit facilities are inadequate and rates of interest are exorbitant, sometimes as high as 30 per cent. The philosophy of the bazaar is to seek the maximum profit on each individual transaction without thought of the morrow. A rumor of war which reaches the bazaar will send prices upward, not gradually but with a great spurt. And the merchants of the bazaar act in concert to reap quick returns on the heels of a rumor. These things can change but slowly in a country like Iran.

3. Government and Social Classes

The groups of Iran's population which have been described in the preceding chapter—the peasants, nomads, and inhabitants of the smaller towns, who have remained almost untouched by industrialization—constitute the great mass of the Iranian people, unchanged, inert, passive. They, together with the landed aristocracy, the wealthy bazaar merchants, and the religious leaders, represent the old Iran.

Effective power in Iran today still remains for the most part where it has always been—in the hands of the Court, the landed aristocracy, wealthy merchants, religious leaders, and the army. The power of these groups, however, has not remained unchallenged, and liberal voices are increasingly heard, even occasionally from among the ruling classes themselves. But the emerging middle class, supported by the growing strength of labor, has undoubtedly furnished the greatest impetus toward democratic reform.

Thus far the demand for reform has not resulted in a significant shift in political power. Numerically both the middle and working classes are still small, but the principal reason for their failure to play a significant role is their lack of organization. Potentially, however, they are of great significance.

The political picture was simpler in the days of Reza Shah, before the present ruler dedicated his government to a strictly constitutional course. Under the old Shah there was no question who wielded power. Today the Court has lost some of its prerogatives, but it is still a potent force in the country.

1. THE COURT AND THE SHAH

Iran has been a constitutional monarchy since 1906. Until that time the Shah was a despot responsible to no one save the religious leaders, who watched over his actions and morals as well as over those of his subjects. The Shah's position was a survival from medieval times, when he was the "shadow of God upon earth," the ultimate authority from which there was no recourse. Even after the Shah's power was curbed by the Constitution he was still regarded by his people much as the Tsar was venerated by the Russian peasants—as "the little father." The enemies of Reza Shah accused him of overriding personal ambition when, after toying with the idea of a republic, he decided to found a new dynasty. Perhaps he understood the temper of his people better than they. For undeniably there exists among the Persians an intangible feeling toward the institution of the Shah, which may be compared with the feeling of some Frenchmen toward the Republic, so well expressed by Charles Péguy as *la mystique républicaine*. There is also a *mystique* of the Shah-in-Shah or "king of kings" in Iran, which enhances the authority of the ruler.

One need only read the Constitution of Iran to realize the great powers left to the monarch. The Shah has the right to introduce legislation in parliament, and the influence which he exercises over it is far from negligible. Half of the sixty members of the Senate, the upper house of the parliament, are appointed by the Shah and half are elected. His court minister is a member of every cabinet, and he has, of course, extensive powers of appointment in the executive branch of government. All bills must be approved by him before becoming law. His influence extends far beyond this through friends and relatives who occupy positions of authority. Several members of the royal family, and Reza Shah had eight children, are active in the political and social life of the country. 'Abd al-Reza Pahlevi, Harvard '47, was appointed president of the Senate when it was formed, and is now honorary head of Iran's Seven Year Plan.

The present Shah, Mohammed Reza Pahlevi, is a serious young man with progressive ideas and high hopes for the future of his country. He was born in 1919; he studied in Switzerland, where he learned French and English, and completed his education as an officer in the Persian army. In 1939 he married the sister of Farouq, king of Egypt, but in November 1948 the marriage was dissolved. He was remarried on February 12, 1951 to the daughter of a Bakhtiyari chieftain. The announcement of this marriage was celebrated with approval by the people, for Article 37 of the Supplementary Fundamental Laws to the Constitution states that the eldest son of the Shah, if born of a Persian mother, shall be the heir apparent to the throne.

After he ascended the throne in 1941, Mohammed Reza Shah

turned over most of his father's fortune to a philanthropic organization which was formed for the occasion and espoused the cause of democratic government. Further, on January 28, 1951, the Shah issued an order instructing the Director of the Pahlevi Endowment Organization to sell all of the cultivated property of the Organization to the peasants tilling the land. The large estates were to be broken up and sold to peasants on long-term installment plans, proceeds from which were to be spent on coöperatives and agricultural projects to benefit the peasants. This revolutionary step in land reform may influence the great landlords to emulate their ruler.

The present ruler is not at all like his domineering, morose father, nor is he weak and vacillating. After he returned from his visit to the United States in December 1949, he set to work to introduce economic and political reforms in his country, to which we will refer later. Generally speaking, he occupies a special position above politics and is revered by his people.

2. THE PARLIAMENT AND BUREAUCRACY

The Majlis, the lower house of the parliament, is the living symbol of the Constitution, and it too occupies an important place in the hearts of the Persians. They are proud of their tradition of constitutional government and Constitution Day is celebrated all over Iran with much fervor and sentiment. The Majlis can hardly be said to be truly representative of the people; it represents very well, however, the interests of the aristocracy and the religious leaders. Iran's revolution occurred before World War I, and was a revolt of the upper classes against the despotism of the Shah. Turkey's revolution, on the other hand, came after World War I and overthrew the power of the Ottoman aristocracy. This is not to say that the Majlis is composed solely of members of the landed aristocracy. Long and bitter denunciations of the aristocracy have been heard on the floor of parliament, and one group of deputies, the "National Front," headed by the popular fiery Doctor Mossadeq, who became prime minister on April 28, 1951, has been especially critical of the conservatives in Iran. Nonetheless the conservative bias of parliament is all too evident.

Although the Constitution provided for a Senate, the latter did not come into existence until the summer of 1949, after a Constituent Assembly had met in February, at the behest of the Shah, and drafted reforms. Many profess to see a threat to the authority of the Majlis, and a strengthening of the Shah's hand, in this move.

It is a significant feature of both the Majlis and the Senate that their members are not required to be residents of the districts from which they are elected. Hence regional problems are frequently neglected in favor of national and international affairs. This feature has led to the justified complaint, on the part of a few individuals, that parliament does not represent the people of the countryside at all.

The cabinet usually consists of thirteen members, including the prime minister, who selects the other members of the cabinet, plus the court minister, who is the representative of the Shah. The cabinet functions much the same as cabinets in Europe; since the end of the war Persian cabinets have had a history similar to their counterparts in France. According to the Constitution, a minister must be a Moslem and an Iranian by birth.

The bureaucracy in Iran, like the bureaucracies of other Middle Eastern countries, is swollen beyond sensible requirements. Salaries are low and continually threatened by rising prices. The growth of the bureaucracy has matched the increase in the city population. Just as peasants have flocked to the cities and have remained there, so the number of those desiring to avoid manual labor by obtaining a desk job in the bureaucracy has grown.

Prior to 1938 Iran was divided into four large provinces and a varying number of smaller units. In that year Reza Shah created a new organization of ten provinces, each with a governor at the head, appointed by the Shah. The provinces were further subdivided into forty-nine administrative districts, which were in turn composed of counties. The counties included several rural districts, which were a number of villages grouped together for administrative purposes. Each village was administered by a head man, usually the choice of the greatest landlord of the district, and in practice his instrument of control. The power of appointment and removal of the officials was centralized in the Ministry of the Interior. So Teheran was not only the center of national government; it was also the center of local government.

The curse of local government in Iran is its utter dependence on the central authority. If a municipality wishes to levy taxes and spend money on local improvements, it must first negotiate with the Ministry of the Interior. In effect the tax system of a community is only an appanage of the national tax system, which has long been in a sorry state. Local initiative has all but vanished primarily as a result of the all-pervading centralization.

In July 1950 the late prime minister, General Razmara, proposed a series of reforms in local government. Under his plan Iran would be divided into eighty-four provinces, each of which would have a provincial council to administer local health, education, and social affairs. The post of governor would be abolished, and county councils would be created to care for village affairs. This attempt to give more power to the local government, while stimulating interest among the people, met with strong opposition in the Majlis, where vested interests opposed any change in existing conditions. Some deputies opposed the plan on the basis that it would disrupt affairs in the country and create confusion. Others argued that it would divide responsibility and make for more abuses than exist under the present system. Proponents of the plan, on the other hand, claimed that if the reform were carried through it would be the first step in building up a political awareness among the people, who would begin to realize that they could influence their government. Razmara took the matter into his own hands, after parliament had recessed in September 1950, and issued an order for the election of provincial councils.

Traditionally the government has been regarded as a master and not a servant, while the exactions of the officials were ordained by Allah. This attitude is changing and, although direct influence of the people on individual deputies is small, there is a growing public opinion with which parliament will have to reckon.

The structure of law and government as described on paper is an enormous advance over conditions fifty years ago. Unfortunately the theory is belied in practice, for nepotism, bribery, and external pressure combine to discourage hopes of reform and progress. Another difficulty, which has already been mentioned, is the independent position of the tribes. The governor of the province of Fars, for example, must make his peace with the Qashqai chieftains. The appointment of a governor hostile to these tribesmen is usually the signal for an attempt on the part of the government to bring them under more control.

3. THE LANDED ARISTOCRACY

Members of the landed aristocracy, for the most part, live in cities on income from their properties in various parts of the country.

Under the traditional Islamic laws of inheritance it was difficult to preserve large family estates intact for generations. The ranks of the aristocracy were never frozen and the history of Iran is replete with Horatio Algers. On the other hand, in recent years the preservation of fortunes has been made easy by the lack of an adequate income tax law. Of course certain families always have been regarded as noble. Princes of the Qajar dynasty are still alive, but they are considered prominent members of the aristocracy by virtue of their culture and education as much as by their wealth and social standing. In debates in parliament in 1950, on the anti-corruption measures of the government, the phrase "the thousand families who control the wealth of Iran," was occasionally heard, but it does not seem to have captured the popular imagination.

4. THE ARMY

Under Reza Shah the army occupied a unique position of power and prestige. The late monarch more than doubled its size (bringing it to over 90,000), reorganized it, and lavished money and attention on it. Just as in Turkey, so in Iran, the army has been the ladder to success of many a peasant or nomad's son. Under the present Shah, however, the army does not enjoy all the privileges it had under his father. On the whole it is a conservative force and a center of opposition to the Communists. The army feels loyal to the person of the Shah above all else, and during the premiership of General Razmara this feeling was strengthened.

5. LABOR AND THE MIDDLE CLASS

By far the greatest number of workers in Iran are the artisans who work in small shops without the aid of machines. The Persians had a well-deserved reputation for fine craftsmanship in home industries, but by the beginning of the twentieth century the inroads of cheap Russian and English machine products had caused a decline in the native crafts. The quality of local products suffered from the competition; cheap European dyes and mass production methods affected the manufacture of the famed Persian carpets. The traditions of good craftsmanship were almost at the vanishing point when Reza Shah attempted to revive them by the establishment of schools for handicrafts. The trend was not halted, however, and the factory had come to Iran to stay. The craftsmen of the bazaar are part of the old pattern, while the growing number of factory workers form a special group.

Iran's three largest industries—oil, textiles, and sugar—employ some 62,000, 29,000, and 4,500 workers respectively.* Estimates of the total number of industrial workers employed by the larger factories vary from 100,000 to 200,000.

What is the condition of the industrial worker in Iran and what is his political importance? Under the terms of the Labor Law of 1946 the laborer was granted most of the legal rights enjoyed by labor in the industrial democracies of the West. The law provides for a 48-hour week, annual vacations with pay, health and aids funds, arbitration of disputes, minimum wages, and so forth. It legalizes trade unions and strikes, and regulates child and female labor. But all this is on paper; administration of the law encounters serious difficulties, many of which are the result of conflict with traditional practices. Because of this, and because of inadequate administrative machinery, enforcement of the law has been limited to the larger factories.

Trade unionism is still embryonic, relatively inarticulate, and politically ineffective. The labor movement is disunited; there are a number of company unions and local organizations but no strong national authority. There is a Ministry of Labor and a Supreme Labor Council, composed of government representatives and labor leaders, to handle labor problems. In 1946 the government was accused of splitting the pro-Communist Iranian Federation of Trade Unions, a member of the WFTU, by sponsoring an independent organization. In any case the pro-Communist union declined in numbers. At the Free World Labor Conference held in London in November 1949, Iran was represented by the *Union Syndicale des Travailleurs et Agriculteurs,* which claimed a substantial majority of organized labor in Iran as members.

Communists have found their greatest support among the workers of the oil company and of the textile industry—especially in Isfahan. The first significant strike in Iran in decades was that of the telephone employees in February 1942, but it was brief and mild. Other workers quickly learned the effectiveness of the strike; in May and July of 1946 particularly violent strikes broke out at the Abadan

* "Agricultural and Industrial Activity and Manpower in Iran," *International Labour Review,* vol. 59 (1949), 554.

oil refinery. In fact there was a wave of strikes in the oil and textile industries, instigated by the Communists. Since the decline of the IFTU there was relatively little labor unrest until April 1951 when a major strike occurred in the oil industry.

There was little unemployment in Iran in the years before World War II, owing to the government's extensive projects such as construction of the railroad, military preparations, and construction of factories. This state continued throughout the war, but after the evacuation of Iran by the Allies there was some unemployment caused by the large number of workers released from service with the armies of occupation. Most of these workers have now been reintegrated into the Iranian economy, but many remember their better-paid jobs with the armies and are dissatisfied with present conditions.

Iran's small middle class—composed of government officials, army officers, merchants, professional men, small businessmen, and so forth—has thus far remained as a whole subservient to the interests of the entrenched ruling classes. Yet it is mainly from this group, as we have said, that the few genuinely liberal and pro-democratic critics of the *status quo* have come. And it is from this same group that leadership and support for democratic reform must largely come.

Political parties in Iran up to now have been utterly unable either to utilize effectively existing democratic sentiment or to promote its growth. In fact there have been no political parties (with one or two exceptions) in our sense of the word at all. Such parties as have existed have always been so unstable and so short-lived as to be virtually without effect.

6. THE RELIGIOUS LEADERS

It is difficult to assess the power of the religious leaders in Iran today, but their influence is certainly strong even though it is behind the scenes. According to the Constitution the official religion of Iran is Islam, according to the Shiite doctrine, which faith the Shah must profess and promote. The religious leaders are represented in parliament and may declare legislation null and void if it conflicts with the principles of Islam, thus acting as a kind of supreme court above the Shah and parliament. (See Appendix I.) The ulema, or learned of the faith, never lost their prestige in Iran as they did in Turkey, although they were roughly handled on a number of occasions by Reza

Shah. In his desire to modernize and westernize the country he put many curbs on religion, but he never attempted complete secularization. In a series of measures over several years he instituted a western legal system, depriving the religious judges of authority in civil cases. He confiscated religious endowments and reorganized and secularized religious schools. The power of the religious leaders was effectively curbed during the lifetime of the strong monarch, but once his hand was removed a reaction set in. One can observe today stricter adherence to religious injunctions, such as observance of the obligatory fast during the month of Ramazan every year, and it seems as though the influence of the conservative clerics is growing. Religion may be regaining lost ground with the mass of people, but it is on the wane among intellectuals, although they may use it to bolster nationalism. On the whole in Iran religion is more important as a social or even political force than in its philosophical or ethical implications. Some claim that it is not secularism which is growing but simply indifference to religion, yet the trend is unmistakable.

Despite this trend, chiefly observable among the intellectuals, religion is still the essence of life for most of the people of Iran. In order to understand better the position of the religious leaders and their hold on the people, it is necessary to discuss in some detail the concepts of religion and law held by the Persians. Though such a discussion of the details of their religion may seem academic to some, a knowledge of them nevertheless is vital for a real understanding of the people, who depend, especially in the villages, on the local religious leaders for education, advice, and guidance.

4. Religion and Law

1. THE OFFICIAL RELIGION

While the West has distinguished between government, law, social behavior, and religion, Islam has known no such separation. Religion covers every aspect of the life of the individual and of the community. There is no distinction between the sacred and profane, and theoretically all of one's actions, from devout prayer to the most menial of tasks, are equally binding under religious law. More than that, Islamic society and the state were created to defend the religion.

Islam is democratic in the sense that it is a brotherhood of the faithful; slave and master, black and white will pray together bending their backs in unison facing Mecca. The equality of all men, however, derives from their relation to God, and this equality implies a religion of simplicity, a religion of rites and duties. One frequently hears from Moslems that Islam has no theology but only duties. The mercy of God is above all, but it must be supplemented by works; one must do the right things. And the Moslem should not attempt to penetrate the mysteries of religion; Allah alone knows them, and man has but to obey the injunctions of his God.

Yet Islam is a religion which encourages meditation in solitude, and no one can tell what a man will think when he is alone and undisturbed. At any hour of the day, one of the faithful may step from the busy street into a mosque, remove his shoes out of respect for his surroundings, and sit in quiet contemplation and prayer until called to his duties outside. It has been often repeated that there is no organized clergy in the Moslem faith. Yet the independent role of the individual seems forgotten when one observes the massed congregation of believers in a mosque on Friday. The almost disciplined rows of worshipers give the impression of an army with officers, ready to fight and die for the sake of the prophet.

Just as in Judaism, so in Islam, it is not theology which is central,
but law. The Moslem moral code is divided into five categories, ranging from forbidden acts to obligatory duties, and the drinking of
wine and the representation of the human form belong to the forbidden. Yet Persian artists painted the figures of men and women in
their miniatures, and the wine of Shiraz, famed in poetry, is still consumed by the worthy citizens of that city. How can this be reconciled
with the precepts of Islam? It is difficult, if not impossible. The answer, however, is partly that the Persians were Persians first and
Moslems afterwards. Further, the answer is to be sought in the revolt
of the Persians against orthodox Islam, their acceptance of a heresy,
and their transformation of it into something more in accord with
their own traditions. This heresy is the schismatic sect of the Shiites.

The Shiite branch of Islam, the state religion of Persia, is distinguished from the Sunni branch, which obtains in the neighboring
states, by many differences in rites and beliefs, and perhaps as many
people have been killed in struggles between the two as there were
Christians killed in the religious wars of the Reformation. The
Shiite movement began as a political revolt after the death of the
prophet. Some Arabs thought that the caliphs, the successors of Mohammed, should be chosen from the family of 'Ali, son-in-law of the
prophet. After the death of 'Ali, who was himself the fourth caliph,
the office of caliph did not go to his son but to a member of another
family. As a result the Shiite movement developed and soon political
aspirations were put on a doctrinal base. But Shiism came to mean
much more; politically it became the rallying point of any opposition to the ruling caliphs. Doctrinally it became mixed with pre-
Islamic Iranian, Christian, and pagan beliefs. From the beginning
the Shiite party attracted romantics and mystics. 'Ali himself came
to be regarded as an idealistic cavalier, a Sir Galahad who was more
sympathetic to many than the businesslike, matter-of-fact Umayyad
caliphs who ruled in place of the descendants of 'Ali.

The fundamental difference between Shiites and Sunnis is the
belief of the former in the transmission of the divine power of proph-
ecy through an apostolic succession. The Shiites could not follow a
book (the Quran) alone; they had to exalt a man ('Ali and his children). Superficially, one might compare the Shiite revolt against
orthodoxy with the Christian development out of Judaism. Many
small sects of Shiism with varying doctrines grew up, but in them all
is belief in a leader, or *imam,* who is the only authoritative source of

knowledge, possessing secret information denied ordinary mortals. More than this, in the official religion of Persia is the belief that the twelfth *imam,* in descent from 'Ali, vanished and will some day re-appear as the messiah to lead his people to salvation. This concept is an ancient one in Iranian religious thought, for in the *Avesta,* long before the birth of Christ, the coming of a savior is predicted. Thus, native Iranian tradition reasserted itself after the Arab conquest.

One prominent feature of Persian Shiism is the ten days of mourn-ing every year to commemorate the death of Husain, son of 'Ali, at the hands of the Sunnis in the year 680. The climax of the period of mourning is the "passion play," which arouses the strongest feelings of the Persians. It is the equivalent of Christmas and Easter rolled into one. Until Reza Shah forbade it, during the procession which accompanied performance of the play, some fanatics would cut them-selves with knives or beat themselves with chains to show their grief at the martyrdom of Husain, and as atonement for their own sins. The play itself is simply the story of Husain's last days before he and his followers were overwhelmed and killed by his enemies. It con-tains passages of real merit, however, and Husain is revealed not only as a sympathetic character, but as a man of thought and insight. For instance, in a moment of resignation, when Husain realizes he is surrounded and cannot escape, he says, "Men travel by night and their destinies travel towards them." Events in the passion play are interpreted as acts of great religious import for the Shiites. Although the public performance of the play was forbidden by Reza Shah, it still continues in private, and, together with the ten days of mourn-ing, is still an integral part of the Persian religion.

Even in this brief survey of the religion of the Persians, which per-force omits much of significance, the popular beliefs of the masses and mysticism must be mentioned. For one must distinguish between the formalistic religion of the books, which was the religion of the educated and the religious leaders, and the popular religion of the common people. Many superstitions of the Persians and many of their ideas and practices regarding birth, marriage, and death are age-old and frequently not in accord with strict Moslem beliefs. Nevertheless they are widely held and followed and are an important part of the popular religion. For example, many Persians believe in various kinds of spirits and supernatural beings. The world is popu-lated with fairies, *jinn,* and myriad unseen creatures, both good and evil.

The influence of the mystics, or Sufis as they are called in the Middle East, on the development of Islam has been of great importance. The personal and emotional approach to religion of the Sufis suited the common folk more than the abstract, legalistic teachings of the orthodox. It was largely due to the missionary work of the Sufis that the Moslem faith, though not in its orthodox form, reached China, India, and the depths of Africa. The mystics taught that one could attain a direct, personal experience of God, which teaching was far more effective than the inculcation of mere obedience to the precepts of the orthodox. One could attain this personal ecstasy by various methods—strict asceticism, prolonged contemplation, or by inducing a trance with music or dance. Brotherhoods of Sufis were formed and their number grew. These were known in Iran as the dervish orders, which were popular all over the Moslem world. In Iran wandering dervishes, or religious mendicants, had a great influence among the common folk, perhaps to be compared to that of the saints of medieval Europe or to the holy men of India, but today their number and importance have declined greatly. Instead secret brotherhoods of religious fanatics have grown. No one knows the strength and influence of secret societies, religious and otherwise, but the tradition is an old one in Iran and is certainly in operation today. It was religious fanatics who assassinated Prime Minister Razmara in March 1951.

2. LAW

In the ancient Middle East there was no distinction between religious and secular law. Law came into being by divine revelation; thus it was authoritarian. With the advent of Islam the same traditions continued, even though the Moslems claimed that Islam nullified all that came before it. The result was a synthesis of the new with the old.

For Moslems the fountainhead of all law, indeed of all wisdom, is the holy Quran, the revealed word of God. It is obvious, however, that the Quran could not provide answers to all of the problems which came up in disputes, not only about religious matters but about purely secular affairs. While there was no priesthood in Islam, there were judges who were of necessity experts in both religion and law. These judges referred their problems to the Quran, and if that failed to provide a solution for them, they turned to the writings about the

customs and practices of Mohammed, the *Sunna,* whence the name
Sunnis. After the death of Mohammed men tried to remember his
words and actions. Thus there arose collections of traditions about
the prophet's acts and sayings which were used by the Sunni judges
to decide cases. About the tenth century after Christ the traditions
of the orthodox were codified, and judges in the future could only
explain the treatises; they could not change or add to them. The
legal structure was thus frozen.

Shiite law, which was the law of Persia, differed from the Sunni in
that the former refused to recognize the great collections of traditions
of the Sunnis, deeming them all spurious. The Shiites maintained that
the *imam* alone received the divine inspiration of Mohammed, and
passed it on through the family of 'Ali. After the disappearance of the
twelfth *imam,* Shiite experts in law could interpret disputed cases in
his absence. Since the Shiites did not develop a body of canonical
law, as did the Sunnis with their collections of traditions, the Shiite
judges had greater freedom in the exercise of judgment. In practice,
therefore, there was greater opportunity for development and adaptation to the needs of the time in the Shiite system of law.

It became obvious in the nineteenth century that Iran would have
to adopt a European legal system if the country was not to remain
isolated and out of touch with the rest of the world. Before the Constitution little had been done to give Iran a modern legal system, although a Ministry of Justice had been created at the end of the nineteenth century. A judicial branch of the government was created by
the Constitution, separate from the legislative and executive branches.
Students were sent to Europe to be trained as lawyers, but progress
was slow in the face of the determination of the traditional "religious"
judges not to give up their prerogatives. By 1931, however, most of
what we know as law, except questions of marriage and divorce, had
been transferred from religious to secular courts.

In 1919 the Ministry of Justice founded a school of law, which was
joined to the University of Teheran in 1935. Modern Persian law, for
the most part, has followed French examples. New civil and criminal
codes, modeled after the French codes, were published in 1926, and a
new penal code, based on the Italian, was adopted in 1939. The collection of common law follows both Shiite and French law, while the
code of commercial law, finished in 1932, is based entirely on European law. There is a hierarchy of courts with a Supreme Court as the
final authority. In the last named the religious leaders are influential.

Although the system is adequate on paper, the inexperience of the judges, as well as the illegal use of prestige and wealth, has led to many abuses.

3. RELIGIOUS MINORITIES

While Shiite Islam is the official religion of Iran, it is not the only religion in the country. There are Sunni Moslems, the Kurds being the largest group of these, but there are also a number of religious minorities which are more distinct as minorities than are the different ethnic groups. Until the development of present-day nationalism, religious loyalties were more important than all others in the Middle East, and the question still asked of foreigners in remote villages is not "What is your nationality?" but "What is your religion?"

There are some 60,000 Armenians in Iran who belong, for the most part, to the national Armenian church, which has its center in the Armenian Soviet Socialist Republic. They are mostly city dwellers and have their own schools, newspapers, and clubs, and they use their own language among themselves. Because of the existence of an Armenian state across the northern border in the Soviet Union, the Armenians have been regarded with suspicion and mistrust by Moslem Persians. After the recent war many Armenians went to Russia at the invitation of the Soviet government, but stories of their reception and life in the Soviet fatherland, which circulated in Iran, indicated that many were decidedly unhappy. One story, which is well known throughout Iran, says that an Armenian told his friends in Iran that he would indicate to them how he liked his new home in the USSR by sending them a photograph of himself. If he were standing in the photograph, it would indicate that he was happy; if he were sitting, it would mean that life was difficult and unpleasant. Several months after he arrived in the USSR his friends in Teheran received a letter with an enclosed photograph in which the Armenian was lying on the ground.

There are about 40,000 Jews in Iran, all engaged in trade and the professions. They speak Persian, although they sometimes write it in Hebrew characters. They have not formed a conspicuous minority like the Armenians and they have not suffered the tribulations which Jews have experienced in the Arab countries.

About 30,000 Nestorian Christians live in the vicinity of Rezaiyeh, in the Lake Urmiah district, as peasants and craftsmen. Some are also to be found in Teheran. They are also known as Assyrians, followers of the ancient, eastern offshoot of the Christian faith.

There may be perhaps 15,000 Zoroastrians left in Iran, where once the state religion upheld the teachings of the ancient prophet. The "fire worshipers" are looked upon with contempt by the strict Moslems, and it is surprising that the tenacious group of Zoroastrians has been able to maintain itself for over twelve centuries in the midst of the Moslem majority. They live today in Teheran, Kirman, and Yezd and they still practice the rite of exposing their dead on a tower. They have been fortunate in their contacts with their coreligionists, the rich Parsis of Bombay, who have contributed much to the well-being of the Zoroastrian community in Iran. Under the reign of Reza Shah they were favored as representatives of the old pre-Islamic culture of Iran, this because of the Shah's nationalism.

One must not forget to mention the Bahais, who number over 200,000, with headquarters in Teheran. They belong to all classes of the population and have contacts with other Bahais throughout the world, especially in America. On the shores of Lake Michigan, in Wilmette, Illinois, stands the beautiful temple which is the center of their activity in this country. The Bahais are not recognized as a religious community by the Iranian government and their lot has not been pleasant. Although there is supposed to be religious freedom in Iran, the religious minorities, especially the Bahais, must be careful in their actions, and attempts at proselytizing sometimes have met with violent hostility from the Moslem majority.

5. Character, Culture, and History

Foreigners have many misconceptions about the Persians, which are matched by the delusions of some Persians about the rest of the world. Toward his neighbors the Persian feels vaguely superior; his faith is different and his culture higher. Toward the Westerners some Persians are deferential, cognizant of the overwhelming material power of the former. Others, have little understanding of the weakness of Iran and overestimate her strength. This attitude was more prevalent before 1941, but even the Anglo-Soviet invasion failed to quench the beliefs of many. There is another, more widespread, feeling, that the ills of Iran are the result of the machinations of foreigners. It would be unwise to dismiss this feeling as mere nationalistic sentiment; it is far more significant. Furthermore, historically it is eminently justified.

Americans should not be surprised that the Persians are not so unitedly pro-American and anti-Soviet as the Turks. Persians exhibit a great diversity of opinion, and they are not wont to keep their opinions to themselves. The black and white interpretations in other countries are frequently a variety of shades of gray in Iran. The desire for quick action and results evinced by Americans is regarded with a mixture of awe, unwillingness to coöperate, and amused contempt by many Persians. The traditional mad dogs and Englishmen have been put in the shade by Americans in Iran, but American initiative by no means endears itself without question to the Persians.

Several Persian traits may puzzle, and sometimes distress, the foreigner. One is the trait stemming in part from the religious doctrine of *taqiye* or dissimulation, which permits a Shiite to pretend that he is a Sunni, or even a Christian or Jew, if he is at any time in danger because of being a Shiite. The ramifications of this practice extend beyond religion. Another is the penchant of the Persians for exaggeration, which has earned for them a bad reputation among their neighbors. Perhaps reasons for these traits could be found in the history and traditions of Iran, but an engineer, impatient to get his job done, cares little for the reasons.

A traveler of thirty years ago would have found much in common externally between Iran and Turkey, but today many of the generalizations which could have been made then about the two countries in common would still be valid of Iran though inaccurate of modern Turkey. It should be borne in mind, however, that the Turks, when they turned their backs on their past, were rejecting a culture which was primarily borrowed, while the Persians have maintained their own. It was easier for the Turks to replace Arab-Persian norms with western models. The traditional culture of Iran, then, is of great importance.

1. THE ARTS

From the most ancient of times Persia has been known as a land of splendor and luxury; not of barbaric ostentation but of magnificence softened by a certain refinement. The art of Iran has always been characterized by a subtle feeling of elegance, never forced, never seeking to impress. There is in the painting, the poetry, and even in the carpets and other creations of the Persian genius, a kind of delicate sensuality which even the stern religion of the Arabian prophet failed to quench. This sensuality is never gross or brutal but highly refined, the product of high civilization. This quality has always been present in the aesthetic conception of Persian art.

Many Westerners think that in Persia everyone reclines on beautiful carpets and recites exquisite poetry between puffs on a water pipe or bites of sherbet. Carpets and poetry, above all else, have spread the name of Persia throughout the Occident. Hand-woven Persian carpets are esteemed by Westerners, but in Iran they hold a special place among works of art in the hearts of the people. They are the expressions of the love of form and beauty by all of the folk. The finest of carpets will often be found in an otherwise poor nomad's tent, and it will be prized above all else by the illiterate tribesman. The intricate patterns frequently have been handed down through generations in families which make their own carpets. Although the Islamic religion forbids the representation of the human form, art has always taken precedence in Persia, where figures of men and women, as well as the more frequent geometrical patterns and floral motifs, appear on carpets and in miniatures. The carpet has become the symbol of the Persian artistic genius in the Occident, but it would be a great mistake to assume that this is the only artistic creation worthy of notice.

The arts of Iran, however, never attained the stage of individuality which they reached in the West. Persian miniature paintings, produced, as they were, under conditions roughly analogous to those which gave rise to western medieval painting, cannot therefore be compared with the painting of, say, a Rembrandt. This is not to imply that Persian painting is any less beautiful on that account, any more than medieval painting is necessarily "inferior" to more recent painting; they are in different worlds.

The Persians not only delight in the lovely designs and the quality of their magnificent carpets, but also of their metalwork, pottery, and other arts and crafts. The beautiful inlaid boxes of Shiraz are not made for the tourist trade, although now commercialism is cutting deeply into the traditions of fine craftsmanship, but rather for the appreciative local citizen. The purely decorative character of Persian art is everywhere perceptible, in architectural design, in painting, and in the crafts. Pottery is especially noteworthy, and Persian pottery of the Middle Ages is hardly inferior to the wonderful ceramic wares of the Chinese. The sense of proportion and the colors are superb in the Persian pieces, even though there is little variety.

The Persians have been accused of a lack of originality in their arts, but originality may be prized too highly. Persian art frequently adapted the models it received from the outside to the special requirements of the Persian genius. Every work of art produced in the country has a special stamp on it, even though it be borrowed from a foreign culture. Nevertheless we owe much to Iran in the Fine Arts, as well as in architecture and landscape architecture. The squinch, the *aiwan,* or arched entrance way, the arrangement of house and garden borrowed by modern landscape architects—all are testimony to the influence of the arts of Iran in the history of civilization.

Long before the Persians appeared in history, domed buildings were erected in Mesopotamia, modern Iraq, but the structures were themselves circular or octagonal. The Persians invented the squinch to enable them to place a round dome on a square building; the spherical pendentive came later. The *aiwan* is a much later development, but it has been the characteristic form of mosque architecture in Iran since the thirteenth century. Nowhere else in the world can one find such magnificent arches facing the mosque courtyards, covered with beautiful tiles which in the sun dazzle the worshiper. The lovely melon-shaped domes, covered with blue tiles, on the old mosques of Iran, are among the most beautiful products the architect ever created.

Another Persian creation in architecture is the garden pavilion with high, slender columns supporting a flat roof and open on one or three sides. Persian gardens are quite formal with straight rows of cypresses and pools of water paved in tile. Some gardens have waterfalls over blue tiles, imparting a cooling atmosphere in the summer.

In considering both painting and architectural ornament, mention must be made of Persian calligraphy, for in Iran as in China the art of beautiful writing is closely tied up with painting and decoration. Western architecture is rectangular and the Latin script is inflexible, but the Arabic script as developed by the Persians fits the curved surfaces and the tiles of Persian architecture. The interweaving of design and inscription on the illustrated page of a book, on ceramics, on carpets, or on their buildings is a characteristic of Persian art which distinguishes it from the arts of neighboring peoples.

There are several features of Persian art which may not be pleasing to the Westerner. One is the abhorrence of a vacuum, the desire to fill every empty space with decoration. Another is the formalism and convention of much of their art. In literature too, design rather than meaning makes the work beautiful to the Persians. Still the Westerner is usually moved by the beauty of Persian art, despite his objection to the prevalence of stereotyped design.

2. LITERATURE

Persian is a clear, melodious language with an unusually rich vocabulary, since it draws heavily upon Arabic to enrich the native words. Thus it resembles English with its Latin and Teutonic blends. Because of the harmony of its sounds and the prominence of vowels, Persian has been called the Italian of the Orient. It is a language admirably suited to poetry because of its large vocabulary with many synonyms, and also the great range of rhyming not to be found in any European language. Furthermore, individual words and expressions are unusually evocative and carry rich emotional overtones.

The Persians share in common with the Arabs a love for the spoken word. Repartee and witty conversation are highly regarded and much cultivated, though frequently the puns, in which the Persians delight, are very bad. The traditional method of education throughout the Islamic East is recitation from memory, and in Iran poets have always stood high in the curriculum.

If an American were to ask for the recitation of his favorite classical English poem instead of a favorite popular song in a night club, it would be considered a joke. Furthermore, it is highly questionable if anyone could fulfill his request. In Iran, however, it is not at all unusual to hear the poetry of one of the great classical poets of Iran being recited in a tea house by anyone present. For poetry in Iran is not the exclusive preoccupation of professors or aesthetes but is rather part of the life of the people. Thus it is not surprising to hear an itinerant shepherd or merchant quote a line from Saadi to emphasize his point.

While classical Persian literature includes other genres, its greatest achievements are undoubtedly poetic. So universal is the love for poetry that despite widespread illiteracy the names of the greatest poets—Firdausi, Nizami, Saadi, and Hafiz—have become household words in Iran. These poets yield the palm to none in beauty of language and regard for form. Whoever said that one can learn about a people best from its poets might well have been thinking about Iran.

Persians have certainly not abandoned their traditional artistic and literary forms for western models. No real synthesis has ever been effected between traditional and Occidental literature in Iran. Her own literature and literary forms are still preëminent. Poetry is being written today as in the days of Saadi and Hafiz, and it differs little in spirit and form, though it is quite inferior. Certainly many works of literature have been translated from French and other European languages, and a few novels have been written by Persians, but the traditional forms are still appreciated more. Persian literature has not been the preoccupation of the aristocracy alone but has roots deep in the people; Saadi's *Rose Garden* is one of the first books read by children everywhere in the country.

3. THE GLORY THAT WAS IRAN

The Persians are a proud people, always ready to recall their past glory. And well they may be, for Iran's contributions to the history of civilization have not been few and her history has not been lacking in great achievements. The influences of bygone civilizations project onto the present scene, and the modern educated Persian is more conscious of his past than the Westerner is of his. While this reverence for the past is commendable in many respects, it also tends to dull men's realization of present needs and future potentialities. It begets a conservative, backward-looking philosophy of life, more concerned with preserving the *status quo,* or even emulating past eras, than with planning for the future. While this aspect of Persian society may be exaggerated sometimes by western interpreters of Iran, it cannot be ignored.

The abundance of ruins where now desolation reigns attests to a once more prosperous land. From historical records it would seem that Iran formerly had a much denser population than it has today, for there exist remains of irrigation canals and abandoned towns in areas which are now deserts. This is not the result of shifts in population for, on the whole, man in the Middle East has been a stationary animal moving little from the home of his ancestors, a fact which has made the work of archaeologists easier.

In the sixth century B.C. the Persians created the largest empire the ancient world had yet witnessed. The "One World" of the Achaemenid kings was a tolerant one in comparison with the former oppressive and even cruel domination of the Assyrians and Egyptians. Far from destroying the local temples or prohibiting the worship of local deities, as was the custom of conquerors in the ancient Orient, Cyrus, first of the Achaemenids, aided and fostered the various religious minorities in his empire.

It was to the age of the Achaemenids that Reza Shah turned for inspiration in his attempts to foster a spirit of national pride. Achaemenid art and architecture, as found in the magnificent ruins of the palaces of the great kings, were adapted to modern buildings. The National Bank of Iran, on Firdausi Avenue in Teheran, is the most striking example of the use of Achaemenid style for a modern structure, while the Ministry of War buildings are perhaps too slavish a copy. In the purge of Arabic words from the Persian language, scholars subsidized by the government searched for ancient substitutes. The glory of the Achaemenids was proclaimed by representing their monuments on postage stamps and on bank notes, a constant reminder to the people of their illustrious ancestors.

Four great waves of foreign conquest have inundated Iran in its long history since the Achaemenids, thus bringing the Persians into intimate contact with four alien cultures: the invasion of Alexander the Great in the fourth century B.C., the Arab conquest of the seventh century of our era, the Mongol invasion of the thirteenth century, and the European wave of the nineteenth and twentieth centuries. Yet Persian culture, though it did absorb those elements of foreign cultures which were compatible with it, always maintained its own unique qualities. After centuries of Greek cultural dominance the native culture reasserted itself under the Sassanian kings. A religious reaction (that of the Shiites) revived Iranian religious tradition against Arab Islam. The Mongols were absorbed by superior culture. Although the Persians have finally resisted European political domination, they are voluntarily, if selectively, adapting western technology, science, and institutional patterns to their own needs. Who can say whether Persian culture will maintain its basic character, as it always has hitherto, or whether ultimately it will be wholly transformed by westernization?

The most important of the four invasions of Iran was that of the Arabs. Their conquest ushered in a new era in the history of the country; it marks the end of the ancient and the beginning of medieval and modern Iran. This is not the place to discuss the amazing expansion of the Arabs from Spain to Central Asia and India, but the regular armies of Byzantium and the Sassanian Empire were unable to stem the Arab tribesmen, fanatic in their faith and confident of victory. It is wrong, however, to assume that the Arabs gave the conquered peoples the choice of conversion to Islam or the sword. The more usual and encouraged form of submission was the payment of tribute and taxes. Three hundred years after the Moslem conquest there were still large areas in Iran where few Moslems were to be found. This is not to minimize the importance of Islam in Iran, not only as a new religion but also as a revolutionary force bringing the promise of a new political and social order. At the same time the proud Persians maintained their native traditions.

About the year 1000 numerous Turkish tribes moved into Iran from Central Asia, and thus began the Turkish invasions, similar to the German invasions of the Roman Empire. These Turkish migrations were to last almost four hundred years and to leave their mark on the country. When one remembers that Iran was ruled by Turkish dynasties for over five hundred years after this time, it is significant that the Persians were able to maintain their identity without succumbing to their masters. As a matter of fact the conquered turned the tables on their conquerors, for the Turkish rulers adopted Persian customs, the Persian language for state affairs, and Persian culture in general.

The movement of Turks into the Middle East was accelerated by the terrible Mongol cataclysm in the thirteenth century. For a long time Mongol rulers dominated Iran, at first as representatives of the great Khan in Mongolia and then as independent sovereigns. It is difficult to determine the effects of the Mongol conquest and rule in Iran. Historians have attributed the decline of Islamic civilization, especially in the eastern part of the Moslem world, to the great slaughter and rapine which the Mongols wrought in Central Asia and Iran. Numbers of flourishing cities were laid waste and libraries and works of art were destroyed, but perhaps more significant was the feeling of insecurity and instability which lasted for centuries after the storm. Perhaps the most significant result of the Mongol occupation of Iran was the permanent Turkification of Azerbaijan and the spread of Turks to other parts of the country. The aftermath of domination by the Mongols was a long period of internecine wars which soon destroyed any benefits of the short-lived unity which the country had enjoyed under their yoke.

In 1502, Ismail, a religious leader from the town of Ardebil in Azerbaijan, proclaimed himself Shah. Claiming descent from the *imams,* he rallied the Shiites around him and with fanatic troops swept the field of rivals. He conquered all of Iran, but in the artillery of the Ottoman Turks he met more than his match. From this time till the nineteenth century Iran and the Ottoman Empire were to dispute control of the Middle East.

It was under Safavid rule that Europeans rediscovered Iran. Alarmed by the growing power of the Ottoman Empire in Europe, the western powers sought to establish diplomatic relations with Iran in the hope that the Shah would attack the Turks in the rear. We still have many interesting accounts of the British, French, Portuguese, and other European envoys to the Safavid court. They came for trade as well as diplomacy, and soon the British outweighed the others in their influence at the Persian court.

The most famous of the Safavids was Shah Abbas, a contemporary of Queen Elizabeth and the Great Moghul Akbar, who adorned his capital Isfahan with some of the most beautiful examples of architecture in the Middle East. In fact, the age of Shah Abbas has become the symbol of all that was beautiful in Iran, and merchants in the bazaars today will invariably claim that their antique art objects date from the time of Shah Abbas, which serves to enhance their value.

After the Safavid dynasty the history of Iran consists of wars and conquests, and only in 1794 did the Qajars, a Turkish tribe, unify Iran and establish their capital at Teheran. The founder of the dynasty was a tyrannical eunuch, who was assassinated and succeeded on the throne by his nephew. He is known in history as the only eunuch who founded a dynasty. With the Qajars the modern history of Iran begins.

6. The Impact of the West

In the nineteenth century Iran's weakness became apparent to the European powers, and she soon became a prey to their ambitions. Russia early took the lead by extending the Tsarist boundary and influence in northern Iran by military force, while Great Britain was not slow in consolidating her position in the south. As a result Russia and Britain have remained the traditional foes of Iran, the former more feared, the latter more disliked. Russian imperialist designs first touched Iran in the eighteenth century when Peter the Great took the cities of Baku and Derbend in the Caucasus from the Persians. In the nineteenth century the Russians in two wars routed the Persian armies and dictated their own terms. By the treaty of Gulistan in 1813 Russia annexed the territories of Georgia, Daghestan and the Caspian seacoast down to the present boundary, and Iran was forbidden to maintain warships on the Caspian Sea, which soon became a Russian lake. The treaty of Turkomanchai in 1828 imposed the Capitulations on Iran and gave Armenia, with its chief city of Erivan, to Russia.

The Capitulations gave the Russian consuls, rather than Persian authorities, jurisdiction over Russian nationals in Iran. This was similar to the extraterritoriality imposed by the European powers on China. Iran's power to levy customs duties on Russian goods was made subject to Russian approval. Most European powers followed the Russians in securing special rights for themselves; it was a bitter pill for the Persians to be kept from being masters in their own house for almost a century, until the time of Reza Shah. The Europeans, enjoying special rights in the country, frequently acted as though Iran were a colonial territory. It is true that they built factories, laid telegraph lines, and founded financial institutions, but these were invariably owned and operated by them and not by Persians. In the years immediately before World War I the Persians seemed to have lost all control and authority in their own country.

The power and despotism of the Shahs made it easy for the European powers to obtain concessions, since they had to deal with only one person, who frequently put his own interests above those of his country. To raise money for growing personal expenses, the Shahs would mortgage state property. Although the tradition of monarchy was well implanted in Iran, the assassination of Nasr al-Din Shah in 1896 revealed the existence of new movements and new ideas among the people. Just as the year 1848 marks a turning point for liberalism in Europe, so the year 1905 marks the end of one era and the beginning of a new one for Russia and for Asia. This is also true for Iran.

On December 30, 1906, the Constitution of Iran was proclaimed. Shortly afterwards oil was discovered in the south of the country. The former event symbolizes the advent of western liberalism and democracy, the latter of western technology and science. Both have profoundly affected Iran, though perhaps in some ways differently from what was foreseen at the time.

The Russian revolution of 1905 may well have had echoes in Iran, but the Persians had long been showing signs of discontent with the extravagances and tyrannical rule of the Shah, who governed by decree. The religious leaders were dissatisfied with his high-handed treatment of religious property and of their special prerogatives. Crowds in the bazaars began to demonstrate against the Shah, at the instigation of the religious leaders, and over ten thousand people, including many prominent merchants, held a sit-down strike in the British Legation compound. To end this the British representatives negotiated between the Shah and the leaders of the "Nationalists" with the result that a constitution was promulgated. Shortly after this act the Shah died and was succeeded by his son, who resolved to regain the powers lost by his father. With the granting of the Constitution the present phase of the history of Iran began; it marked a profound change in the destiny of the nation. It is an event still fresh in the minds of the Persians, for some of the prominent leaders of this revolution are alive and active today.

In 1906 the country was in a bankrupt, lawless state, with provincial governors acting almost completely independently of the central government. With the establishment of a parliament and consequent division of authority, all semblance of central government control in the provinces vanished. In Teheran and other cities people joined either the Shah's camp or that of the partisans of the parliament. The first parliament was, on the whole, a self-constituted assembly of members of the nobility, merchants, and religious leaders. Naturally they represented strong private interests rather than the people as a whole. There were, however, a number of Persians who had been educated in the West or who were strongly influenced by liberal ideas and were devoted to the concepts of representative government, but they were few and powerless and their counsels usually went unheeded.

As a result of the growing weakness of the Persian government, Britain and Russia concluded the infamous Anglo-Russian agreement of 1907, which patriotic Persians remember with bitterness. According to the terms of this agreement Iran was divided into two spheres of influence with a neutral zone between them. Russian interests were recognized as paramount in northern Iran and British in the south. The Iran agreement was one of several ententes which the European powers were forming at this time; it quieted the rivalry of the two countries in Iran but did not end it.

The Constitution and parliament, once established, did not fare too well. In 1908 the new Shah dissolved parliament and took the rule back into his own hands. This move was followed by an uprising of the Bakhtiyari tribesmen, who marched on Teheran, and, together with other supporters of the Constitution, compelled the ruler to abdicate in favor of his young son and retire to Russia. Several years later he again tried to regain power, but his invasion, supported by the Russians, was unsuccessful and he was forced to withdraw. Although the Constitutionalists had triumphed, it was a hollow victory, for the northern part of Iran was still dominated by the Russians, who dictated policy to the Persian government. In the south were the British, whose influence was less obvious and militant, however, for, unlike the Russians, they did not maintain troops in Iran. But the oil fields kept them active and interested in the country.

In World War I Iran was as innocent as Belgium, yet her soil was violated by armies of Russians, British, and Turks, and her citizens were slain by both sides. She remained neutral throughout the war. By 1917 the Turks, with their German officers, had been almost entirely cleared from Iranian territory when the Russian revolution caused the withdrawal of Russian troops. In the north the Turks took advantage of the vacuum thus created to invade Azerbaijan and the Caucasus area, but their own government was distintegrating. In

1918 British troops moved northward, and they even took Baku, which they subsequently had to abandon. It seemed that Britain was in a position to annex Iran, for her old rival to the north was engaged in a bloody civil war. In 1919 a British-Persian agreement was proposed by the British foreign minister, Lord Curzon. The British proposal seemed unobjectionable; it provided for British advisors and aid to Iran, including a large loan. Many Persians believed, however, that it would impose a British protectorate over the country. The weak parliament was ready to ratify the agreement when the people rose in protest and throngs gathered in the bazaars to denounce it. As a result, in 1921 it was rejected by the parliament, which itself, however, gained no additional strength or influence thereby. The country was in chaos nursing the wounds received in the war, and relations with the Russians were uncertain. Soon the Persians were to be agreeably surprised by them.

As early as 1918 the new Soviet government proclaimed a policy of friendship toward Iran, and shortly thereafter they repudiated all Tsarist privileges, including the Capitulations. In addition they canceled all debts which the government of Iran had contracted with the imperial Russian government. The Persians, of course, were happy to have their powerful neighbor withdraw, but they accepted the Soviet acts as long overdue and hoped for even more concessions.

At the end of 1920 diplomatic relations were opened between the two countries and a Soviet ambassador was appointed to Iran. The following year Irano-Soviet relations were formalized by the treaty of February 26. According to this treaty both powers promised non-interference in each other's internal affairs. Iran was permitted to establish a naval force on the Caspian Sea and a number of previous Soviet concessions were put in writing. This treaty has been the basis of Irano-Soviet relations to the present. It was by no means completely in favor of Iran, for the Soviet government reserved the right to send troops into Iran if it felt threatened by anti-Soviet groups who were using, or who might use, Iran as a base of operations. Articles Five and Six of the treaty were utilized by the Soviets in 1941 and still constitute a threat to Iran, in spite of Persian denunciations of Article Six made in April 1949, and again in July 1950 (see Appendix II).

Persian feelings toward the Russians are not easily analyzed. The Russian occupation of northern Iran before World War I had made some friends for them as well as many enemies. The Bolshevik revolution won idealistic adherents in Iran as it did elsewhere in the world, so there was created a nucleus of pro-Soviet Persians. And had not the new Soviet government repudiated the hated privileges of the Tsars in the Shah's domain? Although there was, then, a basis of *rapprochement* between the two peoples, feelings soon cooled. There was not only the traditional fear of Russia and the historic enmity, but a new factor had been introduced by the Bolsheviks which, though it may have made little impression on Atatürk's Turks, colored the feelings of the Persians towards the Russians. This was the anti-religious policy of the Bolshevik government; the "Godless Russians" became a standard epithet for the northern neighbors. That the Soviets could find some support in Iran, however, was made evident by the events in the province of Gilan on the Caspian seacoast.

A strange foretaste of the autonomous Azerbaijan republic of 1946 was the formation of the rebel government of Gilan after the first World War. Soviet troops had followed the retreating White forces across the Caspian to the shores of Iran in 1920 and had disembarked at several ports. Contact was established with a local band of rebels against the Teheran government and a Soviet Republic of Gilan was proclaimed. After the signing of the Irano-Soviet treaty of February 1921, however, the Persians could not understand why Soviet troops remained in Iran. Repeated protests from Teheran to Moscow brought the response that it was no concern of Moscow, but rather of the "independent" Soviet Republic of Gilan. Just as after World War II, the continued presence of British troops in the south gave the Soviets a good excuse to continue their occupation in the north. Eventually, in the autumn of 1921, the Red Army forces were withdrawn and the rebel government collapsed when troops moved against it from Teheran. Iran was at last free of foreign occupation.

With the advent of Reza Shah the impact of the West was felt not only in government circles in the capital, but all over the country. Iran entered a new era in its history; she walked into the arena of world politics alone, without the British or the Russians guiding her steps.

7. Reza Shah Pahlevi

The story of Iran from 1921 to 1941 is the story of Reza Shah. A colonel in the Persian Cossack brigade, which had been organized by the Russians before World War I, he had risen from the ranks and was a favorite with his men. He was an ardent patriot but had lost his respect for the pusillanimous parliament in the capital. Together with a group of liberal young Persians, he marched on Teheran with his troops and overthrew the weak government. His rise after that was swift; he first became commander-in-chief of the armed forces; in 1923 he became prime minister, and two years later Shah. The last ruler of the Qajar dynasty resigned himself to a life on the Riviera, abandoning his throne to a more energetic potentate.

Reza Shah was one of the successful dictators who seized power after World War I. What kind of man was he? Compared to his fellow dictator in Turkey, he is a shadowy figure. It is difficult to give a character sketch of a man who disliked society so much and especially the company of foreigners. He was awkward in the presence of any except military men, and contacts with foreign diplomats were left to the polished court minister, Teymurtash, who was not limited to Persian in his linguistic ability. There was never any doubt, however, who ruled Iran. The Shah is said to have had long periods of melancholy and he was rarely seen smiling. There was little sophistication in this soldier. To his followers he was a formidable figure who could never be opposed. Yet his people respected and admired him for his achievements in freeing Iran from foreign control and direction. In the early years of his reign this was his main purpose, toward which he directed much of his energy.

Until the middle thirties he seemed to be working selflessly for the good of his country. Unfortunately, lust for power and wealth began to dominate his mind until he was not above murder to achieve his ends. He grew more suspicious of his associates and led a more secluded life. His right-hand man, Teymurtash, fell under his displeasure and died an unnatural death. The last years of his reign, till his abdication in 1941, were almost an era of terror for the landed aristocracy. If the Shah coveted an estate, or certain properties, he would not rest until he had obtained it by fair means, or more frequently foul. Many tales are told of the ingenious methods of extortion which the Shah employed. A favorite means of getting rid of a rival was the injection of air bubbles in the blood stream of the victim by the Shah's doctor. In spite of this dark side of the Shah's character, he did much for Iran and a mere list of his reforms and innovations is impressive.

Reza Shah sought to strengthen and unify his country following the example of Atatürk, but he had a much more difficult task. The Turks had been in closer contact with Europe for a much longer time and were better prepared to accept reforms and westernization. Furthermore, Reza Shah failed to form a group of loyal, capable lieutenants to carry out his plans and continue his work after his death. During his reign nationalism became the slogan of the day, and foreign influences in Persian culture were played down as much as possible. The reform of the language and the copying of ancient Iranian motifs in art and architecture have already been mentioned, and there were many other changes in the interest of nationalism. The nationalist movement, however, never attained the strength it did in Turkey, although it has left its mark on the country and people.

Another principle of reform followed by Reza Shah was westernization. Although suspicious of the designs of the European powers on Iran, the Shah had great admiration for western technical progress, especially in the military domain. He made of the army officers a special, favored class, building sumptuous officers' clubs, sending them to Europe as students, and providing them with uniforms which put the garb of the common soldier to shame. The army was reconstructed throughout on western models.

Just as in Turkey, the method of westernization was to build from the top down, which resulted in much waste and many failures. The Shah made a mistake which is patent elsewhere in the Orient. He thought he could transplant the finest factories, hospitals, and other institutions of the West almost overnight to Iran and have them function just as they did in Europe or America. He forgot that even the material manifestations of western culture are not isolated and self-contained, but are the result of building on the knowledge and achievements of centuries of development, forming the warp and woof of western civilization. It should be a maxim that single achievements of western civilization, material or spiritual, cannot be lifted from their milieu and transported to a completely different one and be expected to flourish unless the ground has been well prepared in advance. This is perhaps the principal reason why one sees abandoned factories, grain elevators, and the like in Iran. Many should not have been built.

To give an example, an excellent hospital, supplied with the best medical equipment, and staffed with doctors trained in Vienna and New York, failed to function as it should. It failed because of the lack of understanding that a successful hospital is the result of the cooperation of many people on many levels and not only of eminent physicians. The lack of trained nurses, orderlies, and above all the lack of understanding of the elementary rules of sanitation among the patients, combined to defeat the project. Furthermore, a preventive medicine and public health program is far more important for Iran than elaborate, specialized hospitals. Indeed such a program should be a prerequisite for the hospitals.

Thus a justified criticism which can be leveled against the westernizing reforms of Reza Shah is that they were imposed too quickly, without adequate preparation. The people had no chance to grow into them, and there was lack of foresight in some of them. Future developments were not planned for, and there was little, if any, provision for the eventual evolution of democratic processes. It frequently appeared as though it were the passing whim of the Shah which decided the promulgation of a new reform, with the expectation that it would be put into effect immediately. The Shah once decided that camel caravans were a sign of backwardness; so they were forbidden and they theoretically ceased to exist in Iran.

The Shah's campaign against the religious leaders, the stronghold of reaction and tradition, has already been mentioned. Privileges of the aristocracy were curbed as well, and the use of flowery titles was forbidden. The elegant, but time-consuming, ritual and formality of aristocratic society were gradually discarded. Women were encouraged to emulate their European sisters, but the "emancipation" of women was not received with great acclaim, even by those who enjoyed the benefits. If the number of Turkish women who are prominent in public life may be counted on one's fingers, similar Persian women can be counted on one's thumbs.

Not all the reforms were accepted passively by the populace. Violent opposition in the bazaars frequently resulted from the promulgation of a new decree of westernization, opposition which was sometimes suppressed with force. One riot in Meshed, in the sacred shrine of Imam Reza, the tomb of the eighth of the *imams,* was put down by the machine guns of the Shah's army. The police were instructed to use force in removing the veils from women and the turbans or other non-European headgear from men, after the Shah had so decreed. In short, the Shah revolutionized the social and religious life of his people—on the surface.

The most spectacular venture of the Shah was the construction of the trans-Iranian railroad. The story of this costly undertaking would require volumes, but certain details in the account of its building are of interest. The British and Russians had long dreamed of a trans-Iranian railroad, the former seeking to connect India with the European network through Iran, while the latter hoped to extend their line, already reaching Tabriz, to the Persian Gulf. The Shah heeded neither the British nor the Russians but laid out his own route. Almost every nation in the world participated in the construction of the railroad with personnel or materials, but it was finally completed by a Scandinavian concern. It was finished in 1939, covering a distance of over 870 miles. It is a truly spectacular feat of engineering, with over 4,000 bridges and 200 tunnels, some almost on top of one another. The train must climb from sea level at the Caspian Sea to an altitude of over 9,000 feet in a relatively short distance. The railroad, condemned as the Shah's folly when it was built because of the route it followed, proved of immense value to the Allies in World War II. It is no exaggeration to say that the supplies sent to the Soviet Union over this railroad during the war turned the tide in Russia against the Nazi armies.

The Shah paved the streets in Teheran, improved the highways, and constructed modern buildings in some of the large towns. He made his capital the show place of the nation. His zeal for westernizing Iran, however, sometimes drove him to extremes. Although he had been outside of his native land only once, on a short visit to Turkey to meet Atatürk, he sought to embellish his capital with western institutions he had never seen, such as an opera which was completely out of place in Iran. The opera house still stands an unfinished shell, empty, in the heart of Teheran, and declared unsafe by construction engineers. The airfield and radio station, on the other hand, function well and the Persians are justifiably proud of them.

All of this cost huge sums of money. Reza Shah was resolved not to apply to foreign sources for loans but rather to raise money from the people of Iran. This meant a revision of the economic organization of the country and new taxes. In 1927 a National Bank of Iran was founded and five years later paper money was issued by it. To raise money for the railroad the first government monopolies, on sugar and tea, were instituted in 1924. They proved so profitable that the government embarked on an extensive program of state ownership and control, and by 1941 there were several dozens of monopolies which supplied revenue, among them matches, tobacco, paper production, and textiles.

This growing regimentation of Iran coincided with the rise to power of Hitler. Before the advent of the Nazis, Persian relations with Germany had not been too cordial owing to several minor diplomatic incidents. One of these involved a group of exiled Persians in Germany who had written articles against the Shah, and had neither been arrested nor forbidden to write by the German government. Still there were no black marks against the Germans in the history of Iran; rather many Persians had fond memories of the activities of such Germans as Wassmuss during World War I. And had not the Kaiser's troops almost defeated the traditional enemies of Iran? Furthermore, Germany was far away and had no designs on or special interests in Iran.

Any offended feelings the Shah may have had were soon smoothed by the envoys of the German dictator. Reza Shah could understand and deal more easily with countries like Germany and Italy than he could with democracies, which, incidentally, were less responsive to offenses of *lèse majesté* by their journalists. There is no question that German methods, the efficiency of the dictator, and the regimentation of the people appealed to the late ruler. A secret police was developed in Iran similar to counterparts in the Fascist states, though it was never so oppressive or efficient. Following the lead of the Axis powers, Reza Shah intensified his activities against the Communists. Some were imprisoned; others fled to the Soviet Union, while still others, needless to say, went underground.

Movements of foreigners in the country were restricted and life became oppressive for many of the individualistic Persians. The number of intellectuals who fled from Iran increased, as did suspicion and corruption within the government. There is little evidence to indicate that the xenophobia of the government really went deep into the people, who by no means supported their ruler in all of his plans and deeds. Disunity and dissatisfaction were growing in Iran when World War II began.

8. World War II and Its Aftermath

Trade statistics reveal that in the years immediately preceding the Nazi invasion of the Soviet Union, Germany had outstripped her nearest competitors in trade with Iran. Along with trade, German influence had grown apace, and German technicians, teachers, and merchants were to be found in considerable numbers in Iran. The German embassy, one of the newest and most luxurious buildings in the capital, was the center of the many Axis activities in the country. The tourist trade, too, increased even after 1939, and by the time of the Allied invasion there were several thousand Germans in Iran.

The difference between the Turkish and Persian reaction to the invasion of Russia was one of degree. Both governments and peoples would have been happy to see an Axis victory over their mutual, traditional foe. The Turkish people were probably more united in their anti-Soviet feelings than the Persians, but the Turkish government was more cautious than the Iranian in its dealings with the Allied and Axis powers.

After the German attack on the U.S.S.R. in June 1941, the Shah received several joint Soviet-British notes requesting him to expel the Germans from Iran. His replies were unsatisfactory and on August 25, 1941, Soviet and British forces invaded the country, the Soviets basing their action on the treaty of 1921. The fighting was over in a few days after a token resistance in the south against the British and a complete fiasco in the north against the Red Army. The two great powers rapidly took over the entire country, and on September 16 Reza Shah abdicated in favor of his son Mohammed Reza Pahlevi, the present ruler.

The Persians have no illusions about the events of the autumn of 1941. They know full well that Britain and the Soviet Union were determined to open a supply route to the Red Army across Iran and that the result would have been the same whether their Shah had capitulated or resisted. The Persians can no more be blamed for being anti-British and anti-Russian than they can be blamed for believing in the independence and integrity of their country.

After the occupation of the country by the Allies most of the Germans were interned and returned to Germany; several, however, managed to escape into tribal territory. A pro-Axis group of Persians was formed and plans were made for a fifth-column movement. The defeat of the Axis armies at Stalingrad and El Alamein was a great blow to the underground movement, but German agents were parachuted into the country in the spring and summer of 1943 and sabotage increased, especially against the railroad. Eventually the enemy agents were captured, while at the same time pro-Axis Persians were arrested by the government at the behest of the Allies. The last enemy agents hiding in Iran were surrendered to the British by the Qashqai chieftains in the spring of 1944. Thus ended the German attempt to sever the life line of supplies to the Soviet Union.

After the invasion the Allies immediately began to utilize the transportation system and other facilities in Iran for the prosecution of the war against the Axis. On January 29, 1942, the occupation was legalized by a treaty between Iran, Great Britain, and the Soviet Union, in which the two Allies agreed to respect the territorial integrity, sovereignty, and political independence of Iran, and to defend Iran from German aggression. Iran, on her part, agreed to coöperate with the Allies in the war effort, putting her resources at their disposal. The two great powers pledged themselves to safeguard the economic well-being of the Persians, and they further agreed to evacuate Iran not later than six months after hostilities between the Allies and Germany and her associates had ceased by an armistice. The Americans, who first arrived at the end of 1942, had no treaty or agreement with Iran, but were in the country theoretically under British military auspices. The American troops were primarily railroad and motor maintenance and transport troops and never numbered more than 30,000. The Persian Gulf Command came to an end in 1945 and the United States forces departed by the end of the year, but the British and Russians remained.

The volume of military supplies which passed through Iran to the Soviet front astonished the Persians and they are still conscious of the important role which Iran played in the final victory. Postage stamps were issued in 1950 commemorating Iran's part in the war as a bridge between the Allies. Iran herself declared war on Germany in September 1943, but Persian troops did no fighting.

The Russians handled the transportation of supplies through the area north of Teheran, while the British and Americans were in charge in the south. The Red Army also used northern Iran as a rest and recuperation center for soldiers who had seen severe fighting on the front. The Russians requisitioned what they needed in northern Iran, but otherwise they did not molest the local population. There were some declarations that the Red Army had come to Iran to save the country from Nazi aggression, but they fell on deaf ears. In 1942 and 1943, however, the Soviet Union was fighting for its life and had little time to devote to the welfare of comrades in Iran. That was to come later.

At the end of November 1943 Teheran was astir; something of significance was in the air. It was only after the meeting of Churchill, Roosevelt, and Stalin that the townspeople knew what had happened in their midst. The Teheran Conference is a memorable date in the history of the war, but it was likewise important for Iran. The declaration on Iran, issued at the end of the Conference, at the suggestion of the Americans, reaffirmed the independence of Iran and the desire of the Allies to assist her economically during and after the conflict. (See Appendix III.) The repeated protestations of respect for the independence of Iran by the Allies caused some cynical remarks to be made among the Persians, but the Teheran Declaration was taken as the basis of American policy toward Iran, and in February 1944 both the United States and Britain raised their legations to embassies in recognition of the increased importance of Iran.

The importance of the Teheran Declaration to the Persians was reëmphasized in June 1950 when the then foreign minister, Husain Ala, in a declaration on the three principles of Persian foreign policy, placed the execution of the articles of the Teheran Declaration on a par with adherence to United Nations principles and the consolidation of cordial relations with other states on a basis of mutual respect.

In 1942 crop failures had caused a food crisis, which was augmented by the lack of adequate transportation for civilian needs, by hoarding and black marketeering, as well as by seizures of the Red Army, occupying as it did the granaries of Iran, the provinces of Azerbaijan and Khurasan. Food riots broke out in northern Iran and the situation looked grim indeed. The United States and Great

Britain, in order to prevent anarchy, signed an agreement with Iran to provide food supplies to make up the deficiency resulting from the requisitions of the occupying forces. The Soviet Union also at one time made a gift of grain which was highly publicized in the press, even though the grain, for the most part, came from Iran itself. The food situation remained critical through 1943.

There was not only a food crisis but a financial crisis. The war, for some Persians, had brought good wages working for the occupation forces, but it also brought an unprecedented inflation. By 1944 the general cost of living index had climbed over 1000 per cent above prewar figures, and Teheran had become one of the most expensive cities in the world. More and more bank notes were issued by the National Bank of Iran, a great part of them for use by the Allied troops. The government incurred large debts and people began to lose confidence in the money as well as in the government.

As mentioned above, the Allies monopolized transport and the industrial potential of the country, leaving little for the local population. This was remedied when the United Kingdom Commercial Corporation, an agency of the British government, helped to organize the civilian transportation system of Iran, thus rendering great service to the country. Several American missions also aided the government; these will be discussed in the next chapter.

The war also meant a relaxing of controls by the Iranian government over its own subjects. A number of prominent Persians returned from exile, while tribal leaders were at last able to leave Teheran, where they had been kept as virtual hostages by Reza Shah, to return to their own people. The central authority was weakened and local leaders increasingly took affairs into their own hands. It seemed a repetition of the years after the granting of the Constitution. Politicians became active again and the press was unmuzzled by the collapse of the Shah's censorship and secret police.

The development of the press in Iran after the abdication of Reza Shah deserves special mention; it exhibited in obvious fashion the anarchy into which the country fell. In 1942 newspapers began to appear like flies, and in spite of frequent suspensions of publication by the government, they reappeared time and again to torment the public. Anyone who wished to air his grievances in public would start a newspaper, for the lax laws permitted an unusual degree of slander and vituperation in the press. Over one hundred and fifty newspapers and journals appeared in Iran during the first two years of the occupation. Most of them lasted only a few weeks or months, and, needless to say, the quality of the majority was quite low.

The Iranian government resented attacks upon it in the press and, of course, nothing offensive to the Allies could be printed. To combat the often irresponsible papers the government made liberal use of the power of suspension which it had under martial law, sometimes banning a dozen in one day. The usual practice was for the suspended newspaper to resume publication the following day under a different name. With the foreign legations issuing newspapers in English, French, Polish, and Russian, Teheran was well supplied with news during the war. In 1942 and 1943 the press avoided political issues which concerned the Allies. With the end of the war, and the beginning of tension between the Soviet Union and the western powers, the papers began to join one side or the other. The number of newspapers declined and the press became more stable, but hardly more responsible. The government maintained its right to suspend papers after the war, and in March of 1949 the Majlis passed a Press Law which legalized that right. The severe articles of the law relating to suspensions and arrests caused a sit-down strike of editors in the Majlis in December 1950. They agitated for freedom of the press and consequently, in January 1951, the law was rescinded.

The influence of the press in Iran should not be minimized, for information in the papers is carried by word of mouth to remote villages where no one is literate, yet where the written word is highly respected.

But to return to the events of 1942, there was at that time a reaction against some of the reforms which Reza Shah had imposed on the country. Traditional costumes reappeared on the streets of provincial cities though with little popular response in the capital. Veils were seen more frequently on women and there was a revival of religious sentiment in the country. The religious leaders began to campaign for stricter observance of the injunctions of Islam: conscientious keeping of the monthly fast, the giving of alms, and the like. Mosques which had been opened to European tourists by Reza Shah were closed again to nonbelievers and sentiments of fanaticism spread in the country.

Another feature of the occupation period was the increase in political activity. The new Shah, after his accession to the throne, proclaimed a real constitutional government, and the resulting opportunity for politicians caused a flurry of activity. Although the Constitution had been in force since 1906, there had been no political parties under the dictatorship of Reza Shah, and it was impossible to resurrect the old pre-1921 parties. The young men who had grown to maturity under the dictatorship, however, could not take the lead in a constitutional government owing to lack of experience. It was left to the graybeards to direct the political destinies of the country. They managed to form groups or "fractions" in the parliament of likeminded men, which were not parties however in our sense. Personalities rather than policies or parties were, as they still are, the principal issue in elections, in politics, and in the debates in parliament itself.

The only lasting party started at this time was the Tudeh (Masses) party, which was formed outside of parliament in 1942. Although it was composed of leftist intellectuals and liberals, the party was controlled from the beginning by a hard core of Communists. As the war continued the party became stronger and better organized, and at the same time its Marxist emphasis became more pronounced. It soon became identified with the Soviet line. In the elections for the fourteenth parliament, which convened in 1944, however, the Tudeh party gained only eight seats out of more than one hundred and thirty. The party was naturally strongest in the northern part of the country, which was occupied by the Red Army. Various other parties were formed but none of them had the organization or strength of the Tudeh. Most of them soon disintegrated, to be replaced by other equally unstable parties. This did not mean that the Tudeh party was able to capture parliament; far from it, for the individual deputies would invariably band together and vote against the small Tudeh minority.

During the war there was another party which was of some importance. This was headed by a prominent Persian, Zia al-Din Tabataba'i, an associate of Reza Shah in his march on Teheran, who had been in exile in Palestine, however, from 1921 to 1943. Because of his known opposition to the Russians and his conservatism, he was regarded by many as in the pay of the British. Zia al-Din was a good organizer and had some success in uniting opposition against the Tudeh party, but he was unable to hold the individualistic deputies together on a positive program. He met with the same difficulties which obstruct all attempts to form political parties in Iran: too much suspicion and mutual distrust for concerted action.

By the end of 1944 the "Soviet phase" of the war had begun in

Iran. The Soviet Union began to shift its campaign of vituperation from the Germans against the Western Allies. The newspapers of the Tudeh party began to use the stock words—fascist, reactionary, and imperialist—against Britain first and then the United States. Political activity moved to the international level and outside forces began to exert greater influence on Iranian politics.

As early as the end of 1943 several American and British oil companies had sent representatives to negotiate with the Iranian government for oil concessions in areas of the country outside the Anglo-Iranian Oil Company's territory. The Russians did not remain inactive, and in the autumn of 1944 a large Soviet delegation, headed by Vice Commissar for Foreign Affairs Kavtaradze, arrived in Teheran seeking concessions for oil and other mineral deposits in northern Iran. The Persians were greatly concerned with the Soviet requests, and the government announced it would stop all negotiations for concessions until the Allied troops had left Iran. Many Persians thought that the Soviets had sent their mission to keep the Americans from obtaining any concessions in northern Iran rather than to obtain any for Russia. For American companies had been interested in concessions in the north during the 1920's. But the storm of protest from the Soviets and their minions in Teheran which followed the government's announcement belied that theory. Shortly after this declaration a law was passed in parliament prohibiting any Iranian official from even discussing oil concessions until all foreign troops had departed.

The Tudeh newspapers began a campaign in favor of oil concessions to the Soviets and included an attack on the existing government for its anti-Russian, fascist, and reactionary attitude. The Russians too did not cease to belabor the Iranian government in the press and over the radio. An indication of the ramifications of the oil dispute was a statement in the Moscow paper *Izvestia* attacking the presence of American troops in Iran without a treaty arrangement. This was the beginning of our trouble with the Soviet Union not only in Iran but throughout the world.

During the war the Red Army in northern Iran had refused permission to Persian government officials to visit the provinces. Consequently taxes could not be collected and all activities of the central government were hampered. The Tudeh party was building up its power in the north and in some places the Tudeh officials had more authority than government employees. The central government's protests to the Soviet ambassador that the Red Army was hindering the exercise of authority in the northern provinces went unheeded.

The Tudeh party in Azerbaijan continued its activities, under Soviet aegis, until September 1945, when the Azerbaijan Democrat party was formed, with a program to obtain some measure of autonomy for the northern province. The Azerbaijan Tudeh party was thereupon dissolved and its members taken into the new party. At first the Aberbaijan Democrats only sought concessions from the government in Teheran: an increase of representation from Azerbaijan in the parliament, the introduction of the teaching of Turkish in the schools, and reforms in the provincial government and in taxation. There is no indication that the Soviets in the beginning wanted Azerbaijan to secede from Iran. Rather they hoped to use Azerbaijan as a lever or tool against the central government. Relations between Teheran and the Azerbaijan Democrats, however, continued to deteriorate, and finally, in December 1945, the creation of a rebel government of Azerbaijan was announced in Tabriz. Although government troops had been unsuccessful previously in penetrating Azerbaijan, they were again dispatched, but were turned back by the Red Army only a short distance from Teheran on the road to Azerbaijan.

The establishment of a separate regime for the northern province was hailed by the Soviet radio. The head of the rebel government was a certain Ja'far Pishevari, a seasoned Bolshevik agent. In 1920 he had been Minister of the Interior in the short-lived Gilan Republic, but after the collapse of that government he had returned to the Soviet Union. During the 1920's, under the pseudonym Sultan-zadeh, Pishevari served the Comintern well in the Middle East, but in 1936 he returned to Iran claiming he was a refugee from Bolshevik purges. He was closely watched by the Persian authorities until 1941 when he helped to establish the Tudeh party. He became premier of the Azerbaijan autonomous government and issued proclamations calling on all the people of Azerbaijan to support him. One cannot deny that he met with some response, for many people in the northern province had long resented the exactions of the central authorities. Some thought the provincial government should be controlled by local Turkish-speaking Persians rather than Persians from Teheran. It was frankly recognized that Teheran had grown rich at the expense of the provinces, and there were many justified complaints on the part of the provincial leaders against the drainage of wealth to the capital.

The rebel regime proceeded to carry out a series of reforms. Banks were nationalized, Azerbaijani Turkish was introduced as the official language in place of Persian, and a program for the distribution of land was instituted. A secret police and "people's army" were created as well as other trappings of a totalitarian state.

The Kurds, following the lead of the Azerbaijanis, established an independent republic with its center at the town of Mahabad. The Kurdish republic remained only a side show, but it managed to last a few days longer than the rebel regime in Tabriz itself. The Kurdish republic considered itself an independent nation, for on April 23, 1946, its leaders signed a treaty with Azerbaijani representatives affirming the friendship of the two nations for each other. Although the Kurdish republic did not receive so much attention in the world press as the Azerbaijan regime, the former was perhaps potentially more explosive, since large minorities of Kurds live in Turkey and Iraq, and had the Russians exploited their nascent nationalism, an important international problem might have developed.

The sequence of events following the consolidation of the rebel government of Azerbaijan is highly interesting, and due credit must be given to the wily prime minister in Teheran, Ahmad Qavam al-Sultaneh, for his part in the drama. Qavam was known as a liberal, and when he became head of the parliament in January 1946, the press, which had hitherto been somewhat restrained by government censorship, obtained complete freedom. The result was a deluge of attacks and counterattacks by partisans and enemies of the Tudeh party and the Azerbaijan Democrats. For the Tudeh party did not vanish as a result of the founding of the Azerbaijan republic but continued its work in the rest of Iran. It even supported other local "autonomous" movements in Gilan and Mazanderan, which did not, however, attain much success. During all this time the Red Army continued to occupy northern Iran and to keep foreigners out of the area.

Meanwhile Iran had become the subject of headlines in the world press. On January 19, 1946, the Iranian ambassador in London, on instructions from his government, made an appeal to the United Nations. The Iranian government charged the Soviet Union with interference in the internal affairs of Iran, and with creating a situation which might lead to international friction. The continued presence of Soviet troops was a further complication. The United States, on November 24, 1945, had sent notes to the U.S.S.R. and Great Britain proposing the withdrawal of all Allied troops from Iran by

January 1, 1945. This proposal was rejected by the Soviet government, which reminded everyone concerned that the Red Army could remain in Iran until March 2, 1946, according to the treaty signed between Iran, the Soviet Union and the United Kingdom on January 29, 1942. This rejection was followed by the proclamation of the Azerbaijan republic just before the second conference of foreign ministers held in Moscow in December 1945. That conference was a failure in regard to Iran, and that country then turned to the United Nations.

After much fruitless discussion in the Security Council, the dispute between Iran and the U.S.S.R. was referred to the two parties, with the request that they enter into direct negotiations with each other. Prime Minister Qavam, following the Security Council's recommendation, departed for Moscow, where he remained almost a month. While he was in Moscow the deadline for the evacuation of Allied troops came. The American troops had left before January 1 and the British were out by March 2, but from the Soviets came only a declaration that the Red Army would evacuate the province of Khurasan and a few other areas but would remain in Azerbaijan and the Caspian area until the situation had been "clarified." Great Britain protested, the United States protested, and Qavam protested, all to no avail. Qavam returned to Teheran to find the parliament buildings besieged by the Tudeh party rank and file. Unless a majority of deputies could meet and prolong the parliament it would come to an end on March 11, 1946, and Qavam would take power into his own hands until new elections for the next parliament were held. And parliament had passed a law that no elections could be held until all foreign troops had departed from Iran. Mass demonstrations in front of the parliament kept out many of the deputies so it was impossible to form a quorum. The crowds remained a number of days until March 11 and parliament came to an end. Qavam was now a prime minister without an assembly and thus was in virtual control of the country.

The attitude of Qavam was enigmatic, for sometimes he seemed to oppose the Soviet Union violently and on other occasions he appeared to act in its behalf. When the Red Army continued its occupation, Qavam sent instructions to the Iranian representative at the United Nations, and ambassador to the United States, Husain Ala, to bring up Iran's charge against the U.S.S.R. again. Tempers rose in the meetings of the Security Council, and Gromyko, the Soviet delegate, gained a world-wide reputation for his vetoes and his walkouts. The Russians sought to remove the Iranian question from the U.N. agenda, claiming that it was an affair to be solved by them and the Persians alone. The Soviet attitude served to disillusion the other members of the Council about the intentions of the government in Moscow. This, the first crisis of the U.N., revealed the tactics which the Soviet Union was to use repeatedly in the future.

The Soviet government did enter into direct contact with the government of Iran in the person of Qavam. They exerted pressure on him so that he asked that the complaint of the government of Iran against the Soviet Union be removed from the agenda of the United Nations. Husain Ala refused to request this, believing that Qavam had issued the instructions under pressure. The Security Council debated and finally on April 4 resolved to postpone any further action until the sixth of May 1946, at which time the two governments were to make a report on the status of negotiations between them.

The Soviets had hoped to obtain concessions from the Teheran government as the price for evacuation of the Red Army, and Qavam led them to believe they would succeed. At the end of March the prime minister suppressed the anti-Soviet newspapers and disbanded the organizations of the rightist political leaders. Zia al-Din was arrested and put in jail. On the same day, April 4, that the Security Council postponed their debate on the Iranian question, Qavam concluded an agreement with the Soviet government. The Russians agreed to withdraw their forces by May 6, while Qavam promised that he would submit a proposal for a joint stock Soviet-Iranian oil company to the new parliament, and would work for a satisfactory solution of the Azerbaijan problem. It seemed as though the Soviets had won, but the Persians were soon to reveal that they had other ideas. Qavam realized that first he had to conciliate the Russians and have the Red Army evacuate northern Iran before the Iranian government could clean its own house.

The Soviet evacuation of northern Iran was the result of a number of factors; probably the most important was the belief on the part of the Russians that Qavam had been won over to their side. He had suppressed the anti-Soviet elements and had agreed to a joint oil company, subject to the ratification of parliament. The rebel government in Azerbaijan was growing in strength and there was every reason to suppose that it would maintain its position and even gain at the expense of the Teheran government. The pressure of world

opinion and the debates in the United Nations, although they may
have been responsible in influencing the Soviet government to evacuate Iran earlier than had been planned, were probably of much less
significance than the factors mentioned above. When the Soviet government did announce that it had evacuated all its troops on May 9,
1946, it seemed as though Iran had fallen on the Soviet side of the
fence.

The Soviets now turned to the task of consolidating their position
in Iran and winning support for the coming elections to parliament.
Throughout the summer of 1946 the Tudeh party held a number of
mass demonstrations and sponsored several strikes against the Anglo-
Iranian Oil Company. The strikes were violent, and a number of
people were killed and many wounded in the rioting. It looked as
though the classic pattern of infiltration into the government were
succeeding in Iran when on August 2 Qavam included three Tudeh
members in his cabinet plus a fourth fellow traveler. But the strikes
and the inclusion of the Tudeh members in the cabinet brought forth
a new crisis.

British troops landed in Basra, ostensibly to protect supplies of oil.
Qavam protested, without effect, and shortly thereafter he had a
tribal revolt on his hands in southern Iran. The Qashqai tribesmen
took the lead in forming a coalition which demanded that the Tudeh
members be removed from the cabinet and that certain reforms be
instituted in the southern provinces. The tribesmen captured a number of important towns in the province of Fars and in October
brought the central government to accept their demands. Qavam
dropped the Tudeh ministers from his cabinet and acceded to the
demands for reforms. Anti-Communist forces were encouraged by the
success of the tribes and began to take heart again.

Qavam himself had not been idle during the summer. At the end of
June, he founded his own political party, the Iran Democrat party,
which began to grow by leaps and bounds with the stimulus of government financial support. This party is not to be confused with the
Azerbaijan Democrat party, although Qavam purposely selected the
same name. The Iran Democrats formed a coalition with other progressive groups and soon they outshone all their rivals. The public
demonstrations led by the Iran Democrats put the Tudeh efforts in
the shade. The way was now clear for elections, which were scheduled
to begin in December 1946.

This meant that the central government would have to reëstablish its authority in Azerbaijan in order to supervise the elections. The Soviets were in a quandary; in order to obtain an oil concession agreement of the parliament was necessary, and in order to convene parliament elections would have to be held all over the country, including Azerbaijan. The Azerbaijan rebels declared they would resist if government troops crossed the border into their province, and they began to prepare defenses. If the Soviet Union supported its puppets against the central government the oil concession might never be ratified.

On the international front the Trieste issue was in the news and the gulf between the U.S.S.R. and the West had widened. But at the end of November the Trieste question was settled by a more conciliatory attitude on the part of the Soviets. At the same time the Soviet Union gave more friendly responses than it had for many months, especially in regard to such questions as disarmament and freedom of navigation on the Danube River. Whatever the reason for this easing of tension on the international scene, the Iranian government took it as an opportune moment to send its forces against the autonomous regime of Azerbaijan. A number of days before the march Qavam arrested the leading Tudeh members in Teheran.

There are several versions of what happened in Azerbaijan when the government troops advanced. The story from Teheran is that the government army fought a number of battles with the rebels, defeated them, and advanced to the liberation of Tabriz. The people of Tabriz claim that they rose up against the rebel regime and caused the leaders to lose heart and flee to the U.S.S.R. before the government army appeared. Certain neutral sources claim that the Kurds, and other elements in Azerbaijan, had been won over by the government and had planned to attack the rebels in the rear, who, seeing the hopelessness of the situation, fled. All versions contain some truth; for the people would not have thrown off the rebel yoke if there had not been help on the way. There were a number of skirmishes and there were defections in the ranks of the rebel forces, as well as among the Kurds, which may have been created by government promises. In any event, the rebel regime collapsed so quickly and easily that everyone was surprised. In various towns throughout the province the local populace threw out the rebel authorities. The government army, after it occupied the province, imposed martial law, and in 1950 travel on the roads after sunset in Azerbaijan was still forbidden.

Another story has it that the Soviet ambassador called on the prime minister and the Shah and warned them that the Soviet government would not tolerate any disturbance in Azerbaijan which might threaten Soviet security. This was said to have occurred several hours after government troops had been dispatched to Tabriz and the Persians were able to assure the ambassador that everything would be under control. It is significant that during the regime of the rebel government in Persian Azerbaijan, the frontier with Soviet Azerbaijan was closely guarded by Soviet border guards. Only tried and tested Communists were sent to Persian Azerbaijan from the U.S.S.R.

The Kurdish republic lasted a few days longer than the Azerbaijan regime before government troops arrived and arrested the leaders. Iran was united again and the Tudeh party in the capital had lost its directors by arrest. Now the question of the election arose.

Although the elections began in January it was several months before results were known and the new parliament was not convened until the middle of August. Qavam's Iran Democrat party won a majority of seats, and Qavam was committed to passing the measure establishing the joint Irano-Soviet oil company. The opposition in parliament, however, began to agitate strongly against the oil agreement and the Soviets became annoyed. Twice the Soviet ambassador handed Qavam notes urging him to ratify the agreement in parliament. The Persians became bolder and even some of Qavam's supporters spoke against the agreement. On September 11 the American ambassador to Iran, George V. Allen, made a momentous speech in Teheran in which he assured the Persians of the support of the American people in any choice they made in regard to the oil agreement. This was an important statement by a representative of the American government, and it defined American interest in Iran. Ambassador Allen said:

The United States has no proper concern with proposals of a commercial or any other nature made to Iran by any foreign government as long as those proposals are advanced solely on their merits, to stand or fall on their value to Iran. We and every other nation of the world, however, do become concerned when such proposals are accompanied by threats of bitter enmity or by a statement that it would be dangerous for Iran to refuse . . .

Our determination to follow this policy [to remove the fear of aggression in the world] as regards Iran is as strong as anywhere else in the world. This purpose can be achieved to the extent that the Iranian people show a determination to defend their own sovereignty. Patriotic Iranians, when considering matters affecting their national interest, may therefore rest assured that the American people will support fully their freedom to make their own choice.

Iran's resources belong to Iran. Iran can give them away free of charge or refuse to dispose of them at any price if it so desires.

The British were not so forceful as the Americans in this instance, and the speech by Allen undoubtedly had a great effect in Iranian political circles. Qavam finally submitted the agreement to parliament, but it was decisively rejected by a vote of 102 to 2 on October 22. In December Qavam resigned as Soviet disapproval grew stronger.

The subsequent fate of Qavam is not surprising to anyone who knows the Persian scene. Qavam, in dealing with the Russians, had been faithful to the doctrine of dissimulation, but he had made many bitter enemies as a result. Although a Persian politician of the "old school," an elder statesman, and a wealthy landowner, Qavam had been disturbed by the social and economic injustices in his country. Like some other wealthy intellectuals, Qavam had a strong sense of the reformer. He had been prime minister in 1942, but had been forced to resign after the bread riots, and had failed to accomplish much. For some time he had even supported the Tudeh party, but its subservience to Moscow had disillusioned him. Qavam held to both old traditions and new socialist ideas, and, although he may not have been entirely honest, he was a loyal Persian. After he resigned as prime minister in 1947, his enemies took heart, but it was some time before they accused him openly of misrule and corruption. He was denounced as a traitor, and finally in April 1950 he was deprived of his honorific title, the last part of Qavam al-Sultaneh (pillar of the state) while he was absent from Iran on the Riviera. It was rumored that he was not on good terms with the Shah. In October of the same year, however, he returned to Teheran, where he was greeted at the airport by a crowd of loyal supporters who hoped that the elder statesman would resume his political activities. He is still a highly controversial figure, subject to bitter attack as well as praise on the floor of the Majlis. His career is typical of the ups and downs of a Persian politician.

To return to our story, parliament later in 1948 passed another oil bill which forbade the granting of any new oil concession to foreigners, and declared Iran's intention of obtaining more royalties from the Anglo-Iranian Oil Company. As a result of this, the Soviet government sent a note to Teheran accusing the Iranian government of hostility, and later the Russians protested against American activities in Iran. As the "cold war" was intensified in Germany, and by Soviet consolidations in the countries behind the "Iron Curtain," Iran began to feel the effects. The Soviet radio kept up a barrage of attacks on the Iranian government, on the British, and especially on the Americans in Iran. The Tudeh party, for its part, resorted to a program of soul searching and many members were purged from its ranks. The government assisted it in its purging by arresting a large number of Tudeh members in April 1948. This did not halt the activity of the Tudeh party by any means, and throughout the year, as Soviet pressure continued, the Tudeh party held demonstrations against the growing American interests in Iran.

On February 4, 1949, a Persian journalist emptied his revolver at the Shah as the latter was visiting the University of Teheran for a special ceremony. The Shah was only slightly wounded and the would-be assassin was quickly killed. It was freely rumored in Teheran that the attempted assassination was part of a plot by the Tudeh party to seize power, and that the Soviets were behind it. As a result martial law was proclaimed in Teheran and the Tudeh party was outlawed. At the same time the assassin was said to have had connections with a reactionary religious group; so extremists on both the right and left felt the displeasure of the government. The accusation, from some journalists, that the Russians were behind the plot roused a new storm of protest from the Soviet government, and notes were sent to Teheran protesting the hostile insinuations of the Persians. The Soviets also complained again of American influence in Iran, claiming that the Americans were building up Iran as a base for military operations against the U.S.S.R. They pointed to the Americans who were serving as advisors to the army and gendarmery, and who were active in Iran's Seven Year plan for economic rehabilitation and development.

In the spring of 1949 there were a number of incursions of Soviet troops across the northeastern frontier of Iran in which several Persian soldiers were killed and others captured. The government in Teheran protested and on April 15 threatened to declare the treaty of 1921 null and void. The Persians maintained that Article Six of the treaty had been supplanted when Iran joined the United Nations. The Soviet Union closed four of its consulates in Iran and the future looked ominous.

9. The United States and Iran

Before World War II official interchange between Iran and the United States was relatively slight and insignificant, although formal diplomatic relations between the two countries began in 1883. Yet the United States had a legacy of good will in Iran, developed over many years, which was enjoyed by few other powers. Much of this was due, no doubt, to the fact that America was far from Iran and had no record of interference in the internal affairs of the country as had some of the European nations. There was a positive element in this tradition of good relations, however, which was the work of American missionaries and private individuals in the service of the government and people of Iran.

Most of the contacts which Iran had with the West in the nineteenth century were not conducive to the promotion of friendly relations. Stray merchants and adventurers came to Iran seeking their own gain, while foreign envoys and armies too often regarded the country as a field for exploitation. There were some Westerners, however, who did not regard Iran as a sheep to be sheared. These were the missionaries, primarily American and British.

The first American missionaries were sent to Rezaiyeh in Azerbaijan to work among the Christian Assyrians in 1829. They were followed by other missionaries, who opened new centers in various towns in Iran, especially in the years after 1870. The American missionaries made an agreement with their Anglican colleagues whereby the former worked in the northern part of the country while the British operated in the south. As in Turkey, so in Iran, the missionaries not only preached Christianity and established churches, but they built schools and hospitals which became centers for the diffusion of western culture. Persian teachers and nurses were trained, and they in turn taught others what they had learned from the missionaries. Work was frequently restricted, and for long was confined to Armenians, Assyrians, and other non-Moslems, but the influence of the missionaries spread far and wide, and they earned the appreciation of the common folk which no diplomat could hope to match. During the Soviet occupation and the rebel regime in Azerbaijan, the American hospital in Tabriz continued to function, serving rebel, government supporter, or Red Army man alike.

The growth of nationalism under Reza Shah proved a setback to missionary work. In 1935 Persians were forbidden to attend foreign schools, which soon brought the educational activities of the missionaries to an end. Several years later the two Presbyterian colleges in Teheran were taken over by the government, but the hospitals were permitted to continue their work. Many Persians regretted to see the American schools close, although the effects of their work continued after them. There is no doubt that many of the Persians educated in American schools, and now occupying important government posts, form a strong pro-American group, but their influence, as well as the influence of the missionaries, can be exaggerated.

Three times in its recent history Iran has turned to the United States for aid in solving her economic problems. In 1910 the Iranian government was in desperate financial straits and sought an impartial and efficient economic advisor in the West. America was far away and obviously had no stake in Iran, so the Persians applied to Washington. President Taft sent a Treasury expert, W. Morgan Shuster, to Iran with the understanding that he was an employee of the Iranian government and had no official connection with the United States government. Once on the scene Shuster realized that he could accomplish little in a purely advisory capacity. He therefore requested and received from the Iranian government certain powers to deal with the financial crisis. He organized a gendarmery to aid in the collection of taxes, but immediately met the opposition of the Russians. The latter feared that Shuster would undermine their influence and special privileges in Iran. There were also certain favorites of the Russians who had no intention of paying their taxes and who looked to their northern protector for support against Shuster's gendarmes. The British were embarrassed because they had recommended one of their officers to Shuster to help organize the gendarmery, while at the same time they were pledged to support the Russians by virtue of the 1907 agreement between the two countries. Likewise the international situation was such that they did not wish to antagonize the Tsarist government. Consequently they refused to support Shuster. As a result of Russian pressure Shuster was obliged to resign. He returned to America where he wrote a book appropriately entitled *The Strangling of Persia.*

During World War I foreign armies marched across and fought on Iran's soil with the result that the Persian people suffered great hardships. Finances were in a miserable state and the government again turned to the United States. In the autumn of 1922 A. C. Millspaugh, an economic advisor in the Department of State, went to Iran as the head of an economic mission. But again the Americans were in Iran as employees of the Iranian government with no official connections with the United States government. In the period 1922 to 1927, when the mission came to an end, Dr. Millspaugh was able to effect a series of important reforms. He had extensive powers and was supported by many progressive Persians. Revenues were centralized and the collection of taxes was put on an orderly, organized basis. State monopolies on sugar and tea were proposed by Millspaugh and eagerly adopted by Reza Shah. American engineers and agricultural and financial experts were employed to assist in the huge task of westernization. Reza Shah at first coöperated with the mission, but turned against Millspaugh when his personal plans were opposed. Reza Shah attached more importance to the development of the army than to other reforms and clashed with the American advisor a number of times. Much was accomplished before Millspaugh left, feeling that he could no longer execute his plans. American prestige, however, remained high even after the departure of the mission.

The second World War brought American troops to Iran and an increased interest on the part of the United States government in the Middle East. At the request of the Persian government a number of American missions were sent to Iran; the members of these missions were sponsored by the United States government though employed by the Persians. This was a noticeable departure from precedent and heralded a new stage in American activity in Iran. The War Department sent two missions of American officers to advise the Iranian army and the gendarmery. Colonel H. Norman Schwartzkopf, famous for his work as head of the New Jersey State Police at the time of the Lindbergh kidnapping, performed yeoman service in the gendarmery, remaining in Iran five years at the task. Other American advisors were sent to advise on police administration, irrigation, and health. But most important was the large economic mission.

This third American economic mission to Iran was also headed by Dr. Millspaugh, who arrived in Teheran in January 1943, in the midst of war. The situation had changed considerably since the last time he was in Iran, and the American government was far more interested in this mission than it had been in the others. The purpose of the third mission was substantially that of its predecessors, to reorganize the finances of the country and especially their administration. In 1943 the country was suffering from an inflation which had boosted prices to fantastic heights, and parts of the country were in the throes of famine. The administration of finances was hopelessly chaotic and inefficient; the conduct of government was mired in bureaucratic red tape and graft. Since the Allies had taken over most of the railway rolling stock and trucks for military purposes, and there was a shortage of automobiles, it proved exceedingly difficult for the government to enforce its authority in the provinces.

Millspaugh was given broad executive powers by the Iranian parliament and a five-year contract, but he met strong opposition from many quarters. After considerable difficulties a progressive income tax law was prepared, submitted, and finally passed by the Majlis. Collection of the new taxes, however, proved a formidable job and many members of the mission felt thwarted by the restrictions on their power of action. Vested interests violently opposed the income tax and refused to pay.

Though ultimately unsuccessful, the mission did accomplish something. The amount of grain, and other stock commodities such as sugar and tea in the warehouses was augmented and a steady supply assured. Internal transport was gradually restored to more normal conditions and the distribution of goods was placed on a more equitable basis. To be sure many abuses in the functioning of the economic system went uncorrected, and some shortages remained to plague the nation. In relations with the Persians, members of the mission sometimes made mistakes out of ignorance or lack of tact. Millspaugh had trod on many toes and had earned many enemies for himself, so it was not surprising that parliament repealed the measure granting him extensive powers. In its place a new law was passed transferring much of Millspaugh's authority to various governmental agencies. Consequently Millspaugh resigned and left Iran in February 1945, with most of his mission following him before the year was over.

The mission could undoubtedly have accomplished much more had there not been so many factors complicating the situation, such as the occupation by foreign troops, uncertainty of the relations of the mission to the American Embassy and to the Persian Gulf Command, as well as war conditions generally. Also the Russians, with unconcealed hostility, did everything they could to hamper the mission's work. There have been some recriminations against or by the mission, including a book by Millspaugh himself defending the mission. In view of the inevitable opposition of many Persians, not to mention foreigners, and the understandable friction and jealousy caused by the authority of the mission, it is doubtful whether the mission could have solved the economic problems of Iran in a manner satisfactory to both the Persians and the members of the mission. But the departure of the Millspaugh mission did not terminate the activity of Americans in the economic life of Iran.

Among the American charitable institutions which have continued to perform services for the people of Iran, as well as for the Arab countries, special mention must be made of the Near East Foundation. A nonprofit enterprise, the Foundation has a long and distinguished record of work in public health in various areas. It has conducted demonstrations of health education, sanitation, malaria control, and the like, which have been of inestimable value to the people. In 1944 the Foundation was invited by the Iranian government to conduct a program of rural improvement in the country. Work did not begin for more than a year, but the Foundation was so successful the first year of its operation that its services were eagerly sought by a number of branches of the government. The Ministry of Health in 1949 asked the Foundation to undertake extensive malaria control in Azerbaijan.

The Foundation has been especially successful in its program of rural education, and has made great strides in certain small demonstration areas, teaching the people not only reading and writing but also the basic elements of farming, sanitation, health, and child care. The Foundation has shown Persians how to train teachers to go out in the field and work for the betterment of the poor in villages and among tribes. The Shah, at a dinner given in his honor by the Foundation in New York on November 23, 1949, praised its work highly. It has done much for American prestige in Iran. Although too much can hardly be said in praise of the Near East Foundation, still it must be remembered that its achievements represent only a tiny fraction of what needs to be done.

. . .

One aspect of our foreign policy which is important for the future of United States relations to Iran is the program for aid to underdeveloped countries, better known as the Point Four Program, since it was set forth by President Truman in his Inaugural Address of January 20, 1949, as the fourth of the major courses of United States foreign policy. This was a bold step in the right direction. It was not until June 1950, however, that Congress passed the Act for International Development embodying the program. A sum not exceeding 35 million dollars was authorized under this Act to provide for technical and educational assistance to underdeveloped areas.

The program is twofold: that is, in addition to providing this limited fund for technical assistance, it calls for financial assistance in the form of large-scale investment by both private and public capital, the latter through such agencies as the International Bank and the Export-Import Bank. The success of the program depends largely on the government's ability to encourage capital investment.

United States funds for technical assistance, under this program, will be supplemented by United Nations funds, to which the United States is expected to make a major contribution. For the United Nations has its own Economic Assistance Program formulated by the Economic and Social Council at Geneva in August 1949 and later unanimously approved by the General Assembly.

These programs apply, of course, to all underdeveloped areas and Iran's share in them will necessarily be small. Furthermore, innumerable difficulties confront them, the greatest of which is undoubtedly the attracting of sufficient capital. But even if these programs succeed in encouraging substantial foreign investments to be made in Iran, many problems will remain. How, for example, can we ensure that such investments will really benefit Iran and not result merely in draining off wealth and exploiting the people? There is not space here, however, to discuss or even list all the dangers and obstacles that lie in the path of such an undertaking as the Point Four and Economic Assistance Programs envisage, and excellent analyses of these problems are widely available (see Appendix IV).

Despite some understandable reservations and misgivings, most Persians welcomed the Point Four Program. Indeed, at the Islamic Economic Conference, held in Teheran in October 1950, utilization of such aid was urged by most of the participating countries. On October 19 a credit of $500,000 was obtained by Iran, the first grant under the Point Four Program, for rural improvement in the form of the establishment of demonstration centers and technical training. A month later the Export-Import Bank granted Iran a credit of $25,000,000 for her Seven Year Plan (it has never been ratified), but attempts to obtain a loan of $250,000,000 from the World Bank have met with no success, a fact which has given the Soviets and their minions in Iran ammunition for propaganda.

The growing importance of Iran to the United States was emphasized by the State Department when it created a new Greece, Turkey, and Iran section in the Department shortly after the war. This put Iran in the same category as the other two nations favored by Truman Doctrine aid. In the eyes of some it seemed as though these three nations were grouped together as the important outer core of resistance to Soviet pressure in this area, while the Arab states were the weaker inner group. Some Persians thought Iran should receive military aid as did the other two states, on the theory that a chain is only as strong as its weakest link. Iran, however, was never included in the military aid program, though other assistance was to come later.

In June 1947 an agreement was signed between the United States and Iran for the sale of surplus military equipment. The following year the agreement, for the sum of ten million dollars, was ratified by the Iranian parliament, and the first shipment of arms arrived in Iran in March 1949. American policy had come a long way since 1939, when almost the sole principle followed in Iran was the policy of the "open door" for all businessmen.

On March 18, 1949, after the signing of the North Atlantic Pact, Acheson declared that the pact did not mean a lessening of determination to support the integrity and independence of Greece, Turkey, and Iran. Bevin echoed the same sentiments in the British Parliament on the same day.

American prestige was high, though not so high as in Turkey. American advisors were in Iran. The Voice of America began broadcasts in Persian, relayed through the government radio in Teheran, on March 21, 1949, the Persian New Year's day. On November 16 of the same year Mohammed Reza Shah arrived in Washington by airplane. He came to this country to ascertain if he could obtain aid, and before he left, after a visit of six weeks, a joint statement by him and President Truman indicated that he had received promises of assistance. We promised Point Four aid, more arms, and support of Iran in her applications for loans from the World Bank. The Shah promised that Iran would implement her plan of economic development, and would welcome American investments as well as technical assistance. Future relations between the two countries looked rosy.

But in the summer of 1950 world affairs had taken a turn for the worse, and, although defeats in the Korean war may not have been the cause of the growing estrangement between Iran and the United States, they coincided with signs of a certain coolness. Hopes that American capital might be of substantial aid to Iran's economy faded.

The Persians have never done anything to influence American public opinion in their favor; there is no Iranian information office in this country. Criticisms of America are heard on the floor of the Majlis. In itself this means little, since the individualistic Persians are wont to speak their sentiments openly, but coupled with other developments it is not encouraging. The worsening situation in Iran prompted the Department of State to send as ambassador to Teheran in June 1950, a trouble-shooting diplomat, Henry Grady, who had been in Greece during Truman Doctrine days.

The situation should have improved when reputedly pro-American General Razmara became prime minister on June 26, but at the end of July foreigners were barred from travel in the vicinity of the Soviet border, and on September 3, 1950, several Persian government officials were dismissed for visiting a foreign consul. This was followed by an order forbidding the military attachés of foreign missions from leaving Teheran without the permission of the prime minister. Foreign missions were asked to make all contacts with Iranian government agencies through the Iranian Foreign Office, and all Persian government employees were forbidden to contact foreign missions. Finally in November 1950, the Persian programs of the Voice of America and the BBC were discontinued from radio Teheran. Although the Persians claimed that this had not been prompted by foreign pressure, and meant no change in their foreign policy, speculation was rife. The American press, which had accused Iran of widespread corruption, was rebuked by the Shah in an interview early in December. He also criticized the slowness and meagerness of American aid. It is true that Prime Minister Razmara, in late December, alerted the army against a possible Soviet attack, which was interpreted by some American observers as a gesture to reassure the western powers that Iran was not abandoning them. It is more probable—as interpreted by some Persians—that the move was motivated by internal conditions, and that Razmara intended to gather more strength in his own hands thereby. These actions coincided with an Irano-Soviet *rapprochement*. On November 4, 1950, after extended trade talks, an important barter agreement was signed between the two countries.

American trade with Iran, since the trade agreement of 1943, has been on a most-favored-nation basis, which is not true of Britain, France, and other Western European nations, which have classified Iran's chief article of export (rugs) as an unnecessary luxury item. But Iran has foodstuffs, tobacco, and other products to trade, which the United States does not need. Yet to obtain scarce American dollars Iran must sell these products. The Soviet Union was, and is, Iran's natural market and supplier, but trade with Russia had been at a virtual standstill since the war. Meanwhile Iran's adverse trade balance was becoming worse. According to the Iranian government, during the first five months of 1950, the value of imports was four times the value of exports. So the signing of the barter agreement with Russia was welcomed by the Persians, especially the merchants. A trade agreement was later signed with Western Germany.

The Germans, before the war, had been successful in their trade dealings because they practiced the barter of goods, which worked well in Iran. Such an exchange, however, requires a planned economy, which both the Soviet Union and Iran, to a much lesser extent, have. Soviet Russia has now become Iran's best customer. Prime Minister Razmara, in the Majlis session of November 7, 1950, announced that no new barter agreement had been signed, but only that the agreement of 1940 between the two countries, with several amendments, had been confirmed for execution. The agreement involves some 20 million dollars for each country; the principal items of import from Russia will be sugar, cement, and textiles, while Iran will send rice, tobacco, skins, and other raw materials to the U.S.S.R. At the same time the prime minister announced that the Russians had released the Persian officers and soldiers who had been captured by Soviet border guards during the past several years, and that negotiations were proceeding for the return of Iranian gold blocked in Moscow since the war. The Soviets took advantage of the agreement to augment their propaganda campaign, and it seemed as though the Russian star was in the ascendant.

Fortunately, Iran's relations with her eastern and western neighbors have been, on the whole, cordial. It was Reza Shah's initiative which brought together Turkey, Iraq, Iran, and Afghanistan in the

Saadabad Pact of friendship and nonaggression in 1937. After World War II there were differences with Afghanistan over the water of the Hilmand River, but relations have remained amicable. There exists an Iran irredenta, however, the Bahrein Islands in the Persian Gulf, which, though under British protection, the Persians have never ceased to claim as their own. But Bahrein is rich in oil, ánd, although the question comes to the fore periodically in the Majlis, there seems little hope of satisfying Persian demands.

In the winter of 1950–51 the oil crisis overshadowed everything else in Iran. It had internal political and economic ramifications as well as international importance. Britain's major, and long-term, interest in Iran is oil, and since American oil companies contracted to purchase almost 40 per cent of the production of the Anglo-Iranian Oil Company, Persian oil is also of interest to Americans. Inasmuch as the British have made a huge investment in the AIOC, and the Iranian government depends on revenue from oil for the future development of the country, it is important to investigate the oil company's position in Iran.

The Anglo-Iranian Oil Company was the first of its kind to work in the Middle East, and its difficulties and achievements served as a pattern for the development of others. In 1901 an Australian financier named D'Arcy obtained a concession from the Shah for drilling in a large area including most of Iran except the northern provinces. For several years he prospected unsuccessfully and was ready to give up in despair, when in 1908 a chance drilling came upon a rich field. On the basis of this well the Anglo-Persian (later Anglo-Iranian) Oil Company was formed. Several years later the British government, with Winston Churchill as First Lord of the Admiralty, decided to convert the Royal Navy from coal- to oil-burning ships, and consequently bought 52.5 per cent of the stock.

The Company has had a successful career, and Iran is now the fourth largest oil-producing country in the world. The Company, however, has not been without its difficulties. In 1932 Reza Shah canceled the concession, and only after long negotiations was it restored with provisions more favorable to the Persians. By the terms of this agreement the original area of the concession was limited to 100,000 square miles in the southern part of the country and the concession was to terminate in 1993. Royalties paid to the Iranian government varied, but they constituted a good portion of its total revenue and have enabled it to finance many projects which would have been impossible without the extra revenue.

The AIOC has made extensive investments in southern Iran, including the largest refinery in the world on Abadan island. The activities of the Company, however, far exceed the operations necessary for securing and refining oil. It maintains two fully equipped hospitals and many doctors. Extensive housing projects have been provided for workers, and over a dozen schools in the province of Khuzistan have been built and equipped by the Company. There is no question that oil has brought material benefits to Iran, but it also brought many problems, including the difficult task of integrating the oil industry, operated by foreigners, into the economy of the country.

American oil companies had evinced an interest in concessions in parts of Iran not covered by the British concession after World War I, but nothing came of it. In 1937 an American company explored northeastern Iran for oil but abandoned the concession the following year. In 1943–44 two American companies again tried their luck, but the Persians shortly put an end to the hopes of all foreigners seeking oil concessions. Instead the Iranian government now, under the Seven Year Plan Organization, has its own oil company which has been engaged throughout 1950 in exploring and surveying the country for oil.

Foreigners have been eager to obtain concessions in Iran for several reasons. Most of the oil here, as elsewhere in the Middle East, does not require extensive pumping. This reduces the cost of production in comparison with other oil-producing areas where pumps are needed. Furthermore, average productivity of the Iranian wells exceeds that of oil wells in many other parts of the world. Finally the low labor costs and low royalties have enticed oil companies to seek concessions in Iran.

When the Majlis decided that no more foreign concessions for oil would be granted, it was also agreed that the government would seek an adjustment with the Anglo-Iranian Oil Company for higher royalties. An agreement raising the basic royalty considerably was signed on July 17, 1949, but it was never ratified. Prolonged negotiations gave rise to increased agitation over the oil issue, and the demand for nationalization of oil grew. In the Majlis session of October 19, 1950 Dr. Mosaddeq, chairman of the Majlis Oil Committee, gave the following figures for the expenses of the oil company in 1949:

British income tax	£28 million
Dividends to shareholders	£ 7 million
Royalties to Iran	£10 million
Reserves	£17 million
Operational expenditures	£17 million
Total	£79 million

When he protested that Iran was not receiving her fair share of the profits, he was reflecting a widespread sentiment, a sentiment amply attested by numerous public demonstrations against the AIOC and for nationalization.

On January 2, 1951 the Arabian-American Oil Company announced an agreement to share its profits equally with the Saudi Arabian government, which meant, in effect, that the government would levy a tax of 50 per cent on the profits of ARAMCO. This presaged demands for the revision of agreements between various governments and the other oil concessionaires in the Middle East.

Prime Minister Razmara, in opposing nationalization, declared in the Majlis that Iran did not have enough trained personnel to operate the oil installations herself. Feelings against Razmara, against the British, and indeed against all foreigners, were inflamed and the climax came on March 7, 1951 when the Prime Minister was assassinated by a religious fanatic. The assassin confessed he had shot Razmara because the latter had opposed the nationalization of oil and "had given the country to foreigners." It was too late for the AIOC to offer the Iranian government half of its profits. The day after the assassination the Majlis Oil Committee voted unanimously for the nationalization of oil, and the Majlis and Senate did the same a short time later. It remained for the Shah and the new prime minister, Husain Ala, to concur. Husain Ala, however, resigned on March 27 and the following day Dr. Mosaddeq, leader of the nationalization forces in the Majlis, became prime minister. The Shah signed the measure and the Iranian government was ready to take over the AIOC.

The British government protested that the unilateral action of the Iranian parliament was an illegal repudiation of international obligations, but took no action. Some hoped that an agreement—perhaps a managerial contract between the Iranian government and the AIOC —would be reached. More serious than the oil crisis itself was the resulting deterioration of relations between Iran and the West, as well as the worsening financial situation in the country. The Communists, of course, profited from the growing xenophobia, and fears were expressed that the Soviets might obtain control of Persian oil. When Razmara was assassinated the government was quick to proclaim that Communists were not involved; the Communists did not need to fan nationalist sentiment. The underground Tudeh party, however, became more active, and martial law was proclaimed in Teheran.

The overwhelming sentiment which led to the nationalization of oil, though fostered primarily by nationalists and religious fanatics, was certainly exploited by the Communists in various ways. They sponsored at least one front organization, the "Committee for the Struggle Against Exploitation by the AIOC." They organized mass demonstrations and were behind the wave of riots and strikes which occurred in March and April in several areas, notably at Abadan and in the oil fields. Their aim, of course, is not the same as the nationalist—to secure for Iran the profits of Iranian oil—but rather to disrupt the flow of oil to Western Europe and to intensify growing anti-western sentiment.

But what of the future of the AIOC? It should be understood that the nationalization act approved by the Iranian government applies only to the assets of the AIOC in Iran. Its great tanker fleet and world-wide marketing operations are not included. Since the natural outlet of Iranian oil is Western Europe, the British, with control of transport and marketing, still have a strong bargaining point.

That hope for a satisfactory solution to the oil problem exists is shown, on the Persian side, by the Majlis resolution to set aside 25 per cent of the operating profits of the new national oil company to meet compensation claims of the AIOC. The British, for their part, have indicated a willingness to compromise by proposing the formation of a new oil company in which the Iranian government and the British both would be represented, with an equal sharing of the profits. If compromise proves impossible—and Persian fanatics have claimed they would rather see oil operations cease than permit any British control to remain—then Britain may bring the case before the World Court in the Hague. The dispatch of British troops to Iran to protect AIOC property would lead to new difficulties.

Thus the probability is that some sort of compromise will be arrived at between the Persians and the British. If extremists on either side make such a compromise impossible, Iran will require outside technical aid to carry on oil operations. The United States and Soviet Russia are the only two countries at present able to supply such assistance. Since calling in American or Russian aid is manifestly unfeasible, agreement with the British is virtually mandatory if chaos is to be avoided.

But oil, of course, is produced in other Middle Eastern countries besides Iran, and Iranian oil should not be considered in isolation. The military and strategic importance of Middle Eastern oil is obvious, and its significance for the economic recovery of Europe should not be minimized. And, since ability of the Soviets to wage large-scale war may depend on their securing additional sources of oil, this oil may well be crucial. Some military men argue that in the event of a Soviet invasion of Iran we could destroy the oil wells before the Red Army reached them, and that even if they did put the wells in operation again, difficulties of transportation to the Soviet Union would negate the value of the oil. This view ignores the possibility of a long Russian occupation of the oil fields, and the probability that the Red forces would use the oil primarily for expansion into Asia and Africa. It also overlooks the power of fifth columns, and the possibility—though not probability—that nationalization will drive the West out of all of the Middle Eastern fields. Thus, even though the United States is able to obtain sufficient oil for its own needs from the Western Hemisphere alone, it would be hard to exaggerate the importance of Middle Eastern oil in the event of war with the Soviet Union.

So a solution of the oil problem is vital to Iran, to the stability of the Middle East, and perhaps to the future of the free world. Some Persians think that the Red Army will make capture of the Middle Eastern oil fields its first objective in a war with the western powers. They argue that the American policy of concentrating on the defense of Western Europe is playing into the hands of the Russians, who know only too well the importance of Asia. In any case, the oil crisis is another striking reminder to us that time is running out in Asia.

10. The Present and the Future

Before we turn to a consideration of Iran's future—to an examination, in the context of the deepening world crisis, of her own plans for that future and of what our part in them should be—we should first try to fathom, as accurately as we can, the present Iranian position vis-à-vis the United States and the Soviet Union. *Has* Iran rejected the West and cast in her lot with the Soviets? Despite her recent move in regard to the Voice of America, her barter agreement with Russia, and the nationalization of oil, I think we can say that the answer to this question is "no."

The Director General of Propaganda, when he announced that radio Teheran would no longer relay the programs of the Voice of America, said, "There exists in Iran, as in any progressive country, what is called 'public opinion,' and contrary to the opinion of badly informed individuals, Persian public opinion is alive and at the same time effective. It favored this move." Whether or not public opinion was the real reason for the government's action, the step can probably be interpreted as a moving away, on the part of the government, from a more or less openly pro-American to a more neutral position.

The barter agreement, which we have seen is not a new agreement, was motivated by economic necessities and is a natural, entirely unreprehensible, and not highly significant move. The nationalization of oil too is understandable.

Iran today is a country which would like to maintain its independence, which is looking out for its own best interests, and which refuses to subserve the selfish ends of other nations. For Persians are still saying that they will not be mere pawns on the chessboard of great power rivalry. Even though this kind of thinking seems outdated and irrelevant to us in view of what has happened since 1945, it is still a powerful psychological reality in the minds of the citizens of the small underdeveloped nations of the world. The Persians have ample reason to question the motives of great powers, though hardly any historical justification for questioning ours. Our hands are cleaner in Persia perhaps than anywhere else in the world. The story of Americans in Persia is almost wholly creditable not only in achievement but in intent. But no great power can be above suspicion, and our record in other parts of the world is not so perfect that we should altogether fail to appreciate the qualms of the Persians.

Thus until she is reassured, until tangible and substantial help is more than promised, Iran, though herself anti-Communist, has no choice but to get along with the Russians. Russia is near and America far away. Some Persians view with skepticism American promises to come to their aid at once if they are attacked. They feel that such promises are intended merely as morale-builders. At the same time they know that Britain—notwithstanding the nationalization of oil— has great stakes in Iran, as have the Americans, with their oil wells in Saudi Arabia just across the Gulf. These interests serve to underwrite American promises to Iran, but they are not an unconditional guarantee of assistance. Even though most Persians probably feel fairly sure that America will come to their aid if their country is attacked. it is small consolation to them to know that if their country is invaded World War III will begin. Their desire to live peacefully with Russia, therefore, should not be construed as implying an anti-American or anti-western attitude, any more than it should be taken as implying a pro-Russian. It merely signifies that the Persians fear that in the event of war, regardless of how soon American or United Nations help comes, their country will be overrun. They can hardly fail to have read the lesson of Korea.

What, then, can and should be our role in relation to Iran, an Iran which is still part of the free world, though a relatively weak and insecure part? What is the relevance of Iran and the Iranian situation to the central dilemma of our time, to the struggle of the free world to survive and prosper which must now engage our utmost energies and resources and abilities?

We can divide our role, in Iran as elsewhere, into two parts—a military and a nonmilitary, or what we may call a short term and a long term. On the urgent necessity of adequate defense against the military might of the Soviet Union we are all agreed; on the second aspect of our role there is less unanimity and emphasis. Yet *even now* it is at least equally important and it may ultimately prove decisive. For full and enthusiastic support of our military leadership can be assured only if we simultaneously lead the fight for the ideals of democratic freedom, *and* for the economic and social justice which the peoples of the world demand.

But let us consider first the purely military aspect of the struggle, the half of the battle which must be fought by force alone. Is Iran worth defending militarily and can it be done? We know that her oil is valuable and her geographical location strategic. These two facts alone perhaps define our short-term interest in Iran, or more accurately, they make more urgent the necessity, already plainly evident, of maintaining the present limits of Soviet power. For surely it is not necessary to argue here that we dare not permit the Soviet Union to acquire further territory, beyond its already swollen boundaries, if we are to have any chance of successfully defending the free world.

Nor is it necessary to argue here that it is better, by being strong, to deter Russia from making the attempt to extend her sway than to have to fight to stop her once she has started. To do this it is not only we who must be strong, but all of those countries with whom our fate is inescapably linked must also be strong, strong and united and confident of themselves and of each other. Iran is one of those countries, a vital and valuable asset, cultural as well as strategic. But she is also a tempting prize for an aggressor; she lives in the shadow of Soviet might, and she is very nearly defenseless.

Iran is on the flank of our defense system, as she has been on the fringes of our thinking about the rest of the world. We have the North Atlantic Pact; we have programs of continuing military aid to Greece and Turkey, but we have not as yet integrated Iran, or the Middle East generally, into any scheme of defense. Despite the fact that Iran is of great strategic value and is vital to the security of the whole Middle East, our approach to her problems has remained piecemeal.

Joint military planning is well under way in Western Europe, but in the Middle East we have not even begun to plan for the common defense. We should at least consider the relation of this area to the defense of Western Europe. We should increase military aid to Iran, but we must do more than that. Even more important than increasing aid is promoting overall defense planning for the Middle Eastern area. I believe we should urge the immediate formation of a military pact between Turkey, Iran, and the Arab states, under Anglo-American leadership. Turkey, of course, is far stronger militarily than her eastern and southern neighbors, and we therefore wisely began our military program in Turkey. But should we stop there? Defense

strategy for the Middle East requires coördination and the coöperation of each of its nations. In any such overall defense plan Iran
would play an important part.

I am not advocating the dispatch of American troop units or the
outlay of large sums of money to try to make this area impregnable.
Nor am I proposing that we apportion aid to the Middle East at the
expense of aid to Western Europe. What I am advocating is that we
devote the relatively small amount of money and effort which would
be required to bring about substantial strengthening and improvement, in size and equipment and training, of the existing forces and
that overall defense plans for the area be drawn up making use of
these forces.

We have said that long-term aims must be pursued simultaneously
with purely military objectives. Before we examine what these aims
should be in Iran and what they entail for us, let us look at what the
Persians themselves propose to do to solve their problems.

The course of economic and social progress in Iran for the next
decade has already been blueprinted by the Seven Year Plan for the
development of the resources of the country. The very existence of a
comprehensive plan of this kind is evidence that Iran recognizes the
breadth and complexity of her problems and that she intends to attempt their solution. The original plan was proposed in 1946 and
announced by Prime Minister Ahmad Qavam in the spring of 1947.
A report of a group of American engineers who had been invited by
the Iranian government to study the Plan, the Morrison-Knudsen
report, was submitted to the government in August 1947, and a
Supreme Planning Board was appointed by the prime minister to
draw up a program of development with reference to this report. As
a result of further study it was decided in October 1948 to contract
the firm of Overseas Consultants Inc. (OCI), composed of eleven
American engineering, construction, and consulting companies, to
prepare a detailed plan of development. Overseas Consultants Inc.
was retained, in a consultative capacity only, by the Iranian government to assist in the implementation of the Plan until December 31,
1950, when the agreement was canceled because of lack of funds.
While OCI was gathering material for its survey and recommendations, legislation authorizing the Plan was passed in the Majlis on
February 15, 1949. On August 22, OCI submitted its report to the
Iranian government, a five-volume study entitled *Report on Seven*

Year Development Plan for the Plan Organization of the Imperial Government of Iran.

Three general principles are emphasized by the Report which should serve as guideposts of any program of aid to underdeveloped countries in the Orient. First, any development effort must be applied at the lowest level from the start. This reverses the usual principle of building from the top down. It means that a tractor factory is an absurdity until the peasants have adequate iron hand tools. Further, it means that labor will be unable to meet the demands placed on it unless the workers are healthy, well nourished and feel that they are working for improvements in their own conditions of daily life. The second basic principle is that capital is not a substitute for skill or experience. The power of capital is often exaggerated by Americans in dealing with other countries. It is wasteful, and usually quite futile, to spend money on an enterprise without the necessary skills to carry it through. The third principle is the need for coördination. Those who labor to produce are, at the same time, consumers of the increasing flow of goods, and no single project can be treated in isolation. For example, the construction of a canning factory in Iran requires a host of parallel developments of transportation, communication, and changes in the economic and social life of the community, if it is to succeed.

The Plan itself is formidable in scope and intention. It entails virtually a complete overhauling of the industrial and economic structure of the country. It calls for the expansion and modernization of industry and agriculture and the exploitation of mines and underground resources, especially oil; for improving transportation and communications, increasing exports, improving public health and educational facilities, and generally promoting the well-being and raising the standard of living of the people. If it is carried through successfully, and this is a big "if," the life of every Persian will be affected in some way.

Under the Plan an expenditure of about six hundred and fifty million dollars is contemplated—a huge sum for a country like Iran. About a third of this amount must be obtained through foreign loans, while the Iranian government is to furnish the remainder, at least one half of which will be supplied by revenue from oil.

The Plan emphasizes, as it must, the fundamental importance of agriculture. As noted above, four fifths of the Persian people derive their living from the soil. Only 2 to 5 per cent of these own the land they till; the remainder cultivate land for other people, as tenant farmers or as simple agricultural workers. Under the Plan substantial funds are allocated for irrigation projects, increased cultivation of foodstuffs, and for improvement of farming methods—use of machinery where practicable, fertilizers, better seeds and plants, and so forth —to increase yields per acre. It is also intended to encourage saving among peasants to enable them to acquire their own land.

Thus the lot of the peasant will certainly be improved, but will the basic problem of grinding and hopeless poverty for the vast majority of Persia's people have been solved? Is not radical reform of the system of land tenure necessary at the same time? Should not a program for the redistribution of land be carried out under the Plan, along with the projects mentioned above? Certainly we must admit that the issue of land reform has been one of the most successful cards in the Communist hand in the Orient. If the Persians themselves fail to provide an adequate solution to this problem, they will have unwittingly strengthened the Communist hand.

The Shah himself, as we have seen, has taken the first step in land reform by ordering the large estates which he inherited from his father to be broken up and sold to the peasants cultivating the land as tenants or laborers. This move was acclaimed not only in Iran but in this country as well, and—in spite of the opposition of powerful landlords—it could mean hope for the future.

Only about 20 per cent of the Plan funds have been earmarked for public health, housing, and education. These things are, of course, far more basic than industrial development; their importance can hardly be overstated. Without real progress here Iran's future is uncertain indeed.

It is difficult to determine to what extent plans in most of the varied fields have progressed beyond the paper stage, since reliable information is largely unavailable. Among the projects approved, however, and in some cases begun, during the first year of the Plan are: formation of an Iranian Oil Company, construction of two sugar refineries, extension of the railroad to Meshed, resumption of work on Iran's only steel mill, at Karaj, a village near Teheran, work on which had been interrupted by the war, and the rebuilding of the port of Khorramshahr.

It is still too early to predict how successful the Plan will be. Although ultimately it may accomplish a great deal, it must be said that so far its results have been disappointing. Unfortunately, its first years coincided with a major economic crisis, brought about in part by a series of crop failures and poor harvests. At the same time, as a result of Iran's unfavorable trade balance and the government's conservative fiscal policy, which restricted the amount of money in circulation, the economic situation steadily worsened. Goods piled up in warehouses, factories closed, and unemployment and bankruptcies increased. Plan funds had to be diverted and projects deferred to meet the crisis.

Furthermore, there have been frequent changes in the personnel of the Plan Organization; parliament has not always seen fit to coöperate with it; and the country has not been able to obtain the foreign loans upon which the Plan in part depends. The Organization has been accused of misuse of funds, waste, and inefficiency by deputies in the Majlis.

The difficulties facing any such plan as this are, of course, immense. The lack of persons with managerial and administrative experience in the country poses great problems, as does the lack of industrial and technological skills among the labor force. Want of initiative on the part of businessmen and their reluctance to take risks must be overcome if private enterprise is to have any share, as OCI recommended, in the development of Iran.

Some Persians, and foreigners as well, believe that only a dictator can ensure the success of the Plan and, indeed, is Iran's only means of salvation. Such an idea must be rejected, on many grounds, practical as well as moral, immediate as well as long-range. No matter how attractive or convenient it might momentarily and superficially appear to resort to dictatorship, such a course would be not only risky but futile. For a dictatorship, no matter how able and well intentioned, would be successful only within self-imposed limits. And it would not be self-perpetuating. At its end the Persians would be left, as they were after the downfall of Reza Shah, weak, divided, demoralized, without political experience and consequently dependent. Furthermore, even the positive accomplishments of such a regime would probably be less substantial and permanent than they appeared to be. Things would have been done to and for, not by, the people. Imposed by decree, reform and progress, if evident at all, might be largely illusory.

What is the alternative? Every effort must be made by the Iranians, under their present constitutional government, to carry out the Seven Year Plan; it is vital that it achieve at least a fair degree of success. To ensure the minimum conditions of stability and solvency which will permit the various parts of the program to be completed with even partial success, the Iranians must not only keep their government functioning but they must strengthen it and somehow bring about increased honesty and efficiency and effectiveness. For their government is not now strong and united and effective, nor is it truly representative.

Prevalent corruption in the bureaucracy was recognized by the parliament in the summer of 1950. A law against corruption was passed and a committee was appointed which drew up three lists of government employees: (List A) those who were honest and required; (List B) those who were honest but whose jobs were unnecessary; and (List C) those who were corrupt and undesirable. When List C was made public there was a great uproar in parliament and in the press. The committee was accused of unfairness and of being prone to petty revenge. As a result the anticorruption campaign became a farce and on November 16 the law was rescinded.

Besides political inexperience, one of the gravest of the long-term problems which hamper the conduct of government in Iran is the widespread lack of any real sense of public responsibility. Trust and mutual confidence have been conspicuously absent, as well as respect for law. Failures in the administration of law negate all of the good and adequate laws which may be put on the books. A striking example of this is the failure to pay taxes. The wealthy have been notorious tax evaders and consequently the poor have had to shoulder more than their share of the tax burden through indirect taxes. But this is only one of the inequities with which the government must deal.

Some of their age-old traditions—cultural, social, and religious—are undoubtedly anachronisms in the new social and economic structure which the Persians wish to build. Many of these are real handicaps to further development and must be modified or discarded. The strong tradition of individualism, which still makes personal attachment to a chieftain or leader more comprehensible to many of them than allegiance to an abstract principle or to an impersonal government, is one of these. Child labor is another.

To say that they must adapt themselves and their traditions to the needs and uses of modern democratic society is not so say that they must reject their past. On the contrary, they must be careful to preserve their uniquely valuable cultural heritage. To live, as Persians, but in the modern world, they must select from their own past and from the West what is germane to their aspirations for the future.

The Persians, then, are engaged in a heroic effort to govern themselves, at which activity they are still notably inexpert; at the same time they are undertaking the herculean task of expanding and modernizing their entire economy. They have these two immense jobs to do, both in the face of formidable and perhaps insurmountable difficulties, at a moment when the whole of western civilization, to which in a sense they have apprenticed themselves, and with which they have identified their political interests, is in dire peril. It is their great misfortune to have embarked on these great undertakings at a moment in history when the time for leisurely evolutionary development is not permitted them.

Why all this matters to us, why Persia's internal stability, well-being, and development—economically and politically—are of genuine concern to the United States should perhaps be amply apparent by now. It will certainly be apparent to all those who, like me, believe two things: (1) that, whether we have war or peace, we cannot easily afford to lose another man, another factory, another inch of ground to the Russians, and (2) that the best way to keep Iran from falling into Soviet hands is to help her government and her economy function effectively and *for the increasing benefit of all her people.*

Even if space were not limited, this point of view could not be argued convincingly to those who believe that we can get along even without Western Europe, or indeed that we do not need any friends or allies. I can only urge that we weigh carefully our chances of survival without even one of the present members of the non-Communist world.

Assuming then, to save space, that there is general agreement on the first of these two points, let me very briefly indicate some of the arguments in favor of the second. If and when Russia decides to risk all-out war, we shall obviously have no choice but to take up the challenge and fight. If she decides, however, to continue to gain all she can by methods short of war, only an unstable and demoralized Iran will invite "liberation." Such liberation could be effected in one of two ways: through the standard or so-called classic pattern of infiltration and engineered coup or through invasion by a small force, on the pretext that Persia's instability was a threat to the Soviet Union or that she was harboring anti-Soviet forces or agents. Either of these two methods might assure the Soviets the unimpeded use of

Persia's territory and oil without the risk of general war, but *neither would be tried unless her weakness invited such an attempt.*

Iran is not the most fertile soil on which the Communists are working, even though the internal situation is explosive. Yet it would not pay to overlook or minimize its potential dangers any more than it would pay to exaggerate them. Iran shares a 1500-mile border with the Soviet Union; and we must not forget that, through the Tudeh party and the use of trained agents, Russia is carrying on a systematic, skillful, unremitting campaign of subversion, which not only reaps the benefits of popular disaffection but also sows the seeds of hatred and revolution.

It is precisely because they capitalize on legitimate grievances that the Communists' threat is so deadly, especially in the so-called "backward" or underdeveloped countries. Out of such grievances they produced the revolutionary sentiment which is now an Asiatic phenomenon. In short, although they exploit dissatisfaction, the Communists do not *create the bases* of popular discontent. They do not have to.

It is because communism has become the only hope in many lands for reform, for relief from centuries-old oppression and poverty, that the way to combat it—we are speaking here of the idea of communism, not the military might of the Soviet Union—is to offer a better hope. To do this is to deprive the Communists of a far more valuable and powerful weapon than any in the military arsenal. Thus one cannot be successfully anti-Communist without at the same time being pro-something else. Not just pro-democratic, unless we imply by democracy radical social and economic as well as political reform. We must not offer democracy to the East merely as a series of political and social institutions and practices that, at least as we know them, are ill adapted to Asiatic soil.

Thus, to combat communism within her own borders, to neutralize its appeal (which is to defeat it), Iran must have not only order and stability but economic and social *progress,* progress which is to be measured not by a proliferation of gadgets, machines, and luxuries— the "trimmings" of a mass production economy—but by the increase and equitable distribution of the simple necessities of life, by food, sanitation, and preventive medicine, better housing, better agricultural methods, and so forth.

If the Persian government is unable to provide these things, is unable, in short, to implement its Seven Year Plan, we would do well to help her, to offer help, that is, in excess of what can be provided

under the Point Four Program with its United Nations counterpart.
Unless we make good our promises of assistance, unless we give more
assistance as it is needed and requested, we run the risk of allowing
Iran's hopeful plans for the future to be grounded on the sands of her
own financial, technological, and administrative limitations and inexperience. If that happens ideal conditions for the growth of communism will be created, and Iran may well be lost to the free world.

The Gordon Gray *Report to the President on Foreign Economic
Policies* (Washington, D. C., November 10, 1950) provides an excellent general guide for American economic policy in underdeveloped
areas. While recognizing the great obstacles to economic development in the Middle East, the Report states, "Even limited (economic) progress might reduce their (Middle Eastern nations') vulnerability to Soviet political infiltration and pressure." Limited progress would almost certainly reduce their vulnerability. In the same
vein as this report is the proposal to expand the activities of the ECA
to cover the entire world.

From a recognition of the potency of the Communist appeal, we
can learn the nature of our most dangerous antagonist, in Iran as all
over the world. For we find that we are engaged in a contest with an
idea; knowing that the best defense is offense and recognizing the
power of martyrdom, we know that an idea cannot be defeated by
mere opposition, by suppression, or condemnation, but that it can
only be defeated by a better idea. But having a better idea is not
enough; it must be *communicated,* and must be made relevant and
meaningful to the lives of the people it seeks to influence. Here we hit
America's weakness and her failure. And her one big job.

We know that we have something better to offer the world than
Russia has. Not slavery but freedom, not oppression but opportunity,
not hatred and bitterness and fear, but confidence, trust and love,
not war but peace. Are we so sure however that we are really offer-
ing these things? Have we really kept our best ideals uncorrupted
by partial and conflicting and temporary interests? Have we really
isolated and defined the essential and universally valid nature of the
democratic ideal? Are we sure that we do not often offer the spurious
coin of accidental, external forms and formulas for the genuine gold
of democratic ideals? Democracy as we know and practice it is a
haphazard growth, containing within itself deep and irreconcilable
contradictions, developed almost by pure contingency on American
soil; it cannot be transplanted unmodified to another soil and be

expected to flourish with equal vigor and equally beneficial results.

At any rate, whatever the reasons for the failure and without venturing into philosophical deeps, we can safely say that our genius in the practical and technical spheres has been matched by a colossal ineptitude when it comes to formulating and communicating ideas.

For this big job—to wage war on the ideological front—two things are needed: effective propaganda and good public relations, both designed in every case with a specific country in mind. In turn, to carry out these two recommendations, two things are needed: hard thinking and intimate and exact knowledge and understanding of those we seek to influence.

A third ingredient, money, is also needed, of course, but success or failure on this front is not primarily a matter of money, of the scale on which we conduct the campaign. It is a matter of thought, of effort, of skill and tact and good will, of willingness to learn, of unrelenting labor. It sounds arduous, but we must not forget what is at stake—a matter of survival.

To wage a propaganda campaign in Iran, to conduct a successful public relations program there, we must know Iran and the Iranians far, far better than we do. We must train men, specialists, of whom we have far too few, to work there, to serve her, to serve us there. We must increase public interest and understanding; promote increasing cultural interchange, through the exchange of students, teachers, business and professional men, and others. The initiative in promoting better relations is ours: we must meet the Persians more than half way.

Under several headings, then—military and economic aid, technical assistance, political support and friendship and encouragement, maintenance and growth of cultural and social ties and interchange, expansion of propaganda and public relations programs—can we sum up our positive program for Iran. The details of these various aspects of policy cannot be given here, not only because of lack of space, but because they must be developed gradually, by experts in each of the fields, on the spot and as occasion arises.

We must never sacrifice long-term ideals for immediate gains, which will prove largely illusory if we corrupt idealism with expediency. This means that we must never be tempted to support dictatorship in the hope that thereby internal strength and stability will be ensured. Only through a government which is responsive to the popular will and which serves the interests of the whole population can Iran's future be secured. We should also refrain from unjustified and useless criticism of the government and the people.

And this above all: whatever we do, we must do for the good of Iran and of all her citizens. She must be treated as a sovereign nation, deserving of our respect. If we do this, we shall actually at the same time be serving our own interests; there is no conflict between her good and ours and that of the whole non-Communist world. We must avoid not only the reality of any form of exploitation but also even the appearance of it. Whatever we do, officially or privately, we must be sure that no partial or special interests, Iranian or American, are served.

The program of which I have tried to suggest only the aims and outlines is, perforce, exceedingly general, and it is not immune to the charge of an excess of moral fervor and idealism. It all may seem pitched in too exalted a moral key. The skeptics and cynics will decry it as impractical and unrealistic, the defeatists as too ambitious, impossible of attainment. Yet I believe that it is eminently practical and realistic to be truly disinterested and to aim high, in this grave hour. I have tried to suggest that idealism has even a military value. The Communists offer the hope of earthly salvation, which neither they nor we could possibly fulfill. Dare we offer anything less than our very best?

Many will say that it is too late to try to save anyone but ourselves, that we must devote what time remains and all our resources to our own defense or at most to the defense of Europe and perhaps certain areas in the Pacific. Certainly we have lost much time and it may well be too late—too late even to rearm, let alone embark on the less tangible, though surely more economical, programs of common defense. But one thing is certain: even if there were less chance of success than there is, defeat would be sure if we resigned ourselves to it and gave up.

The difficulties, in Iran as at home and everywhere else, are enormous. The challenge is immense. But let us meet it; let us not retreat into a miserable, ignoble, and unworthy defeatism. Let us not lose by default, but, serving our best aims and our best selves, let us try. Let our failure, if we fail, be because we tried to do too much, not too little.

If we do this, we shall not fail.

Appendix I. The Supplementary Fundamental Laws to the Constitution: Articles 1 and 2

The influence of the religious leaders on the government may be seen from the English translation of the first two of the Supplementary Fundamental Laws to the Constitution of October 7, 1907, which, incidentally, are also good examples of Persian documentary style.

Article 1. The official religion of Iran is Islam according to the orthodox Ja'fari doctrine of the church of the twelve *imams,* which faith the Shah of Iran must profess and promote.

Article 2. At no time must any legal enactment of the sacred National Assembly, established by the favor and assistance of His Holiness, the *Imam* of the Age (may God hasten his glad advent), the favor of His Majesty the Shah-in-Shah of Islam (may God immortalize his reign), the care of the Proofs of Islam (may God multiply the likes of them), and the whole people of the Iranian nation, be at variance with the sacred principles of Islam or the laws established by His Holiness the Best of Mankind * (on whom and on whose household be the blessings of God and His peace).

It is hereby declared that it is for the ulema † to determine whether such laws as may be proposed are or are not conformable to the principles of Islam; and it is therefore officially enacted that there shall at all times exist a committee composed of not less than five *mujtahids* or other devout theologians, cognizant also of the requirements of the age, which committee shall be elected in this manner: the ulema and Proofs of Islam shall present to the National Assembly the names of twenty of the ulema possessing the attributes mentioned above, and the members of the Na-

* Mohammed.
† The learned doctors of theology.

tional Assembly shall, either by unanimous acclamation, or by vote, designate five or more of these, according to the exigencies of the time, and recognize these as members, so that they may carefully discuss and consider all matters proposed in the Assembly, and reject and repudiate, wholly or in part, any such proposal which is at variance with the sacred laws of Islam, so that it shall not obtain the title of legality. In such matters the decision of this ecclesiastical committee shall be followed and obeyed, and this article shall continue unchanged until the appearance of His Holiness the Proof of the Age (may God hasten his glad advent.)

Appendix II. Irano-Soviet Treaty of 1921: Articles 5 and 6

According to Article Five, of the Irano-Soviet treaty of 1923, the two High Contracting Parties undertake: *

(1) To prohibit the formation or presence within their respective territories, of any organization or group of persons, irrespective of the name by which they are known, whose object is to engage in acts of hostility against Persia or Russia, or against the Allies of Russia.

They will likewise prohibit the formation of troops or armies within their respective territories with the aforementioned object.

(2) Not to allow a third party or organization, whatever it be called, which is hostile to the other Contracting Party, to import or to convey in transit across their countries material which can be used against the other party.

(3) To prevent by all means in their power the presence within their territories or within the territories of their Allies of all armies or forces of a third party in cases in which the presence of such forces would be regarded as a menace to the frontiers, interests or safety of the other Contracting Party.

Article 6 provided: If a third party should attempt to carry out a policy of usurpation by means of armed intervention in Persia, or if such Power should desire to use Persian territory as a base of operations against Russia, or if a Foreign Power should threaten the frontiers of Federal Russia or those of its Allies, and if the Persian Government should not be able to put a stop to such menace after having been once called upon to do so by Russia, Russia shall have the right to advance her troops into the Persian interior for the purpose of carrying out the military operations necessary for its defense. Russia undertakes, how-

* The text is taken from A. H. Hamzavi, *Persia and the Powers* (London, 1946), pp. 71–72.

ever, to withdraw her troops from Persian territory as soon as the danger has been removed.

In an exchange of letters, the Soviet ambassador in Iran assured the Iranian government that Articles Five and Six . . .

are intended to apply only to cases in which preparations have been made for a considerable armed attack upon Russia or the Soviet Republics allied to her, by the partisans of the regime which has been overthrown or by its supporters among those foreign Powers which are in a position to assist the enemies of the Workers' and Peasants' Republics and at the same time to possess themselves, by force or by underhand methods, of part of the Persian territory, thereby establishing a base of operations for any attacks—made either directly or through the counter-revolutionary forces—which they might meditate against Russia or the Soviet Republics allied to her. The Articles referred to are therefore in no sense intended to apply to verbal or written attacks directed against the Soviet Government by the various Persian groups . . .

Appendix III. The Anglo-American-Soviet Declaration Concerning Iran

Teheran, December 1, 1943

The President of the United States of America, The Premier of the U.S.S.R., and the Prime Minister of the United Kingdom, having consulted with each other and with the Prime Minister of Iran, desire to declare the mutual agreement of their three Governments regarding relations with Iran.

The Governments of the United States of America, the U.S.S.R. and the United Kingdom recognize the assistance which Iran has given in the prosecution of the war against the common enemy, particularly by facilitating the transportation of supplies from overseas to the Soviet Union. The three Governments realize that the war has caused special economic difficulties for Iran and they agreed that they will continue to make available to the Iranian Government such economic assistance as may be possible, having regard to the heavy demands made upon them by their world-wide military operations and to the world-wide shortage of transport, raw materials and supplies for civilian consumption.

With respect to the postwar period, the Governments of the United States of America, the U.S.S.R. and the United Kingdom are in accord with the Government of Iran that any economic problem confronting Iran at the close of hostilities should receive full consideration along with those of other members of the United Nations by conferences or international agencies, held or created, to deal with international economic matters.

The Governments of the United States of America, the U.S.S.R., and the United Kingdom are at one with the Government of Iran in their desire for the maintenance of the independence, sovereignty, and territorial integrity of Iran. They count upon the participation of Iran, together with all other peace-loving nations, in the establishment of international peace, security, and prosperity after the war, in accordance with the principles of the Atlantic Charter, to which all four Governments have continued to subscribe.

(Signed)
Winston Churchill
J. V. Stalin
Franklin D. Roosevelt

Appendix IV. General Information about Iran*

AREA: about 628,000 square miles.

POPULATION: The Iranian census commission reported that in 1950 the total population of the country was 18,771,538 (*Ettéla'at*, February 5, 1951). According to some observers this figure is several millions too high. The population of Teheran is about one million.

PETROLEUM PRODUCTION AND ROYALTIES PAID BY THE ANGLO-IRANIAN OIL COMPANY TO THE GOVERNMENT OF IRAN

Year	Tons (thousands)	Royalties (dollars) †
1945	18,311	22,672,780
1946	19,858	28,733,900
1947	20,195	28,617,030
1948	24,871	36,963,160
1949	26,807	54,360,670
1950 (to November 30)	28,805	

(Under a new agreement, if it is accepted—which appears doubtful now—the Iranian government will receive $75,231,177 in royalties for 1948 and $92,247,751 for 1949, retroactively.)

* Sources: Ali Moarefi, *The Iranian Seven Year Plan and its Monetary Effects* (Washington, D. C., 1950), and *The Anglo-Iranian Oil Company, Annual Reports.*

† These figures have been converted from pounds sterling at the rate of £1 = $4.03.

278 *Appendix IV*

IRANIAN FOREIGN TRADE
(in million *rials*); one *rial* = ca. $.03

Year	Imports	Exports	Per Cent of Exports to Total Foreign Trade
1945–46	3,106	1,698	35.34
1946–47	4,115	2,570	39.63
1947–48	4,705	2,324	33.06
1948–49	4,115	1,798	30.41

ESTIMATED LAND UTILIZATION (1948–49)

Major Land Uses	Area in Acres	Per Cent of Total
Land in farms		
Crop land		10.15
Pasture, woodland, villages, etc.		1.47
Total	46,949,000	11.62
Land not in farms		
Forests and ranges	69,188,000	17.11
Cities, roads, railroads	4,942,000	1.22
Wasteland	283,176,600	70.05
Total	357,306,600	88.38
Grand Total	404,255,600	100.00

Appendix V. Suggested Reading

1. **Introductory**: There is no lack of general books on Iran, but writings on special subjects are few and hard to find. For general information about the Middle East, and Iran in particular, the publication *The Middle East: A Political and Economic Survey* (London: Royal Institute of International Affairs, 1950), 516 pp. is a reliable guide. More concise, containing a Who's Who of the Middle East, yet with less attention to Iran than to the Arab states, is the book *The Middle East* (London: Europa Publications, 1950), 375 pp. Fortunately a *critical* bibliography of "Recent Books on Iran" has been published by T. Cuyler Young in the January 1950 issue of *The Middle East Journal* (Washington, D. C.), and I do not attempt to duplicate his efforts here. This journal contains a quarterly chronology of events in the various Middle Eastern countries and an excellent bibliography of periodical literature.

A good factual survey of Iran—history, geography, art, economic life, and the like—is provided in the book by Donald N. Wilber, *Iran: Past and Present* (Princeton, 1948), 234 pp. More concerned with the intellectual and spiritual life of the Persians is the general work of William Haas, *Iran* (Columbia University Press, 1946), 273 pp. Lighter reading, and with interesting anecdotes about the regime of Reza Shah, is the volume by E. Groseclose, *Introduction to Iran* (Oxford, 1947), 257 pp. Especially useful is the book by Sir A. Wilson, *Persia* (New York, 1933), 400 pp. Other general works will be found in the bibliography of Young.

2. **Land**: In addition to the work of Wilber, the book by W. B. Fisher, *The Middle East: A Physical, Social and Regional Geography* (New York, 1951), 514 pp., is to be recommended, although emphasis in it is primarily on the Arab states. There have been a number of interesting articles about travels in Iran since the war in *The Geographical Journal* and *The National Geographic Magazine*. Excellent photographs of the land may be found in *Life* magazine for May 20, 1946, pp. 61–67.

3. **People**: For anyone interested in the old Persia, the novel by James Morier, *Hajji Baba of Isfahan,* provides a realistic picture of the life of the people in the early nineteenth century. The best account of the activi-

ties and beliefs of the common people before the first World War is the detailed book by Edward G. Browne, *A Year Amongst the Persians* (Cambridge University Press, 1927), 594 pp. A survey of the problems facing the peasants and any government seeking to ameliorate rural conditions is found in H. B. Allen's *Rural Education and Welfare in the Middle East* (London: H. M. Stationery Office, 1946), 24 pp. Life in a village in Iran is described by L. J. Hayden, "Living Standards in Rural Iran," *The Middle East Journal* (April 1949), pp. 140–150. The forthcoming book by Ann K. S. Lambton, *Land Tenure in Persia*—to be published by the Royal Institute of International Affairs—will be a sociological study of the peasant and his ownership of land. On ownership of land see the article by G. Hadary, "The Agrarian Reform Problem in Iran," *The Middle East Journal*, 5 (1951), pp. 181–196.

There is no general survey of the tribes of Iran. Several articles concerned with the tribes today are: O. Garrod, "The Nomadic Tribes of Persia Today," *Journal of the Royal Central Asian Society*, 33 (January 1946), pp. 32–46; V. Minorsky, "The Tribes of Western Iran," *Journal of the Royal Anthropological Institute*, 75 (1945), pp. 73–80; and concerned with the Kurds, K. A. Bedr Khan, "The Kurdish Problem," *Journal of the Royal Central Asian Society*, 36 (July 1949), pp. 237–248. The story of the migrations of the Bakhtiyari tribes has been told by Merian C. Cooper in the book *Grass* (New York, 1925), 362 pp. A motion picture film was made by Cooper of the Bakhtiyaris with the same title.

On the opium question see Groseclose's book, pp. 207–216. For a description of the cities of Iran, with photographs and historical notes, the book by L. Lockhart, *Famous Cities of Iran* (Brentford, Middlesex, 1939), 115 pp., is to be recommended.

4. Social Classes: There have been few publications concerning the court of the present Shah Mohammed Reza Pahlevi, and one must search in more general articles for information about it. A spotlight was turned on the court by the article on Iran in *Time* magazine for February 5, 1951, pp. 20–26. Persian newspapers questioned the alleged strong influence on the Shah by his sister Princess Ashraf, as asserted by *Time*. No biography of the youthful monarch has appeared, and the influence of court activities on national politics has not been assessed by any writer. The Shah's itinerary in the United States was followed in detail by *The Iran Review* for November–December 1949 and January–February 1950. This is a new review of the Irano-American Society, published in New York.

The Constitution and important pacts and treaties of Iran can be found in the book by Helen M. Davis, *Constitutions, Electoral Laws, Treaties of States in the Near and Middle East* (Durham, N. C., 1947). The formation of the Senate and changes in the Constitution are described by the article "Recent Constitutional Changes in Iran," *Journal of the Royal Central Asian Society* (July 1949), pp. 265–266. Debates in the Majlis may be followed in the air-mail edition of the Teheran newspaper *Ettéla'at,* which is published three times a week in Persian and English.

The Ministry of Labor in Iran publishes a journal in Persian and French, *Majalleh-i-Kar,* which gives information on the condition of labor in various industries. In addition, the International Labour Office in Geneva issues surveys of labor throughout the world. The *International Labour Review* has a number of articles on Iran.

The influence of the religious leaders today is well described by John Elder in "The Moral and Spiritual Situation in Iran," *The Muslim World* (Hartford, Conn., April 1948), 100–112. See also the article by W. M. Miller, written from the missionary point of view, "The Religious Situation in Iran," *The Muslim World,* 41 (April 1951), pp. 77–87. Of interest is the booklet *Islam in the Modern World* (The Middle East Institute, Washington, D. C., 1951).

5. Religion and Law: An excellent account of Islam is given by H. A. R. Gibb in his small, readable *Mohammedanism* (London, 1949), 206 pp. Included in his book are discussions of the Shiites and modern trends in the Islamic world. The Shiite religion is treated in some detail by D. M. Donaldson, *The Shiite Religion* (London, 1933), 393 pp., while magic and superstition among the masses are discussed by his wife Bess Alan Donaldson in *The Wild Rue* (London, 1938), 216 pp.

There is no general account of religious minorities in Iran. More information is available about the Bahais than Zoroastrians, Christians or Jews. Information on the Babis and Bahais may be found in E. G. Browne's book noted above and in the *Encyclopaedia of Islam.* For American missionary work see the book by Groseclose, and for British work the article by W. J. Thomson, "Curtain Up On Iran," *World Dominion and the World Today* (London, September 1948), pp. 269–272.

6. Character, Culture and History: The book by William Haas gives a good insight into Persian character. Persian art has been treated by many writers; perhaps the best known is A. U. Pope and his monumental *Survey of Persian Art* (Oxford, 1938–39) in six volumes. For reproductions of the masterpieces of Iranian art see R. Ettinghausen and E. Schroeder, *Iranian and Islamic Arts* (The University Prints; Newton, Mass., 1941). The influence of Persian art on modern design, especially of textiles, is revealed by the publication *Persian Art and Design Influences from the Near and Middle East* (New York, 1948), 40 pp. Specially to be noted is Nilla C. Cook, "The Theater and Ballet Arts of Iran," *The Middle East Journal* (October 1949), pp. 406–420.

A brief survey of Persian literature may be found in R. Levy, *Persian Literature* (Oxford, 1923), 112 pp., while the most complete account is the four-volume work of E. G. Browne, *A Literary History of Persia* (Cambridge University Press, 1906–1924).

A short summary of Persian history is given by Sir E. D. Ross, *The*

Persians (Oxford, 1931), 142 pp. The history of the Achaemenids, the first empire in Iran, is told by A. T. Olmstead, *History of the Persian Empire* (Chicago, 1948), 576 pp. A general history of Iran from the earliest times to 1930 is the two-volume *A History of Persia* (London, 1930) by Sir Percy Sykes.

7. The Impact of the West: The history of Iran in the nineteenth century is adequately treated by Sykes (above) although there are many works on specific subjects. Sir Arnold T. Wilson's *A Bibliography of Persia* (Oxford, 1930) lists many of the books and articles relating to the nineteenth century; unfortunately the book lists publications by author, alphabetically. The revolution and founding of the Constitution is best described by E. G. Browne, *The Persian Revolution of 1905–1909* (Cambridge University Press, 1910), 470 pp. The two detailed volumes on Persia by G. N. Curzon, *Persia and the Persian Question* (New York, 1892), should not be omitted, for they give a good picture of the country at the end of the last century. The first World War in Iran is treated in a number of books from both sides of the conflict. Special mention might be made of the story of the British expedition to Baku by L. C. Dunsterville, *The Adventures of Dunsterforce* (London, 1920), 323 pp.

8. Reza Shah Pahlevi: A good biography of the late ruler is badly needed. The biography by Mohammed Esad-Bey (London, 1938) leaves much to be desired. An account of the reign of Reza Shah may be found in L. P. Elwell-Sutton, *Modern Iran* (London, 1941), 234 pp. The general books by Wilber, Haas, and Groseclose all devote considerable space to the reign of Reza Shah.

9. World War II and Its aftermath: The political situation during and after the war is well described by A. K. S. Lambton, "Some of the Problems Facing Persia," *International Affairs* (April 1946), pp. 254–272.

Two entertaining books on the impressions of American and British soldiers in Iran during the war have appeared; one is Joel Sayre's *Persian Gulf Command* (New York, 1945), 140 pp., which first appeared in *The New Yorker* magazine. The other is Cecil Keeling's *Pictures from Persia* (London, 1947), 186 pp., which contains some delightful illustrations. The official story of the British forces in Iran and Iraq has appeared: *Paiforce: The Official Story of the Persian and Iraq Command, 1941–1946* (London, H. M. Stationery Office, 1948), 137 pp.

Russia's interest in Iran since World War I has been treated in an excellent book by George Lenczowski, former Press Attaché at the Polish Legation in Teheran during the late war, *Russia and the West in Iran 1918–1948* (Cornell University Press, 1949), 383 pp. He has treated of the Communists in "The Communist Movement in Iran," *The Middle East Journal* (January 1947), pp. 29–45.

The Kurdish revolt was covered by an eyewitness, A. Roosevelt, "The Kurdish Republic of Mahabad," *The Middle East Journal* (July 1947), pp. 247–269, while a succinct account of the crisis in Azerbaijan, with the speeches of American, British, and Soviet leaders at the United Nations meetings, is given by A. H. Hamzavi, *Persia and the Powers* (London, 1946), 125 pp. On internal politics read L. P. Elwell-Sutton, "Political Parties in Iran: 1941–1948," *The Middle East Journal* (January 1949), pp. 45–62. A general discussion of Iran's problems, internal as well as external, is provided by T. Cuyler Young, "The Race between Russia and Reform in Iran," *Foreign Affairs* (January 1950), 14 pp.

10. The United States and Iran: The missionary endeavor in Iran is treated in Groseclose's book and occasional reports in *The Muslim World*. The stories of the three economic missions to Iran are told in the following books: W. Morgan Shuster, *The Strangling of Persia* (New York, 1912), 423 pp.; A. C. Millspaugh, *The American Task in Persia* (New York, 1925), 322 pp.; and A. C. Millspaugh, *Americans in Persia* (Washington, D. C., 1946), 293 pp.

Dangers to "Point Four" success in Iran (or the Middle East) are explained in the interesting article by G. Hakim, "Point Four and the Middle East," in *The Middle East Journal* (April 1950), pp. 183–195. A companion article in the same journal (July 1950), pp. 296–306, by A. Z. Gardiner, "Point Four and the Arab World: An American View," however, leaves many questions unanswered. Halford L. Hoskins points out considerable obstacles in the way of such a program in his article, "Point Four with Reference to the Middle East," *The Annals of the American Academy of Political and Social Science* (March 1950), pp. 85–95. See also the interesting article by George G. McGhee, Assistant Secretary of State for Near Eastern, South Asian and African Affairs, "Economic Development and the Near East," in the forthcoming volume of the Harvard University Press, *The Near East and the Great Powers*. These articles represent only a sampling of the literature on "Point Four," for much has appeared in journals and newspapers on the general question of aid to underdeveloped areas. *The Gordon Gray Report to the President on Foreign Economic Policies* (Washington, November 10, 1950), 131 pp., is commendable for its forthrightness in stating the problems and proposing economic aid to Asia on a basis similar to ERP. Pages 52–54 and 56–59 are devoted to the Middle East and the obstacles to development. This report is strongly recommended as the sanest view of an American economic approach to the area. A detailed account of taxation, budgetary problems, and recent fiscal history—with many tables—may be found in the United Nations publication *Public Finance Information Papers: Iran* (New York, March 1951), 102 pp.

Information on oil in the Middle East, including Iran, can be found in the book by R. F. Mikesell and H. B. Chenery, *Arabian Oil* (Chapel Hill, N. C., 1949), 201 pp. The booklet published by H. M. Stationery Office by N. S. Roberts, *Iran, Economic and Commercial Conditions* (London,

1948), 50 pp., is a survey of the economy of Iran just after the war. The yearly *Reports* of the Anglo-Iranian Oil Company give considerably more information than mere oil production figures.

11. The Present and the Future: Iran's Seven Year Plan has received considerable publicity. Besides the report of Overseas Consultants mentioned in the text, the following articles might be mentioned: a series of articles on Iran by J. M. Bee in the journal *Great Britain and the East* (London, 1950); in the July issue, pp. 27–29, he discusses the Seven Year Plan; "U. S. Engineers in Iran," *Fortune* (February 1950), pp. 70–73, which is perhaps overoptimistic; S. Rezazadeh Shafaq and J. D. Lotz, "The Iranian Seven Year Development Plan," *The Middle East Journal* (January 1950), pp. 100–105—giving the facts of the plan. Maurice Hindus speaks of the Seven Year Plan in his moving book *In Search of A Future* (New York, 1949), 270 pp. It is an impassioned and worthy plea for the less fortunate peoples of the world.

On American policy we have the monthly survey of *Current Developments in United States Foreign Policy,* and a stimulating booklet of 60 pages, *The Security of the Middle East: A Problem Paper* (Washington, 1951), both put out by the Brookings Institute. The Gordon Gray Report sheds light on political policy in this area as well as economic, for they are indissolubly linked. The Middle East Institute published the addresses of their Fourth Annual Conference, entitled *Americans and the Middle East: Partners in the Next Decade* (Washington, 1950), edited by H. A. Kitchen. It contains much of interest to the Iranian situation.

For the rest one must turn to *The New York Times, Ettéla'at,* or the *Christian Science Monitor,* for events are moving rapidly in Iran today, and one can keep abreast only through newspapers. The above bibliography not only neglects many publications in English, owing to limitations in space, but also all of the valuable Persian, Russian, French, and German material, much of which is necessary for an understanding of the many approaches to Iran and her problems today.

INDEX

Abadan, 190, 255, 257
'Abd al-Reza Pahlevi, 194
Abdul-Hamid II, Sultan, 53, 63, 141
Achaemenid Empire, 214
Adana, 19, 23, 30
Adrianople. *See* Edirne
Aegean Islands, 12
Aegean Region, Turkey, 21, 30
Aegean Sea, 5, 12; World War II in, 99
Afghanistan, 91, 190
Afyonkarahisar, 18
Agriculture, Turkish, 22, 23f., 30–32; Persian, 183
Akbar, Moghul, 216
Alexander the Great, 214
Alexandretta. *See* Iskerderun and Hatay
'Ali, 203, 206
Allen, George V., 242–243
Allied Powers after World War I, 58f.
Alphabet, Latin, in Turkey, 7, 80f.
American University of Beirut, 142
Anatolia, plateau of, 18–20; eastern frontier of, 20–21; history of, 38f.; called Rûm, 48
Anglo-Iranian Oil Company, 177, 240, 254f.
Anglo-Persian Oil Company, 254
Anglo-Russian Agreement, 220
Ankara, 7, 30, 66; becomes capital, 73
Antakya, 12, 14
Antalya, 19, 22, 23
Anti-Taurus Mountains, 19

Arab conquest, 215
Arab States, Turkish relations with, 6; in World War II, 100–101; Turkish attitudes towards, 129f.
Arabian-American Oil Company, 256
Arabic language, in Turkey, 80f.; in Iran, 190, 214
Architecture, Turkish, 125; Persian, 211–212
Ardahan, 17; demanded by Russia, 99
Ardebil, 216
Aristocracy, landed, Persian, 197–198
Armenia, Soviet, 17, 66, 207, 218; classical, 23; autonomous, 65
Armenians, of Hatay, 16; nationalism of, 60f.; massacres and deportations of, 60–61; returned to Russia, 17; of Istanbul, 96f.; missionaries to, 140f.; of Iran, 207
Army, Ottoman, 53; Turkish officers' corps, 53, 65; Turkish, 65; Persian, 198
Arpa River, 17
Art, Turkish, 125; Persian, 210f.
Asia Minor. *See* Anatolia
Assyrian Christians, 208
Atatürk, Mustafa Kemal (Pasha), 7, 62f., 72, 84, 223–224; his reforms, 73f.; benevolent dictatorship, 76–77; name, 80; death, 86–87; will, 88; funeral, 89; as party chief, 104–105
Austria-Hungary, 54
Avesta, 183, 204
Azerbaijan, 177, 182, 188, 216, 231, 236f., 241f.

Baghdad Railroad, 14
Bahais, 208
Bahrein Islands, 254
Bakhtiyaris, 188; Queen of Iran, 194
Baku, 218, 221
Balkans, 5, 101, 127–128
Balkan Entente, 86, 91
Balkan Wars, 63
Baluchis, 190
Basrah, 240
Batum, 17
Bayar, Jelal, 81, 90, 103; in 1950 elections, 108f., 138
Bazaar, Persian, 180, 191f.
Beirut, 142
Beyliks, 48
Black Sea, 5, 11–12; coastal ranges of, 19; region of Turkey, 21, 30
Bombay, 208
Bosporus, 12, 100
Bristol, Admiral Mark I., 139
Bulgaria, Turkish frontier with, 13; Turkish attitudes towards, 128
Bureaucracy, Turkish, 43–44, 95; Persian, 195–196, 266
Bursa, 48

Caliphate, 52, 75
Capitulations, Turkish, 68, 97; Persian, 218
Caspian Sea, 5, 179, 181, 187, 218, 226
Caucasus Mountains, 20, 218
Central Anatolian Region, 21–22, 30
Chakmak, Marshal Fevzi, 111
Chauvinism, Turkish, 84, 111–112, 126
Christianity, 40, 203, 207
Chrome, 28, 99
Churchill, Winston S., 98, 99, 254
Cilicia, 19
Cilician Gates, 17
Civil liberties, Turkish, 105–106
Coal, 28
Communications, 33–34
Communism, Turkish prejudice against, 56, 103, 119, 130; in Iran, 177, 199–200, 268f.
Constantinople. *See* Istanbul

Constitution, Ottoman, 53; Persian, 191, 193, 219
Copper, 28
Crimea, 54
Currency, Turkish, 109–110
Curzon, Lord, 221
Cyprus, Turkish desire to regain, 111, 127, 135
Cyrus, 214

Daghestan, 218
Danube, 5
Demavend, Mount, 181
Democracy, in Turkey, 77, 100, 102f., 138; in Iran, 269f.
Democrat Party, Turkish, 103f., 108f.
Derbend, 218
Dervish Orders, in Turkey, 78, 136; in Iran, 205
Deserts, Persian, 180–181, 182
Diyarbakïr, 28
Doğu Bayizit, 17
Dönme's, 96

Eastern Anatolia Region, Turkey, 23, 30
Eastern Question, 50, 54–55
Economic Coöperation Administration, 146
Edirne, 13, 48
Education, in Turkey, 83f., 111–112, 114; Americans in, 140f.; in Iran, 206, 213
Egypt, 50, 129, 131
El Alamein, 230
Elburz Mountains, 181
Elections, in Turkey, 7; in Iran, 240–241, 242
Electorate, Turkish, 76, 78; in 1946, 104, 108; in 1950, 104, 108f., 112; peasants in, 109
England, 97; Turkish view of, 134; *see also* Great Britain
Erivan, 17, 218
Erjiyas, Mount, 18
Eskishehir, 18, 19
Étatism, Turkish, 34–36, 43, 85f., 102, 103, 176
Euphrates River, 20

Europe, impact upon Turkey, 49f.; Turkish attitudes towards, 132f.
Exchange of Populations, 69f.
Export-Import Bank, 250f.
Exports, Turkish, 24–25; Persian, 253

Family life, Turkish, 117
Far East, 175
Farouq, King of Egypt, 194
Fars, 188, 190, 197
Fascism, alleged in Turkey, 7
Fertile Crescent, 20
Firdausi, 213
France, Turkish relations with, 14–16; in Eastern Question, 54; in Hatay, 14f., 66; Turkish attitudes towards, 133; and Iran, 216
French language and culture in Turkey, 80–81
Frontiersmen, Anatolian Moslem, 48

Gallipoli, 5, 63
Gardens, Persian, 179–180
Gaziantap, 23
Gediz River, 21
Georgia, Soviet, 17; autonomous, 65; and Iran, 218
Germany, in Eastern Question, 55–56; in World War II, 91–92, 99; Turkish attitudes towards, 133; in Iran, 227
Gilan, 181, 222, 236
Grady, Henry, 252
Gray, Gordon, 269
Great Britain, and Turkey, 16, 54, 66, 92, 103, 143, 144; and Iran, 176, 216, 218f., 229f. *See also* England
Greece, Turkish relations with, 6; Aegean Islands of, 12; frontier with Turkey, 13; nationalism of, 59; invades Anatolia, 59f.; anti-Greek riot in Istanbul, 111; Turkish attitudes towards, 128; and North Atlantic Pact, 150
Greek language, 40
Greeks of Istanbul, 96f.
Gromyko, 238

Gulistan, Treaty of, 218
Günaltay, Shemsettin, 108

Hafiz, 213
Hamlin, Rev. Dr. Cyrus, 141
Hatay, Sanjak of, 14–16, 89
Herodotus, 152
Hitler, 7, 227
Hittites, 84
Housing, Turkish, 32; Persian, 184
Husain, 204
Husain Ala, 231, 238, 256

Imam, twelfth, 204
Imam Reza, 226
India, 175
Indian Ocean, 182
Industrial revolution, 49
Industry, Turkish, 34–36; Persian, 198f.
Inönü, Ismet (Pasha), 68, 76, 89f., 95, 103; President, 88; at Cairo Conference, 98; as party chief, 104–105; in 1950 elections, 108f.
Iran, Turkish relations with, 5; Turkish frontier, 16–17, 175–176; Turkish attitudes towards, 128–129; and North Atlantic Pact, 150; survey of, 175f.; geography, climate, resources, 179f.; peoples, way of life, 183f.; tribesmen and minorities, 187f.; town life, 190f.; social classes, 193; court and Shah, 193f.; parliament and bureaucracy, 195f.; landed aristocracy, 197–198; army, 198; labor and middle class, 198f.; religious leaders, 200; Shiism, 202f.; law, 205f.; religious minorities, 207f.; national character, 209–210; arts, 210f.; literature, 212f.; history, 213f.; and western powers, 218f.; attitudes towards Russia, 221–222; Reza Shah, 223f.; and World War II, 230f.; Anglo-Russian Occupation of, 230–231; American participation, 230f.; object of Russian hostility, 235f.; Azerbaijani state in, 236f.; Kurdish state in, 237; United Nations acts, 237f.; situation re-

stored, 242f.; United States and, 245f.; missionaries in, 245–246; Shuster in, 246–247; Millspaugh in, 247–249; Point Four in, 250f.; attitudes towards U.S., 252; Razmara, 252f.; relations with Moslem states, 253–254; oil crisis in, 254f.; U.S. in, 259f.; Russia in, 267f.
Iran Democrat Party, 240
Iraq, 16, 65
Iron, 28
Irredentism, absence of in Turkey, 14, 20–21; in Persia, 254
Irrigation, Turkish, 26–27; Persian, 185f.
Isfahan, 186, 199
Iskenderun, 12
Islam, Turkish, 40–41, 45, 46, 75–76, 81, 135f.; Persian, 200–201, 202f.
Ismail, Shah, 216
Israel, 5, 130f.
Istanbul, 5, 7, 30, 48, 96f.
Istanbul American College for Girls, 142–144
Italy, 15, 65, 66, 143
Izmir, 12, 19, 30; Greeks land at, 59, 67; American College at, 142–143
Izvestia, 235

Jews, in Turkey, 96, 130f.; in Iran, 207
Jinn, 204
Judaism, 203

Karabük, 28, 35–36, 102
Karaman, 18
Kars, 17; demanded by Russia, 99
Karun River, 186–187
Kayseri, 18
Khans of Persian Tribes, 187
Khurasan, 182, 188, 231
Khuzistan, 187
Kirman, 208
Kızıl Iramk River, 18
Konya, 18
Köprülü Grand Vezirs, 49
Koran, 81, 203, 205; see also Quran
Korea, Turkish forces in, 7, 150; war in, 252

Kurdistan, 16, 23
Kurds, in Turkey, 78–80, 115; in Iran, 176, 188, 207, 237
Kütahya, 21

Labor, Turkish, 121; Persian, 198f.
Laicism, Turkish, 75–76, 96f.
Land reform, Persian, 195, 263–264
Land tenure, Turkey, 119; Iran, 185
Lausanne, Treaty of, 68f.
Law, Turkish, 68–69, 77–78; Persian, 205f.
League of Nations, 15, 86
Leninakan, 17
Literacy, Turkish, 43, 82
Literature, Turkish, 123f.; Persian, 212f.
Livestock, 27
Lurs, 188

Macedonian Question, 63
Mahabad, Republic of, 188
Majlis, Persian, 195f.
Mardin, 14
Marmara Sea Region, 21, 30
Mast (Yoghurt), 184
Mazanderan, 181–182
Mecca, 202
Mediterranean Sea, 5, 12; coastal ranges, 19
Mediterranean Sea Region, 30; see also Southern Anatolia Region
Mehmed II, Sultan, 49
Memur class, Turkey, 41–42
Menderes River, 21
Menemenjioğlu, Numan, 99
Merich River, 13
Meshed, 226
Middle Class, Persian, 200
Millet system, 46–47
Millspaugh, A. C., 247–249
Minerals, 27–28
Minorities, of Turkey, 69, 76; and Varlık Vergisi, 95f.; civil liberties of, 107; present status of, 113f.; of Iran, 187f.
Missionaries, American, in Turkey, 140f.; in Iran, 245–246
Mobility, social, 44, 116, 120

Mohammed, 203, 206
Mohammed Reza Pahlevi, 194–195, 244, 251f.
Mohammedanism. *See* Islam
Mongol invasion, 215
Montreux Convention, 69, 100
Mosaddeq, Dr., 195, 255
Moscow, 91, 238, 239
Moslemization, 59, 61, 67, 70
Mudros, Armistice of, 58

Napoleon, 50
Nasir al-Din Shah, 219
Nation Party, Turkish, 104, 111
National Front, Persian, 195
Nationalism, in Ottoman Empire, 47, 51; Turkish, 47, 52, 57, 66f., 75, 102, 114–115, 122; Persian, 224
Near East Foundation, 249
Near East Relief, 139
Nestorians, 207–208
Nile River, 5
Nizami, 213
Nomads, Persian, 183, 187
North Atlantic Pact, 150f., 251

Oil, Turkey, 28; Iran, 177, 219, 242f., 254f.
Operation Bootstraps, reforms in modern Turkey, 72f., 77
Opium, 184–185
Osman Bey, 48
Ottoman, culture, 46–47; literature and language, 80f.; mentality persists, 96f., 105, 147–148
Ottoman dynasty, 48, 75
Ottoman Empire, 34, 46–47, 48f.; and Iran, 216
Ottomanism, 52, 54

Pakistan, 190
Pan-Islam, 52, 54, 77; Turkish attitudes towards Arab states, 129f., 132
Pan-Turkism, 52–53, 54, 83f.
Parsis, 208
Pearl Harbor, 94

Peasants, Turkish, 26–27, 30–32, 38f., 42f., 65, 71, 116, 118f., 136; Persian, 183f.
Péguy, Charles, 194
People's Republican Party in Turkey. *See* Republican Party
Persia. *See* Iran
Persian culture, 190
Persian Gulf, 5, 175, 187
Persian Gulf Command, 177, 230f., 249
Peter the Great, 218
Philo-Hellenism, 59
Pishevari ja'far, 236
Point Four, 148, 250f., 269
Police, Turkish, 106–107; Persian, 227
Politics, Turkish, 90; Persian, 200
Pontic state, Greek, 65; Portuguese, 216
Pozantǐ, 19
Press, Turkish, 124–125; Persian, 232–233
Protestantism, 140f.

Qajar dynasty, 198, 217, 223
Qashqai's, 188, 190, 197, 230
Qavam al-Sultaneh, Ahmed, 237f., 240, 241, 242, 243, 262
Quran, 203, 205; *see also* Koran

Railroads, Turkey, 33; Iran, 226
Rainfall, 22
Ramandağ, 28
Ramazan, 201
Razmara, General, 197, 198, 205, 252, 256
Reforms in Ottoman Empire, 51
Republic of Turkey, 34, 71; government of, 73f.
Republican Party, Turkish, 89, 102f., 108f.
Reza Shah, 175, 176, 187, 191, 194, 196, 198, 200, 204, 208, 218, 223f., 232, 254, 266
Rezaiyeh, 207, 245
Roads, Turkey, 32–33; Iran, 226
Robert, Christopher, 141
Robert College, 141f.

Roosevelt, Franklin D., 94, 98, 99, 143

Rûm, 48, 80

Russia, relations with Turkey, 5; Turkish frontier, 17; Turks in, 53, 84; Turkish attitudes towards, 54f., 86, 127–128; Armenia's "protector," 60; in World War II, 91f., 94; renews hostility towards Turks, 99–100, 143, 144f., 149; relations with Iran, 176–177, 218f., 229f.; hostility towards Iran, 235; and oil questions, 258; policy of, 260f., 267f.

Saadi, 213

Safevid dynasty, 216

Sakarya River, 19

Salonika, 13, 63

Samsun, 65

Sanjak of Alexandretta. *See* Hatay

Sarajoğlu, Shükrü, 91, 95

Sassanian dynasty, 215

Saydam, Dr. Refik, 95

Schwartzkopf, Col. H. Norman, 247

Security Council, 238

Seistan, 182

Seljuks, 47–48

Senate, of Iran, 195–196

Seven Year Plan, Persian, 255–262f.

Shah of Persia, 193f.

Shah Abbas, 216–217

Sheref, 103; Shiism, 200, 202f.

Shiraz, 203, 211; Shuster, W. Morgan, 246–247

Smyrna. *See* Izmir

Social Classes, Turkey, 115f.; Iran, 193

Southern Anatolia Region, 22–23, 30

Southeastern Anatolia Region, 23, 30

Stalin, 91

Stalingrad, 230

Straits Area, 5, 92–93

Straits Question, 69, 99

Student movements, Turkish, 111–112

Sufism, 205

Suleiman the Magnificent, 49

Sultan-zadeh. *See* Pishevari

Sun-Language Theory, 83–84

Sunna, 206

Sunni Islam, 203

Syria, 14–16

Tabataba'i, Zia al-Din, 234, 239

Tabriz, 117, 226, 236, 242

Taqiye, 209

Tarsus, 19

Taurus Mountains, 19, 23

Teheran, 196, 208, 226

Teheran Conference, 99, 177, 231

Teheran Declaration, 231

Teymurtash, 223–224

Thrace, eastern. *See* Turkey in Europe

Tigris River, 16

Townsmen, Persian, 183, 190f.

Trakya. *See* Turkey in Europe

Trans-Iranian Railroad, 226

Tribes, Persian, 183f., 187–188, 232

Trieste, 241

True Ottoman group, 46–47, 64–65

Truman Doctrine, 144f., 251, 252

Tudeh Party, Persian, 234, 235, 236, 237, 240

Turkey, international relations of, 6f.; outstanding characteristics of, 8f.; area, 11; frontiers, 11f.; geography, 18f.; regions of, 21f.; natural resources, 23f.; exports, 24–25; mineral resources, 27–28; population, 28f.; public health, 28–29; villages, 30f.; Étatism, 34–36; history, 38f.; ruling group of, 41f.; nationalism, 47; westernization, 47f.; attitudes towards Russia, 54f.; after World War I, 58f.; Greek invasion, 65f.; Treaty of Lausanne, 68f.; Republic, 71; Operation Bootstraps, 72f.; opinion of 1923, 72; Kurds, 78–80; alphabet changed, 80f.; education, 83f.; international relations before 1939, 86; Inönü President, 88f.; in World War II, 90; neutrality, 92; Varlïk Vergisi, 95f.; later phase of World War II, 98f.; object of Russian demands, 99–100; roles in two World Wars, 100f.; position in 1945, 101–102; Democrat Party, 102f.; never a police state, 105f.;

Index

1950 elections, 108f.; social order, 113f.; Turkish view of selves, 123f.; view of world, 126f.; of Moslem world, 129f.; of Europe, 132f.; religion in, 135f.; relations with U.S., 139f.; American missionaries in, 140f.; American education, 141f.; American policy towards, 143f.; Truman Doctrine, 144; America's interests in, 145–146; business mores, 147–148; value to U.S.A., 148f.; North Atlantic Pact, 150f.
Turkey in Europe, 11
Turkification, 45–46, 59, 61, 67, 70; of Azerbaijan, 216
Turkish Information Office, 151
Turkish Language, 40, 44–45, 80f.; in Iran, 182, 188
Turkism, 52–53
Turkistan, Russian, 99
Turkomanchai, Treaty of, 218
Turkomans, 188
Turks, 29, 44–45; in Iran, 215–216
Tuz Gölü, 18

Uludağ, 21
Ulukïshla, 18, 19
Umayyad Caliphs, 203
United Kingdom Commercial Corporation, 232
United Nations, 134–135, 237f., 244, 250
United States, occupying force in Turkey, 58, 139; lend-lease to Turkey, 94; and Varlïk Vergisi, 97, 101, 103, 143f.; aid to Turkey, 110;

Turkish attitudes towards, 134, 138; interests in Turkey, 145–146; private enterprise in Turkey, 147–148; in Iran, 177; Shah's visit, 195; occupies Iran, 230f.; Persian attitudes towards, 252, 259f.
Urfa, 23
Urmiah Lake, 207

Varlïk Vergisi, 95f., 101, 113, 131
Van, Lake, 16, 20
Vienna, 49
Village, Turkish, 30–32; Persian, 185
Village Institutes, Turkish, 120–121
Voice of America, 251–252; 259

Westernization, in Turkey, 50f.; and Atatürk, 64, 71, 74; in Iran, 222, 223f.; slackens, 233f.
Wilson, Woodrow, 139
Women, Turkish, 78, 114f.; Persian, 225
World Court, 257
World War I, Turkey enters, 54, 55–56; conclusion, 58–59, 100; and Iran, 220–221
World War II, 7, 89, 90, 100, 200, 229f.

Yezd, 208
Young Turks, 53f., 63

Zagros Mountains, 188
Zoroaster, 183
Zoroastrians, 208